KU-226-990

Contents

Note

Part of Chapter Six is collectively written by the author with Anna-Nina Koduah, Carys Afoko, Emma Heard, Fionn Greig, Julia Betancour Roth, and Keishaun Decordova Johnson.

Dedication

This book is dedicated to young people and youth workers around the world who are creating, reclaiming and reimagining youth work as a grassroots practice for equality, freedom and collective life.

List of tables

List of abbreviations

CWDC   Children's Workforce Development Council (now defunct)

CYWU   Community and Youth Workers Union (now part of Unite)

JNC   Joint Negotiating Committee (a body that oversees the framework for grading youth work jobs and accrediting professional youth work courses in England and Wales)

IDYW   In Defence of Youth Work campaign

LGBT   Lesbian, gay, bi and trans

NCS   National Citizen Service (government-funded summer scheme for school leavers)

REYS   *Resourcing excellent youth services* (policy document, DfES, 2002)

VOY   Voice of Youth (youth work cooperative)

Acknowledgements

This book has taken three years to research and two years to write, but draws on a much longer involvement in youth work as a young person, volunteer, youth worker and campaigner. Many young people, colleagues, activists, friends, family members, students, teachers, researchers and others have inspired me and informed my thoughts during this journey, and I thank them all, even if I cannot name everybody.

The book is based on research undertaken for a PhD in the Sociology of Education, completed at King's College London's Department of Education and Professional Studies. The department, and specifically the Centre for Public Policy Research, has been a supportive and stimulating place to study and work. First, I am deeply grateful to my two wonderful supervisors, Sharon Gewirtz and Alan Cribb, who were empowering, trusting, thoughtful, kind and challenging at just the right times. They have improved my research and writing more than I can say.

Next, I want to thank Olie Brice, who encouraged me to do a PhD and write this book. He has read and discussed nearly everything I've written, as well as cooking delicious food, playing fantastic music and being great company. Thanks, too, to my other family members and friends, especially Mum and Max – thank you for everything – and Dad, who very helpfully and carefully proofread my thesis.

Thank you to my viva examiners, Jean Spence and Ken Jones, and to the anonymous peer reviewers of this book and of the book proposal. I deeply appreciate your knowledgeable and thoughtful feedback, which has certainly helped me to improve the book, even if I have not followed all of your suggestions! Thanks also to colleagues who read and commented on a draft chapter – particularly Pat Mahoney, Hayley Davies, John Owens, Ada Mau, Becky Taylor, David Pepper, Effrosyni Nomikou, Sally Beckwith and Heather King – and to others who read and provided feedback on parts of the PhD thesis that the book is adapted from – including Meg Maguire, Bernard Davies, Tony Taylor, Ian McGimpsey and Jenny Potter.

My deepest gratitude to the brilliant youth workers who participated anonymously in this research – thank you for your time, thoughtfulness and insight. Huge thanks to everyone in Voice of Youth (VOY) for being an amazing inspiration, especially Anna-Nina Koduah, Carys Afoko, Emma Heard, Fionn Greig, Julia Betancour Roth and Keishaun Decordova Johnson for taking part in the collective writing process; to my other fantastic VOY colleagues over the years including Beatriz, Bev, Chizoma, Dreiw, Falon, Habiba, Jerome, Lita, Lorenzo, Lucy, Mauve, Rochell, Sarah, Shekeila, Sus, Tasha, Tom; to all the brilliant young people from Lea View, Jack Watts and Manor; and to everyone else who has been involved or supported VOY in any way.

Thank you so much to Pauline Lipman and the 'Counter-hegemonics'; to Samira Bakkioui; to Graeme Tiffany, Steve Bramall and SAPERE; to friends at In Defence of Youth Work, Youth and Policy, the Federation for Detached Youth Work, and the National Coalition for Independent Action; and to colleagues and young people through the years in London, Manchester and Bath. Thanks to my youth workers when I was a young person, especially Emma, Paddy and Paul from BDEC (whose approach still informs my practice today), and to teachers who inspired a love of learning, especially Kate Sapin, John Best, Howard Gibson and Clive Symons. Thank you to Alice Nicholas for amazing facilitation of the creative weekend workshop 'Passion and resistance', to participants of that workshop, and to everyone else who has taken part in workshops and discussions relating to this research.

Thank you to all at Policy Press, especially Isobel Bainton, Rebecca Tomlinson, Jessica Miles, Jo Morton and Andy Chadwick, and to copy editor Kathleen Steeden, who have been supportive, thoughtful, efficient and effective. It is a privilege to work with a publisher that aims to make a difference rather than a profit.

The research undertaken for this book was funded by a studentship from the Economic and Social Research Council (ref. ES/101800X/1).

ONE

Introduction

'I've been doing voluntary youth work since October and it's at the local youth club ... I'm there four times a week ... I don't *have* to be there that often but I *love* it ... I *literally* spend the evening going from group to group chatting to people, anything they want to talk about. If I see people on the computer I'll go, "How's your day been, how's everything going?" They come to me, they chat to me. ... I think the face-to-face time is what keeps you real, it's what keeps you wanting to do it.' (Nevaeh, volunteer youth worker)

'It's the changing nature of youth work over the last ten years, we've seen a massive change. And it's all targeted work, now. It's all, I mean, I just remember a young person not long ago in club just saying to me, "I feel like I'm in class again." And it struck a chord with me because I knew exactly what he was on about. Because we were trying to get him to engage in stuff that they'd probably be doing in school. ... We need to get back to grassroots.' (Leo, part-time youth worker)

How do youth workers maintain their passionate commitment to working with young people, while negotiating policy changes that seem to detract from their distinctive methods and approach? This is the central question arising from the three years of qualitative research on which this book is based. The words of Navaeh and Leo, two of the volunteer and part-time youth workers who took part in the research, evoke the passion and the resistance felt by a great number of grassroots youth workers in relation to their everyday work with young people. This book explores how youth work is experienced by its least senior practitioners, who do the overwhelming majority of face-to-face youth work and yet whose voices are rarely heard in policy or research.

The book is written in the context of an unprecedented threat to publicly funded youth work in England, as well as in the wider UK and beyond. Massive public spending cuts in the wake of the 2008 financial crash have created a climate of extreme insecurity – not only for young people, workers and organisations, but also for youth work as a distinctive practice. Government figures showed that spending on English youth services had been cut by a third towards the end of the 2010–15 UK Coalition government's term of office (Barton and Edginton, 2014). The real impact has been greater than these figures suggest, as many decades-old local authority youth services and community organisations have closed altogether, while most others have drastically reduced their activities (CYWU, 2011; Davies, 2013; Taylor, 2015). Even before the 2015 election was won by a Conservative government promising further cuts, three quarters of local authorities surveyed by the government expected that 'all or nearly all' funding for young people's services could be cut within five years (Cabinet Office, 2014, p 15). This destruction of youth services is likely to affect large numbers of young people; according to one analysis of the 'Understanding Society' dataset, 38% of young people aged 10–15 have attended a youth club at least once a week (NCVYS, 2013, p 2). However, young people's voices are often excluded when decisions are made to close down local facilities (see, for example, North Devon Journal, 2014).

In times of such unprecedented change, this book calls for a renewal in grassroots youth work. The word 'grassroots' is used here to evoke an approach to youth work practice that is young person centred, primarily informal, and often rooted in neighbourhoods, social identities or shared interests. Practitioners and researchers across Europe have defined such practice as 'open youth work':

> The purpose of Open Youth Work is to offer young people, on the basis of their voluntary involvement, developmental and educational experience which will equip them to play an active part in our democratic society as well as meet their own developmental needs. Open youth work can take place in youth clubs, youth projects, youth centres, youth houses as well as on the street (through detached youth work). (ECYC, undated)

Open youth work (also known in the UK as open access youth work) tends to have an 'open door' policy. It either welcomes all young people in a defined age group, or provides a space for specific groups such as young women or young disabled people. In open youth work spaces, young people choose *when* and *how* to engage, can come and go without sanction, and ideally have a high level of ownership over what goes on. This has become an increasingly distinctive practice as other spaces (such as schools and the streets) have become more closely governed and controlled. Youth clubs are often particularly important for young people in low income families who have limited space at home.

Spending cuts have been detrimental to open forms of youth work, as organisations with reduced budgets tend to focus on targeted youth support (Cabinet Office, 2014, p 16). This is consistent with a longer policy trend predating the financial crash, in which formal and structured interventions are preferred over open and flexible forms of youth work, partly because the latter are less able to predict and quantify their outcomes in a marketised model of public services (IDYW, 2011). This is not to diminish the value of targeted youth support work, but rather to emphasise the importance of open spaces that facilitate social relationships, informal contact with supportive adults, a range of activities, and a sense of community and belonging. Such environments are important for these intrinsic reasons, as well as for creating a basis of trusting relationships that enable some of the most marginalised young people to begin to trust adults enough to access support. However, youth clubs and street-based projects are at particular risk of closure, disadvantaging the mainly black, working-class and low income young people who tend to use them (Pidd, 2013; Unison, 2014b).

A renewal in grassroots youth work will rely on skilled, experienced and reflective youth workers who ally themselves with the young people they work with, and think critically about what they are asked to do. It will mean youth workers reclaiming elements of their practice that have been attacked in recent years, while also reimagining what youth work might become in the future. Young people have a vital role to play in these processes, and it is important to include them at all levels of decision making. Without youth workers to create the spaces for long-term trusting relationships with young people, however, it is doubtful whether many young people will have a real say in the future of youth work. While research on young people's perspectives of open youth work is of great importance and value (see, for example, Coburn, 2012), this book makes no apology for a focus on the voices of grassroots youth workers at a time when their practice is at risk of disappearing altogether.

This book examines the experiences and perspectives of part-time and volunteer youth workers, drawing on theory and original research to inform and strengthen grassroots practice for the future. For youth work to thrive and succeed, it is essential to value and give voice to its practitioners, many of whom are still young people themselves, and many of whom come from disadvantaged and minority communities. The policy pressures and tensions discussed here are based in the specific working cultures and practices of part-time and volunteer youth workers in England. However, they are likely to resonate beyond part-timers to full-timers and managers, beyond England to other contexts where youth work exists, and beyond youth work to other fields that are facing challenges to person-centred practice in an increasingly market-oriented policy context. This introductory chapter aims to set the research in context, both for those readers who are already familiar with youth work practice in England, and for those who are not.

What is youth work?

> Youth and community work is about dialogue, about conversation. What do youth and community workers do? Listen and talk. Make relationships. Enable young people to come to voice. 'Conversation' conveys a sense of the mutual learning which the practice at its best enables. The roles of educator and learner are each present in informal education. (Batsleer, 2008, p 5)

I have been a youth worker for over twenty years and yet I still hesitate when people ask me what youth work is. I very much like Janet Batsleer's description, above, for its focus on community and dialogue; however, an answer along those lines is sometimes met with puzzlement. Perhaps people wonder how someone might be paid for conversations, or how such a thing could ever be funded! And yet, Batsleer's characterisation of youth work is important precisely *because* it emphasises aspects of the practice that are difficult to capture and observe. If you visit a youth club, you might not immediately 'see' the dialogue, relationship and learning. Youth work can look and sound chaotic, and sometimes it is. However, it is underpinned by a coherent approach to working with young people that has developed over many decades.

Youth workers work professionally with young people to create and claim spaces for conversation, fun, challenge, relationships and collective learning. Youth work is practised in diverse places, including much of Europe, North America, Australasia, Hong Kong and South Africa, although its particular character differs between these contexts. In England it happens predominantly (but not only) in purpose-built youth clubs, community centres, village halls, religious buildings, parks, sports fields and on street corners. Its key features are that young people's perspectives are central to the process; young people become involved by choice rather than being compelled to attend; and there is an element of informal education, of learning through conversation, relationships and activities (Davies, 2015). Skilled and reflective youth workers are crucially important to this process, and can be seen as the most vital resource for good youth work.

The origins of youth work in the UK can be traced back to the eighteenth and nineteenth centuries, when churches and voluntary groups set up Sunday schools and 'ragged schools', early experiments in education for poor people that were much less formal than mainstream schooling and included learning through outings and social activities (Smith, 2013). In the mid-nineteenth century, when mass schooling became more formalised and 'adolescents' began to be identified as a specific group in need of particular services, organisations such as the Young Men's Christian Association (YMCA) and Girls Friendly Society were formed to meet the social, health and educational needs of young men and women in clubs, shelters and settlement houses. Educational and support work at this time was strongly underpinned by the ideologies of empire and Christian faith, often aiming to rescue, discipline and moralise the growing numbers of working-class young people in urban areas (Davies, 1999a).

Contemporary formulations of youth work in the UK draw on this rather colonial history, as well as on alternative frameworks, including radical experiments in play and social work (Paneth, 1944; Bazeley, 1969), feminist girls' work (Batsleer, 2013b; Spence, 2014) and Black perspectives in youth work (John, 1981; Williams, 1988). Thus youth work in the UK has a particular history and character, which is also informed by various related practices around the world, including youth development and after-school work in the US and Canada, youth work in Australasia, social pedagogy and social animation in Europe, and social street work in Brazil. In turn, British youth work theory and practice has been influential elsewhere, including in Australia, the US and Northern Europe (Bessant, 2012; Heathfield, 2012; Forkby and Kiilakoski, 2014).

Youth work's methods and approaches are widely contested in the UK, and there is a rich vein of literature debating its defining features (Davies, Bernard, 2005; Sercombe, 2010; IDYW, 2011). For example, there has been criticism of the move towards employing youth workers in settings where young people are required to attend such as schools and the criminal justice system (IDYW, 2011; Davies,

2015). Some commentators argue that youth work in such settings is not problematic as long as the relationship between worker and young person remains negotiated (Ord, 2009; Coburn, 2012). In contrast, I align with the view that such projects may benefit from practitioners trained and experienced in youth work, but that work in compulsory settings should only be named as youth work if it is clearly able to demonstrate the voluntary principle: that young people have a free choice over whether to engage, and can leave without sanction. A notable proponent of this argument is the campaigning network In Defence of Youth Work (IDYW), which was set up in 2009 to defend a practice based on the following cornerstones:

- the primacy of the voluntary relationship, from which the young person can withdraw without compulsion or sanction;
- a commitment to a critical dialogue and the creation of informal educational opportunities starting from young people's agendas;
- the need to work with and encourage the growth of young people's own autonomous networks, recognising the significance of class, gender, race, sexuality, disability and faith in shaping their choices and opportunities;
- the importance of valuing and attending to the here-and-now for young people as well as to their 'transitions';
- the nurturing of a self-conscious democratic practice, tipping balances of power in young people's favour;
- the significance of the worker themselves, their room for autonomy, their ability to fashion an improvised, yet rehearsed practice (IDYW, 2014a).

This last point, the significance of the youth worker, is emphasised by young people as centrally important to their experiences of youth work:

> youth workers are trying to bring out, like make you realise your self-worth and your potential but not just for your academic side, it's about you as a person ... I think in a way every time you meet with them you always come away feeling good about yourself ... the just whole atmosphere of the group makes you come away feeling good and that you can succeed. (Lucy, young person quoted in Spence and Devanney, 2006, p 43).

Lucy's explanation, here, is echoed by research from the US, in which urban young people identify good relationships with youth workers as a vital element in their attraction to, and continued participation in, after-school settings (Strobel et al, 2008). Thus the focus of this book on youth workers (rather than on young people) is justified by previous research on young people's views about what is important in youth work. The particular emphasis of this book is on part-timers and volunteers, who in the UK carry out the majority of face-to-face youth work with young people and yet whose voices are rarely heard in policy or research.

Part-time youth workers, past and present

Part-time youth workers generally concentrate on face-to-face work with young people rather than managerial activities, usually working on evening, weekend and school holiday sessions. Many smaller youth organisations are run entirely by volunteers, or by volunteers working alongside a handful of paid part-time employees, while local authorities and larger organisations tend to employ a hierarchy of full-time professionally qualified managerial staff, part-time support workers, and volunteer assistants. Part-time and volunteer youth work tends to correlate with a relatively low status and a more basic level of training. In contrast, full-time youth workers are often managers of staff, projects and buildings, and usually have recognised youth and community work qualifications at bachelor's or master's level.

According to the most recent data, volunteers make up nearly nine tenths of the workforce in all sectors, while two thirds of paid staff in local authority youth services are part-timers (Mellor and McDonnell, 2010, pp 8, 11). The same report showed that part-timers were more likely than their full-time and senior colleagues to be women and from minority ethnic backgrounds.[1] Despite their predominance in the field, however, the last significant research to focus on part-timers is now over 30 years old (Bolger and Scott, 1984).

In the early days, there was little need for the 'part-time youth worker' designation because there were very few full-time paid youth leaders (Davies, 1999a). This began to change in England and Wales during the Second World War, when local authorities were required by law to coordinate youth activity and contribute towards the salaries of 'full-time leaders' (Board of Education, 1939). As the UK government's interest in youth work grew, a clear distinction began to be drawn between these full-time leaders and their part-time helpers (Roberts, 2004). This separation became more explicit after the publication of the Albemarle Report (Ministry of Education, 1960), a foundational policy document that heralded a significant expansion of local authority-funded youth work in England and Wales. In the wake of Albemarle, youth work training was expanded and consolidated into two separate routes: a 'professional' course at the newly opened National College for the Training of Youth Leaders, and a localised part-time training route aimed at volunteers. This differentiation in training formalised a distinction between full-time and part-time workers that persists today.

Although the difference in status between part-timers and full-timers has changed surprisingly little since the Albemarle Report, the limited available data seems to suggest a shift in the motivations and demographic composition of part-time youth workers. Part-time youth work was once seen as a 'spare-time' activity, undertaken for reasons of altruism, religious calling and self-fulfilment. A 1970s study based on interviews with 200 full-time, part-time and volunteer youth workers suggested that most part-timers and volunteers had day jobs, and that they were more likely to come from professional backgrounds than were their full-time colleagues (Lowe, 1975). This counterintuitive finding might partly be explained by the number of teachers who worked part-time as youth workers in the 1960s and 1970s, having been specifically sought to address shortages in the youth workforce at that time, whereas combining teaching with youth work is relatively uncommon today.

By the 1980s, volunteering or working part-time had become the first steps on a path towards youth work as a career in its own right. Youth work retained a sense of altruism, but as it was somewhat professionalised it became an attractive career option for women, working class people and members of ethnic minorities in particular. This was demonstrated by a trade union survey in 1982, which found that the majority of part-timers relied on youth work for their main source of income (Davies, 1999b). No longer 'helpers' supplementing a day job, it now seemed that most part-timers lived on the low wages they received for this work and saw youth work as their main occupation.

The trade union survey created an impetus to campaign for improvements to pay and conditions for part-timers (Davies, 1999b). In 1985 a part-time workers' caucus was formed in the Community and Youth Workers Union, and a part-timers' conference was organised (Nicholls, 2009). The union campaigned for the harmonisation of full-timers' and part-timers' terms and conditions, and pro-rata equivalent pay was eventually agreed in 1996 (Nicholls, 2012). This was presented by the union as a significant victory, and undoubtedly made a difference for some; nevertheless, part-timers remain over-represented on the lowest grades of the pay scale because they tend to be employed in the least senior positions.

Aside from the union's interest in pay and conditions, policy and research attention on part-timers has focused almost entirely on training as the route for improved practice. As concerns were raised in relation to the quality and consistency of part-time training in the 1970s, the government instigated a review. The subsequent report, *Realities of training* (Butters and Newell, 1978) is fascinating in its depiction of the culture and ideological basis of part-time youth work courses, although it provides little insight into the actual working experiences of part-timers. A panel was established in 1983 to review part-time training, and a further report, *Starting from strengths* (Bolger and Scott, 1984), identified part-timers as a somewhat subordinated group who felt neglected, under-valued and unheard:

> Part-time youth workers, paid or unpaid, occupy a contradictory position. They work face to face with young people and so are at the centre of what goes on: but they are more often than not at the periphery when it comes to many of the decisions and discussions that affect their work. (Bolger and Scott, 1984, p 7)

This paradox rings true more than 30 years after it was written, as this book will go on to demonstrate. Although *Starting from strengths* was the last significant study to focus specifically on part-time youth workers, more recent research has included the views of a small number of volunteers and part-timers alongside those of full-timers and young people (Spence and Devanney, 2006; Tiffany, 2007; Davies and Merton, 2009, 2010; Lehal, 2010). These studies emphasise part-timers' particular vulnerability to the current policy context. In particular, one study of 12 youth services found that part-timers:

> could seem seriously demotivated by the target culture, claiming that at their level its dilemmas were felt most acutely. They talked of pressure to get the numbers through and of crude counting and measuring by managers interested only in outcomes often unconnected with their practice – or young people's everyday realities. (Davies and Merton, 2009, p 14)

Similarly, Lehal (2010) found that part-timers disliked target-driven paperwork because it took them away from direct work with young people. These suggestions of an experience and critique that is particularly acute among part-timers seemed to warrant further investigation, and it is in this context that the research informing this book was planned.

Research methods

The study that underpins this book started with an open question: how do paid and unpaid part-time youth workers experience their work in a changing policy context? The focus on part-timers is a matter of emphasis: a research decision to privilege the views of those practitioners who undertake most face-to-face youth work, and who are more likely to be young, and from disadvantaged and minority groups. The focus on part-timers is also motivated by personal experience and commitment; I have been a youth worker for my entire adult life, mostly a part-timer, working for a variety of youth, community and play organisations in three different areas of England. The research aimed to create spaces for part-time and volunteer youth workers to reflect critically on their work and share their views and experiences with others, and to this end follows a qualitative methodology which is discussed briefly here, and in greater detail in the Afterword to this book.

The research was based on the detailed and critical analysis of interviews, focus groups and youth work practice carried out from 2011 to 2014 as the study for my PhD.[2] The research aim was to explore in depth the views and experiences of a diverse range of part-time youth workers in England, building detailed contextual understanding in relation to local and national policy changes affecting their work. Most of the data in this book comes from in-depth interviews of up to three hours with 21 part-time and volunteer youth workers, and from a series of three focus group discussions, each lasting two hours, involving a further eight part-timers and volunteers. The quotations throughout the book (unless otherwise attributed) are from these interviews and focus groups.

These workers volunteered to take part in response to a recruitment email and poster I sent to a range of youth organisations and networks. They were working in various cities, towns and villages, mainly in the South East and North West of England, with a smaller number in the South West and North East. They came from a variety of backgrounds, and were involved in a diverse range of youth work, most working in youth clubs, street-based youth work and/or specific projects such as LGBT groups. The majority had become youth workers as young people, and more than half were still in their twenties. Short descriptions of each research participant are provided at the end of this book; the names used throughout the book are pseudonyms chosen by the participants.

Alongside the findings from interviews and focus groups, the study is significantly informed by three years of participant observation as a youth worker in a charity (from 2011 to 2012) and as part of a small youth workers' cooperative (from 2011 to 2013), both in inner-city London. I drew on practitioner ethnography and auto-ethnographic methodologies to record observations, experiences and discussions in reflective diary entries, some of which are included in this book as research diary excerpts. During the course of the research, I realised that effective anonymisation of my main research site (the cooperative) would be impractical because I am publicly associated with this organisation. As a consequence, I avoided including fieldnotes that could be seen as containing sensitive information about young people.

After discussion with colleagues and young people, it was agreed that my main research site – Voice of Youth in Hackney – would be named rather than being kept anonymous.[3] One advantage of this naming was that young people and youth workers involved in setting up the cooperative could be publicly recognised within the book. After discussing how we would like Voice of Youth to be represented, we decided to organise two focus groups, lasting around two hours each, in which young people and youth workers involved in running the cooperative would discuss the principles and practice of the organisation. These conversations were recorded, transcribed and co-edited, and presented as an edited dialogue in the style of Freire and Shor's (1987) 'talking book' (see Chapter Six).

Participant observation in Voice of Youth brought the advantages of familiarity, including depth of relationships and breadth of involvement, as well as enabling a detailed examination of an unusual and innovative youth work organisation. However, the clear disadvantage was that it became ethically problematic to include the perspectives and experiences of young people who participated in Voice of Youth's groups, owing to the difficulties of effectively anonymising young and potentially vulnerable participants in such a small organisation. As a creative response to this barrier, I have included material from practice in the form of narrative vignettes at the beginning and end of Chapters Two to Five. These vignettes draw on my experience over many years (rather than focusing only on participant observation in Voice of Youth). Although the characters are fictionalised and do not represent real people, the words and actions of the young people and youth workers are similar to those I have observed and experienced.

In using collectively edited dialogue, research diary excerpts and narrative vignettes, and in drawing on my own experience as a youth worker, I recognise that the written style of this book is somewhat unconventional. There is a tension between traditional scientific writing and the more reflexive style adopted here. However, creative approaches to academic writing are by no means new or unusual in educational research (see, for example, extensive uses of fiction in Clough, 2002; Gillborn, 2008; and Ladson-Billings, 2012; and poetry in Khan, 2013), and are consistent with the feminist, poststructuralist and anarchist influences on this study. I aim to write in and through the tension between academic convention and authenticity, emphasising the rigorous and internally consistent nature of the reflexive approach used in the research and writing of this book, while acknowledging its limitations.

In a similar way, there are both advantages and disadvantages to being an 'insider researcher': a part-time youth worker researching part-time youth work. Inspired by the liberatory pedagogy of Paulo Freire, I have approached the study not as an empty vessel in search of pure facts, but as a committed and experienced youth worker aiming to develop 'critical capacity, curiosity and rigour' (Freire 1998, p 33). I make no apology for taking sides, and am influenced by activist scholarship, an orientation towards research which contributes to struggle against dominant ideologies and encourages public conversations about theory and practice (Lipman, 2011). I recognise that this insider and activist orientation carries the risks of confirming preconceived ideas, making assumptions and failing to take alternate views into account. It is ethically and politically important to be explicit about the perspective and values that influence this study, while also being reflective, questioning and self-critical (Gewirtz and Cribb, 2006). I have aimed to develop a reflexive orientation throughout the research and the writing of this book, in the knowledge that readers will often have different views, depending on their own perspectives.

Before moving on, it is important to acknowledge other limitations to this research. First and most important, its focus on practitioners means a potential neglect of young people's perspectives. I believe that it was a valid choice to focus on part-timers for the purposes of this research project, especially as research across different country contexts tends to emphasise the importance young people place on having good youth workers (Møller et al, 1994; Strobel et al, 2008; Coburn, 2012; Paddison, 2015). When I started this research, young people and full-time youth workers were somewhat represented in the literature, while the views of part-time and volunteer youth workers were almost entirely neglected. However, there is a developing tendency for educational research to focus on the perspectives of practitioners rather than young people, partly due to perceived barriers around institutional ethical review (Sikes, 2012). Should I be fortunate enough to undertake further research on youth work, I plan to involve young people as co-researchers from the beginning, as a contribution towards redressing this balance.

The second limitation of the research is the specificity of its context. The study was based in England rather than the whole of the UK because it focuses on the effects and enactment of policy, and most policy relating to youth work in Scotland, Northern Ireland and Wales is devolved to those jurisdictions. I recognise that this focus risks adding to a certain English dominance in youth work writing. However, the book aims to be of wider interest and relevance, and many of the issues considered here speak beyond the English context (see, for example, Verschelden et al, 2009; Sercombe, 2010; Fusco, 2013; Fusco et al, 2013). Having met with practitioners from many countries, I know that youth workers have a hunger to learn from each other beyond their own communities and national boundaries. English youth work should not be seen as an isolated practice; it is greatly inspired by research and stories of educational practice elsewhere, from Freire's (1988) radical literacy education in Brazil to bell hooks' (1994) anti-racist and feminist teaching in the US. I have attempted to focus on dilemmas that will resonate beyond England, and to avoid excessive jargon and assumed local knowledge, while retaining a focus on the specificity of contemporary policy and practice in English youth work.

Policy, passion and resistance

The main themes of this book are captured in its subtitle: 'policy, passion and resistance in practice'. The study started from a concern about policy and its effects on youth work practice, whereas the themes of passion and resistance became increasingly central during the process of research. I have made a deliberate decision not to adopt or propose a fixed and over-arching theoretical framework that explains 'once and for all' how policy, passion and resistance work in grassroots youth work settings. Rather, I see them as fluid in relation to the particular contexts that youth workers and young people find themselves in, and I draw on a range of critical theoretical perspectives to understand how they work in this context. Policy, passion and resistance are the threads that weave in and out of the following chapters, sometimes more or less prominent, often overlapping or tangled together and rarely disappearing from view. Here I outline my theoretical starting points in relation to these core themes.

Drawing on the work of critical education policy scholars, policy is understood in this book as a process of struggle, contestation and negotiation (CCCS, 1981; Ozga, 2000; Jones, 2003). This is in contrast to a 'common sense' view of policy as the straightforward proposal and implementation of plans of action, an interpretation that neglects how policy is enacted in everyday practice through 'jumbled, messy, contested, creative and mundane social interactions' (Ball et al, 2012, p 2). I have already briefly discussed the dramatic scale of closures and redundancies under the 2010–15 Coalition government, which led to many local youth services closing or reducing their provision (Cabinet Office, 2014). No major political party pledged to restore funding or support for grassroots forms of youth work during the campaign for the 2015 general election, which was won by a Conservative Party planning further cuts to young people's welfare and services (Mackie, 2015).

While it is important to acknowledge the influence of the 2008 financial crash and its global impact on public spending, an exclusive focus on this 'most visible' area of change can risk obscuring the broader direction of travel. The current phase of cuts, closures and redundancies are presented by governments as unfortunate but inevitable, a matter of responsible financial management in times of austerity (Hall and O'Shea, 2013). However, the so-called financial 'crisis' has not disrupted the major political parties' ongoing devotion to the market; rather, in the years following the crash, social inequality and traditionalist values became more deeply embedded (Jones, 2010).

The current situation is particularly bleak for youth work, but it is not necessarily helpful to view it as new or exceptional; rather, today's policies represent considerable continuity in terms of a longer-term erosion of the post-war welfare settlement, and a more significant role for the market in all public services. In this process, spending cuts implemented under the Coalition government were accompanied by 'payment by results', competitive tendering and insecurity. The austerity agenda dramatically reduced public expenditure, while intensifying the move towards private financing and forms of social investment that use business models (Youdell and McGimpsey, 2015). The current policy settlement can be seen as a break from the 1997–2010 New Labour government's 'third way', which invested in social welfare including youth work while imposing extensive performance targets. Conversely, current policy can be viewed as a logical progression in New Labour's marketisation of public services. The policy mechanisms discussed in this book – the marketisation of youth work, the exploitation of emotional labour, the intensification of top-down performance management and the use of surveillance mechanisms – are of particular importance at the current time. However, they all have roots in the New Labour years, as well as in earlier Conservative administrations under Margaret Thatcher and John Major, and look likely to continue for the foreseeable future.

It is clear that such policy developments are not particular to youth work. Research demonstrates an increase in administration, top-down management, target cultures and market mechanisms for a range of occupational groups, including educators (Gewirtz et al, 2009), social workers (Banks, 2011), voluntary sector employees (Rochester, 2013), museum staff (Tlili et al, 2007), careers advisors (Chadderton and Colley, 2012) and probation officers (Justice Select Committee, 2011). Nor are the changes specifically English; market imperatives and financial pressures have combined to put immense pressure on youth work wherever it exists. In North America, researchers have referred to an 'accordian effect' in which pressures from above and below combine to 'squeeze out' quality:

> Top-down pressures and growing expectations to do more with less at a time of decreased resources and swelling bottom-up pressures are putting the squeeze on organisations like never before witnessed (in our lifetimes). Youthwork practitioners are in the middle caught in stressful attempts to keep up and keep on. They are despairingly and tirelessly working to push up, push back, and hold on. (Fusco et al, 2013, p 8)

Such despairing and tireless commitment was palpable in the accounts of the youth workers who took part in this research. In difficult times, the youth workers I spoke to were consistently more positive and optimistic than I had expected. I had not foreseen the themes of passion, love and care as being central to this study, possibly because I had taken them for granted. Despite my own passionate attachment to youth work and care for the young people and colleagues I work with, I had not previously identified these feelings as worthy of remark. This changed in the process of the research, and positive emotional attachments to youth work and young people came out so loudly and strongly from the interviews and discussion groups that it became vital to position them centrally to the book. Youth workers' passion is not necessarily consistent or continuous; workers experience a wide range of often ambivalent emotions, both in their direct work with young people, and in relation to administrative, managerial and organisational influences that often derive from government policy. At some moments, youth workers' passion for their work encourages them to go along with policies against their principles in order to preserve their job and keep services open for young people; at other times it seems to fuel their resistance to dehumanising policies.

Passion and resistance, then, do not exist in opposition to one another, and neither are they simply two sides of the same coin; they are interrelated orientations towards the everyday struggle of practice. Broad ideological forces such as the move towards market mechanisms can be seen in specific contexts, where policies often become 'inflected, mediated, resisted, misunderstood, or in some cases simply prove unworkable' (Ball, 2008a, p 7). Such messy and contested policy enactments were much in evidence during my research, and many practitioners opposed or questioned the dominant direction of youth work policy. While only a minority were involved in traditional forms of resistance such as strikes, demonstrations and collective campaigning, many more were engaged in what might be termed 'everyday resistance to everyday power' (Ball, 2013, p 148).

Resistance is understood throughout this book in a relatively open sense: as words, thoughts or actions that involve opposition to or subversion of the status quo (Hollander and Einwohner, 2004). Youth workers' resistance encompasses vocal challenge, avoidance, disengagement and discontent. It also involves developing counter-discourses that challenge dominant understandings; experimenting with alternative ways of working; and building critical alliances with young people, workers in other occupations and activists. It is unlikely that individual youth workers solely 'comply with' or 'resist' policy; rather, they are often engaged in both compliance and resistance simultaneously, passionately trying to keep projects alive while contesting aspects of what policy requires them to do.

Outline of the book

The central concern of this book is the world of grassroots youth work practice, how policy interacts with practice and how youth workers respond and resist, and each of the chapters looks at this concern from a different angle. While the chapters proceed in a logical sequence, they are also designed to work independently, and can be read individually or in any order.

Chapter Two, 'The marketisation of youth work', focuses on how neoliberal policies have become dominant in the everyday practice of youth work. According to this logic, simply 'working with young people' is not enough; even volunteers and small organisations need to be able to sell their work, both metaphorically and literally. The market demands more from unpaid and low paid workers, while making their work vulnerable and precarious. At a time when the entrepreneur is a celebrated 'ideal', social enterprise is valorised over 'old' public sector and community organisational forms. The chapter explores some of the ways that grassroots youth workers experience and respond to this context: protesting against youth service cuts, setting up social enterprises, working in precarious circumstances and engaging in entrepreneurial forms of voluntary work.

'Passionate practice' is the starting point of Chapter Three. In challenging times, it is striking that grassroots youth workers talk consistently about their work in terms of love, commitment and care. Emotional engagement might be seen as intrinsic to youth work and necessary for building relationships with young people; it can also be seen as a form of self-exploitation at a time when youth work is governed by market principles and cost-cutting. The chapter explores the continuing relevance of emotional labour (Hochschild, 2003), the theory that workers' emotional efforts are controlled and exploited by employers in the pursuit of profit, as well as newer theories of emotion management (Bolton, 2005). These ways of understanding workplace emotions are particularly important at a time when organisations in all fields demand passion from their workers, and when the distinctions between private, voluntary and public organisations are breaking down. The chapter closes with a discussion of the potential role of passion and love in resisting the commodification of youth work.

In neoliberal societies, there is consistent policy rhetoric about the need to strip away intrusive state interference in local activities. Despite this, most of the grassroots workers in this study experience extensive performance management systems, including databases that track individual and organisational performance against targets and outcomes. The workers in this study see target cultures as obstructive, distracting and even demeaning of good youth work, although they may also experience these mechanisms as a seductive opportunity to feel successful in an individualised and competitive system of judgement. Chapter Four, 'Target cultures and performativity', draws on theories of performativity as formulated by Stephen Ball (2003, 2013) and Judith Butler (1990, 2004) to consider how target cultures change not only *what youth workers do* but also *who they are*. The roles of authenticity and shame are discussed in relation to performativity and youth workers' identities. The chapter closes with a consideration of the different ways in which grassroots youth workers challenge systems of audit and measurement that they see as particularly inappropriate.

Chapter Five, 'Surveillance on the street', explores youth work's uncomfortable role in the tracking and surveillance of young people, focusing on detached (street-based) youth work. Detached workers have historically been situated at a distance from systems of state control and tend to see themselves as informal educators, working on young people's terms and on their territory. But can the street be considered as 'young people's territory' in the context of the increasingly authoritarian and privatised management of formerly public space? And can street-based youth workers legitimately claim to be 'detached' from systems of control when they are called upon to contribute to the policing and surveillance of the street? This chapter reflects on how part-time detached youth workers take part in and resist systems of control and surveillance, and discusses the potential for an alternative approach.

Marking a change in both style and content, Chapter Six, 'Practising differently', focuses in detail on the small grassroots organisation where I have worked and volunteered during the course of this study. Voice of Youth is a workers' cooperative set up in 2011 by young people and youth workers based on principles of critical youth work, equality and cooperation. At the centre of the chapter is a series of collectively written dialogues between part-time and volunteer youth workers from Voice of Youth, discussing how their idealistic principles work in practice and thinking about the dilemmas, challenges, joy and excitement of running a youth work cooperative without bosses or managers. This is followed by a discussion of what can be learned from this case study, and the possibilities and limitations of idealistic and radical organisations as a form of prefigurative practice.

Despite the serious challenges facing youth work, the passionate part-time and volunteer youth workers in this study provide a basis for hope. Chapter Seven, 'Reclaiming and reimagining youth work', begins with a summary of the study's findings. It then returns to the central themes of policy, passion and resistance, which suffuse the working lives of grassroots youth workers, and draws together some of the ways in which workers are engaged in everyday action to challenge systems and practises that they disagree with. Even in a highly challenging context, this study provides evidence that grassroots youth work can – and often does – take young people's side, challenge oppression, oppose tick-box and pathologising methodologies, and question the centrality of market logic. The book finishes with a series of recommendations for policy and practice.

This book is intended to be useful, not only in contributing to a research community, but also for the many practitioners who are interested in using theory and original research to inform and enrich their work. While the book is rooted in the specific practice of youth work, many of its themes are likely to resonate with a broader range of workers in education, welfare and other settings who are facing similar struggles and challenges, and who may be responding and resisting in similar ways. There are many whose work is affected by conditions outside their control, and who sometimes feel too busy, tired and demoralised to know whether and how to negotiate, refuse, circumvent, fight and create alternative ways of working. For these people (of whom I am one), the book does not provide a blueprint of 'what to do'. What it does instead, I hope, is draw on a particular world of practice to provide theoretical and empirical resources for recognition, critical reflection, creative thought, collective discussion and inspiration.

Notes

[1] This data should be taken as indicative. The Children's Workforce Development Council (CWDC) report (Mellor and McDonnell, 2010) draws on data from a variety of sources, making it difficult to give accurate or comparable figures on the demographic profile of the youth workforce. Figures are likely to have changed due to substantial cuts in youth work since the financial crash in 2008, since when the CWDC has been closed, and similar data has not been collated more recently.

[2] This study was funded by the Economic and Social Research Council and approved by King's College London's ethical review panel.

[3] An amendment to the institutional ethical approval, allowing the research site Voice of Youth to be named, was duly sought and agreed by the panel.

TWO

The marketisation of youth work

> **One warm summer evening ...**
>
> A few young men and two youth workers take turns kicking a ball against the youth club wall, sometimes calling out a joke or friendly insult to one another. The ball narrowly misses an older man walking past but he doesn't seem to notice, continuing unsteadily on his way. 'Urgh, he's disgusting,' says one of the young men. 'He sleeps at the bus stop next to my nan's.' Some of the group members laugh or stare. Youth worker Jo says quickly, 'Shush Danny, he might hear you. If he's homeless or something then his life's hard enough without people being unkind.' 'Well tough. It's like my uncle says,' Danny responds, louder, 'if someone's not a success in life it's their own fault.'
>
> A couple of the group nod and mutter agreement. Wondering how much to share, Jo's colleague Ricky says tentatively, 'My mate was homeless when he was younger. I don't reckon it was his fault, he had a lot of bad luck.' Ready for a break and a chat, the young men start to gather round. The ball is left lying in the gutter as they talk about people they know and things they've read in the papers, about poverty, relationship breakdown and illness, discussing and disagreeing about how much choice they'll have themselves over what might happen to them in the future. After a while some of the group lose interest, going round the corner to smoke. Looking at Jo, Danny says, 'Maybe It's not that guy's fault but whatever, he stinks, he should at least get a wash!' The remaining members of the group laugh as Danny kicks the ball high in the air and the game is resumed. Not joining in with the laughter, Ricky and Jo glance at each other, noticing that the moment has passed. They'll bring this up again another time.

This book is written in times of austerity, when two successive governments have made significant cuts to local services and welfare budgets, and homelessness and youth unemployment have soared. During this time, youth services have been disproportionately affected, either closed down or severely cut back in most areas of the country (Barton and Edgington, 2014; Taylor, 2015). These cuts tend to be targeted at open access forms of provision, leading to redundancies and the widespread closure of youth clubs (Cabinet Office, 2014; Unison, 2014b). Since 2010, there has been a steady stream of increasingly familiar stories, such as this one:

> Devon County Council is considering slashing its youth service budget by nearly £1m. ... The council's 34 youth centres could be outsourced to community and voluntary groups. The council said in a statement the 'fundamental change' in the youth service was 'aimed at early help and prevention ... This targeted approach means the county council would no longer manage or run more traditional centre-based activities aimed at universal support for all youngsters.' (BBC, 2014)

The Devon example is typical in the scale of its cuts, the refocusing on targeted rather than open access work, and the exclusion of young people from decisions that affect their lives:

> It was a 'sad day for democracy' as young people were stopped from speaking at Devon County Council's budget meeting yesterday, a North Devon councillor said ... The group was left downtrodden when councillors voted against them having their say. They were there protesting against a consultation which is proposing to close 34 youth centres across Devon. (*North Devon Journal*, 2014)

Such dramatic spending cuts form a demoralising backdrop to contemporary discussions of youth work in England. Even if some cuts and closures are reversed, the current period of disinvestment will leave a legacy of loss. The infrastructure of local government youth services that has existed for over sixty years was often fragile, but has now been shattered. Decades-old local voluntary sector organisations have been forced to close or drastically reduce their services, leaving gaps in the lives of young people and communities at a time when their services are most needed.

As well as recognising the significance of the spending cuts, this chapter also focuses on the underlying marketisation of youth work: the trend towards market mechanisms and values in youth work organisations and the accompanying move towards targeted and individualised youth support, which can more easily 'prove' its worth in a marketplace. Market mechanisms and values are coded as enterprise and 'choice'; this rhetoric tells us that we can all be successful if we knuckle down, take risks, network, improve ourselves and aim for the top. The implicit message here is that we have only ourselves to blame if anything goes wrong. This is clearly demonstrated in the demonisation of the welfare state, in which the idea of welfare as a universal good has given way to a very different image of benefit cheats and feckless people avoiding a hard day's work. These ideas are promoted by politicians who celebrate 'hard-working families' and demonise 'scroungers', contrasting the 'deserving strivers' with the 'undeserving skivers' (Williams, 2013). Such discourse is a deliberate strategy on the part of the state to shape public opinion, and moves with ease from policy documents and political speeches to public discourse through the media and on the street corner (Hall and O'Shea, 2013).

In the vignette at the beginning of this chapter, I borrowed Danny's phrase 'If someone is not a success in life it's their own fault' from the official evaluation of the National Citizen Service, a summer programme for young people introduced by the Coalition government (NatCen, 2012, p 37). The proportion of young people agreeing with this statement increased after they had taken part in the 2011 programme, a result that the evaluators saw as 'encouraging' evidence of young people's feelings of control over their lives (NatCen, 2012). An alternative reading might point out that the statement locates responsibility with the individual, neglects social context, blames vulnerable people for their problems, and lacks any sense that categories of failure and success are inevitably problematic (de St Croix, 2012). I have certainly heard young people – and youth workers – saying this kind of thing, and I understand why they might do so; thoughtful and critical youth workers, however, would aim to challenge the idea that individuals are entirely responsible for their life circumstances.

The widespread cuts and closures decimating youth services also seem to carry a hint of blame, as if their loss is the fault of those involved in them. Coalition government minister Nick Hurd justified youth service cuts by saying that some of the services were 'ok to lose' because they were 'crap' (quoted in Hayes, 2013). This echoes the 'blame' discourse aimed at welfare recipients; the public sector is painted as incompetent and disposable. In contrast, 'good' modern youth workers are imagined as enterprising subjects who are creative and ambitious as they compete for contracts, inspiring young people with dreams of 'making it' as an entrepreneur.

Policy as it affects youth work today is dominated by the structural consequences of neoliberalism: 'the individualisation of everyone, the privatisation of public troubles and the requirement to make competitive choices at every turn' (Hall and O'Shea, 2013, p 12). Neoliberalism is both 'in here' and 'out there' (Peck and Tickell, 2002, p 383), seeping into the everyday lives of young people and youth workers:

> This works by neo-liberalising us, by making us enterprising and responsible, by offering us the opportunity to succeed, and by making us guilty if we do not – by making us into neo-liberal subjects enmeshed in the 'powers of freedom'. This happens not primarily through oppressions but through anxieties and opportunities, not by constraints but by incitement and measurement and comparison. This happens in mundane ways as we work on ourselves and others in conditions of 'well-regulated liberty'. (Ball, 2012, p 145; drawing on Rose, 1999, p 73)

I would like to reflect for a moment on this evocative quotation in which neoliberal governance is understood as the 'powers of freedom' (an account inspired by Foucault's theories around governmentality). The anxieties, opportunities, incitement, measurement and comparison emphasised here are conspicuous in the accounts of workers in my study and in my own practice experience, as will be discussed in this chapter. It is seductive for young people and youth workers alike to think that we are in control of our own destinies – that hard work will inevitably be rewarded with success. Theories of governmentality are vital in understanding how we are all attracted to ideas of self-efficacy, and how even people with restricted opportunities in their own lives (like Danny in the vignette) may claim that people are responsible for their own success or failure.

While acknowledging the importance of this understanding, however, I am wary of denying the role played by constraints and oppressions. Restrictive forces are all too apparent when the poorest bear the largest share of cuts (Duffy, 2014), when disproportionately heavy policing and sentencing is used against protesters and rioters (Cooper, 2012), when young people in working class and ethnically diverse areas see their clubs and projects closed (Pidd, 2013), and when grassroots youth workers are poorly paid and precariously employed. The theoretical approach in this chapter (and throughout the book) combines understandings inspired by Foucault, which usefully emphasise our own role in how we are governed, with a Gramscian interpretation of neoliberalism as a process of consent, coercion and resistance (Hall and O'Shea, 2013; Lipman, 2013). A combination of these frameworks is necessary in understanding the seductive and yet oppressive incursion of market mechanisms and values into youth work.

This chapter, then, explores both the 'freedoms' and the constraints of neoliberal marketised youth work, blending 'macro' policy analysis with a focus on the 'micro' – the everyday working lives of grassroots youth workers. The first half of the chapter analyses how the ideology of neoliberalism and the promise of enterprise have come to dominate youth work under the 2010–15 Coalition government, through the seemingly harmless rhetoric and mechanisms of the Big Society. The second half of the chapter draws on data from my research to explore four of the positions taken up (willingly or less willingly) by youth workers in this context: protesting against youth service cuts, setting up social enterprises, working in precarious circumstances and engaging in entrepreneurial forms of volunteering. The conclusion reflects on whether and how it might be possible for youth workers to challenge market values while also finding themselves implicated in them.

Youth work in the Big Society

> There are the things you do because it's your duty. Sometimes unpopular – but you do them because it is in the national interest. And yes, cutting the deficit falls into that camp. But there are the things you do because it's your passion. The things that fire you up in the morning, that drive you, that you truly believe will make a real difference to the country you love. And my great passion is building the Big Society. (Cameron, 2010)

A Coalition government came to power in the UK in 2010, led by the right-wing Conservative Party and supported by the centre-left Liberal Democrats. The Big Society was launched soon afterwards by Prime Minister David Cameron, presented as a plan to strengthen local neighbourhood groups, volunteering and social enterprise (Conservative Party, 2010). Although the idea met with widespread indifference and scepticism among the public (Anderson, 2011; Hudson, 2011), it provided a clear expression of the government's desire to save money and privatise services through a 'celebration' of the local, the entrepreneur and the volunteer. As such, it is a useful banner under which to discuss the retrenchment and marketisation that characterised youth work during the 2010–15 government term, a crucial period of change that has altered the face of youth work for decades to come.

When the Coalition government took office in 2010, most local authorities had in-house youth services that provided youth centres, street-based projects and targeted youth support, often also playing a role in supporting voluntary sector youth work and training youth workers. Most local authority youth services were formed shortly after the 1960 Albemarle Report (Ministry of Education, 1960; Davies, 1999a, 1999b). In five short years of Coalition government, many were dissolved or changed beyond recognition. A government survey confirmed that 10% of councils had no youth service team whatsoever by 2014 (Cabinet Office, 2014), while those that survived were estimated to have lost around a third of their funding (Barton and Edgington, 2014). Some councils contracted out entire youth services to private or large voluntary sector providers, while others disposed of open access provision such as youth clubs while (at least initially) keeping targeted youth support in-house.

In this context, neighbourhood youth clubs were often the first to go (Williams, 2011). One fifth of councils said they planned to close *all* of their clubs or transfer them to external providers (Pidd, 2013) and four fifths predicted that little or none of their youth service budget would be spent on open access youth work within three years (Cabinet Office, 2014, p 15–16). This loss of open access youth work does not demonstrate its lack of importance but rather its unprofitable nature. Often working with small and changing groups, and led by young people's rather than adults' agendas, open access youth work is difficult to convert to a market system. Anti-oppressive projects working with young women and black, disabled and LGBT young people are in a similarly precarious position (Lepper, 2015). In a market system, 'successful' youth work is that which can prove its potential to make good returns on investment (whether state, private or charitable). This marks a distinctive shift to governance by financial investment rather than through a welfare state (Youdell and McGimpsey, 2015).

The celebration of market values and the valorisation of enterprise in contemporary youth policy represents continuity as well as change. Enterprise was presented as an economic necessity by the 1980s Thatcher administration, and youth workers at that time were funded by employment creation schemes to contribute to the 'construction of the respectable, patriarchal, entrepreneurial subject' (Hall, 1988, p 8; see also Ingram, 1987). From 1997, New Labour continued the Conservative Party's post-welfare project of aligning policy with capitalist values, albeit with some elements of social democracy (Gewirtz, 2002). In youth work settings this meant more funding, although resources were concentrated on individualised, short-term and 'diversionary' youth work, to the detriment of open access clubs, girls' work and anti-racist projects (Davies and Merton, 2009, 2010). Private companies began to enter the field, and charities and local authorities increasingly adopted methods and attitudes from the business world.

The current phase of what might be termed neoliberal youth work, then, goes back at least three decades.

Neoliberal youth policy

Neoliberalism can be summed up as an almost religious ideology in which the private and the market are necessarily good, and the public is seen as bad (Apple, 2013). In practice, it is both complex and contested; its contours vary in place and time and it is 'neither monolithic in form nor universal in effect' (Peck and Tickell, 2002, p 384). Its dynamism is one of the factors in its success, which means it can be supported by a broad-based alliance of pro-market, traditional conservative authoritarian and managerialist interests, with enough social democracy thrown in to retain widespread consent (Hall, 1988; Gewirtz, 2002).

Emphasising maximum market freedom and low taxation, neoliberalism is often associated with a small state; but a small state should not imply a weak one. As Wacquant (2013, p 8) argues, neoliberalism entails 'the construction of a strong state capable of effectively countering social recalcitrance to commodification and of culturally shaping subjectivities conforming to it'. Neoliberal states play a vital role in creating the conditions for capitalism, acting as both 'regulator and market-maker' (Ball, 2012, p 15), while ensuring strong social control through policing, the military, prisons, border control, surveillance, anti-protest laws and the weakening of trade unions. These authoritarian elements of the neoliberal state are themselves created as markets (Davis, 2005). Even policy-making itself is an opportunity for profit (Ball, 2012); for example, management consultancy firm PricewaterhouseCoopers (2006) played a key role in youth policy by recommending the outsourcing of youth services. Through such changes the state becomes smaller and 'at the same time more extensive, intrusive, surveillant and centred' (Ball, 2008a, p 202).

The neoliberal state's interest in education and youth policy is primarily economic: the training of creative and compliant workers, the promoting and normalising of entrepreneurial values and thinking among young people, and the outsourcing of education and youth services. This was apparent in New Labour's brand of neoliberal youth work, which was directed towards social control and diversionary activities, made somewhat measurable and comparable through a crude system of outcomes and targets (see Chapter 4), and run by charities and local authorities that operated as if they were businesses. The Coalition government slashed funding (apart from its investment in the National Citizen Service) and moved further and faster in the structural and ideological privatisation of youth work. Whereas there was little or no private sector presence in youth services a decade ago (PricewaterhouseCoopers, 2006), the market is now firmly embedded in both policy and discourse.

The words 'enterprising' and 'entrepreneurial' crop up repeatedly in policy documents, suggesting that youth workers are required to become skilled mediators and advocates of a market system. Youth workers today must be 'entrepreneurial and responsive' (House of Commons Education Committee, 2011b, p 17), able to 'articulate clearly to commissioners the impact of the services they provide and be enterprising in seeking opportunities to replicate their proven practice' (DfE, 2011, p 16). The government told local authorities to commission out youth services rather than continuing to provide their own, and encouraged employees 'to spin out into independent enterprises' (House of Commons Education Committee, 2011b, p 17). In Kensington and Chelsea, for example, youth workers avoided redundancy by agreeing in 2014 to leave the local authority and set up a public service mutual; in return they were guaranteed funding for five years, after which they will be required to compete with other organisations (RBKC, 2014). The extensive programme of cuts forms an almost hidden backdrop to the more positive rhetoric of enterprise that is foregrounded in policy documents, but which serves in every case to justify and accelerate change.

Changing structures

Writing about youth work some 30 years ago, Bolger and Scott (1984) noted that,

> A very prominent contemporary argument seeks to legitimate the bleeding away of hard won state-funded welfare. In its place will come the volunteer and the commercial entrepreneur.

This prescient quotation emphasises a long-term erosion of the post-war welfare settlement, and could easily be used in relation to changes that took place under the guise of David Cameron's Big Society. The Big Society ostensibly focused on volunteering and community activity, but was explicitly underpinned by the idea that 'the state has become too big and is crowding out private sector interests' (Higham, 2014, p 122). Policy rhetoric emphasised the idea of neighbours looking after their own services, but in reality it was large businesses that benefited from the Big Society while voluntary sector groups lost out (Civil Exchange, 2013). As local authority youth services were decimated, volunteers were expected to plug the gaps (Davies, 2014). This may not have been a realistic aspiration, as M.G. Khan eloquently points out:

> Now, the Big Society volunteer is expected to run the youth centre, the library, the school, the hospital, the parish or ward council, the neighbourhood watch, as well as any housing association they may be connected to ... But how many Big Society volunteers will come back to a youth club where they have been told, in no uncertain terms, to 'fuck off' the week before by a young person? (Khan, 2013, p 3)

Whether youth clubs are run by paid workers or volunteers, there has been a substantial shift in what a youth work organisation looks like and how it is constituted. The movement away from local authority youth services and the voluntary sector has created a growing number of overlapping categories, and as I pursued my research, the lines between private and public were difficult to discern:

> When I look at the websites of youth organisations it is often unclear whether they are charities or businesses, 'for profit' or 'not for profit'. They aim for branding that marks them out as unique, but they all look rather similar: professional logos, consistent colour schemes, and arty photographs of visibly 'diverse' groups of young people doing the kinds of activities you would see on a corporate team-building day (often climbing, jumping or building something – clichéd images of upward progress). Reading on, they all seem to do 'innovative' work with 'vulnerable' or 'disadvantaged' young people, and 'encourage them to succeed' by 'delivering programmes' focused on 'enterprise and employability'. There are sections on 'investment opportunities', 'corporate fundraising' and 'our youth enterprises'. There are headshots of 'our directors' (white men with snappy biographies emphasising their business credentials) and 'our team' (managers always more numerous and visible than frontline staff). Whether charities or private companies, today's youth work organisations portray themselves as dynamic, forward-thinking and business-like. (Research diary, March 2014)

As Ball (2012, p 71) argues, 'Traditional lines and demarcations, public and private, market and state, are being breached and blended in all of this and are no longer useful analytically as free-standing descriptions.' Diversification is not neutral and the direction of travel is clearly towards a social investment model, to which end the Coalition government commissioned the Young Foundation to 'assess the youth sector social market', recommending the increased use of social finance products: '"soft" loans at sub-commercial rates or very long repayment terms; as well as riskier products that mimic equity, like loans with performance-related interest' (Young Foundation, 2011, p 3).

Outsourcing giant Serco became a dominant player in the field through its short-lived involvement in the National Citizen Service (Puffett, 2012b), while large national charities acted as 'predators' and undercut established neighbourhood youth organisations to win local authority contracts (Bell et al, 2013). Charities are 'increasingly difficult to distinguish from the commercial enterprises whose forms and practices they have adopted' (Rochester, 2013, p 85): they merge and form consortia, spend large proportions of their income on managerial staff, institute target-setting and staff appraisal systems, compete for quality marks, and place youth workers on lower wages and insecure contracts. Such changes require a new language:

> Those who lead voluntary agencies became known as 'chief executives', their committees of management were increasingly referred to as 'boards', and, in an attempt to respond to calls for them to be more 'business-like', they increasingly saw themselves as businesses and their beneficiaries and funders as 'customers'. (Rochester, 2013, p 5)

In youth work, as in the wider education field, 'the boundaries between government and state, public and private, processes and results, common wealth and individual profit, charity and benefit, are made increasingly indistinguishable' (Olmedo, 2013, p 6). While youth work is not a 'pure market economy' as such, many of the principles, practices and ideologies of the market are normalised and increasingly taken for granted.

These developments are particularly visible in the development of the National Citizen Service (NCS), a flagship policy of the Big Society that constituted the Coalition government's main investment in youth services at a time when established youth services were being cut and closed down. The NCS was presented as David Cameron's vision for an updated national service, inspired by his experiences at Eton where he took part in the cadets and visited elderly people (Winnett and Kirkup, 2010). Intended to promote 'British values', it takes the form of a short summer programme of team-building and social action for school leavers (Booth et al, 2014). Young people and youth workers have enjoyed taking part, but understood in its wider policy context the NCS represents an insidious attack on youth work (de St Croix, 2011). It has been criticised for its high per-person cost at a time of cuts to cheaper year-round provision for all young people (House of Commons Education Committee, 2011a; Hillier, 2013) and yet is cited by ministers as proof of the government's support for young people and youth activities:

> We passionately believe in the value of youth services for young people. That is why we have developed the National Citizen Service, which has an evidence base to support the value that it gives to young people. (Hurd, 2014)

The 'evidence base' mentioned here is key: it is an essential aspect of making work with young people legible in the market. Using quantitative evaluation, social research company NatCen (2012, 2013) assessed statistically significant impact and used this to monetise the effects of the NCS, estimating its 'social value' at between 1.5 to 2.8 times its cost. NatCen calculated this figure by adding up the 'value' of young people's volunteering at £3.68 per hour, and projected additional earnings as a result of increased confidence in teamwork, improved communication and leadership, and greater take-up of educational opportunities (NatCen, 2013, p 44). The inclusion of the latter, valued at up to £46.3 million, is somewhat perplexing given that there was no statistically significant impact from the programme on the proportion of participants intending to study and neither was there evidence among the previous year's participants to show an increased uptake of educational opportunities (NatCen, 2013, pp 36, 47).

However dubious the calculations, the monetised NCS becomes a market opportunity (Hillier, 2012a) and thus a mechanism for privatisation. Public sector youth services were not invited to tender for the NCS, and contracts were awarded only to private and voluntary sector organisations. The lead provider for the first two years was the Challenge Network, which has strong links to the government's first Big Society advisor Nat Wei and was set up specifically for the purpose of running NCS (Mahadeven, 2009). Although registered as a charity, the Challenge Network is led by corporate managers from companies including Poundland, McKinsey, Rio Tinto and Deloitte (Challenge Network, undated). The Challenge retained substantial contracts in the 2012 round of tendering, but the largest number was won by a consortium led by the multimillion pound company Serco (Hillier, 2012b).

The shadow state

The involvement of Serco in the National Citizen Service illustrates that youth services have become a potentially profitable market (although perhaps not profitable enough, as Serco pulled out of the NCS after its first two-year term). Two thirds of Serco's international income comes from UK government contracts (National Audit Office, 2013) but its activities are difficult to research: 'its contracts with government are subject to what's known as "commercial confidentiality" and as a private firm it's not open to Freedom of Information requests' (Harris, 2013). We do know, however, that it has been accused of beating refugees (Corporate Watch, 2012), fraudulently charging for electronically tagging offenders who were dead or in prison (Farrell, 2014), locking up prisoners all day without exercise, and falsifying data for its GP management services (Harris, 2013). Despite these concerns, established youth work networks and large voluntary sector organisations – including the National Youth Agency, UK Youth and Catch 22 – were willing to work in partnership with this company to deliver the NCS (Hillier, 2012b).

The government spends £187 billion annually on private sector contractors (National Audit Office, 2013, p 8), much of which is spent with 'strategic suppliers', including Serco, Atos, Capita and Group 4. Unaccountable profit-making firms continue to dominate the UK's public sector even after numerous scandals, bringing the idea of democracy into question:

> A 'shadow state' is emerging, where a small number of companies have large and complex stakes in public service markets, and a great deal of control over how they work. Transparency and genuine accountability are lacking ... It has left the Government buying services in a market and using contracts that are far too heavily weighted in favour of the companies they are buying from, and their shareholders. (Williams, 2012, p 5)

Within a short time period under the Coalition government, services for young people were made marketable through the disposal of unprofitable youth clubs and their replacement by programmes that can be converted into a calculable return on investment. As already noted, the direction of change is not new; local authorities and charities have been using business methods and moving from open access to targeted youth work for some years (Davies, 2013). Neither has change been total: during my research I encountered local authorities and voluntary organisations that continue to value youth clubs, street-based work and empowerment groups. However, recent years have seen a marked acceleration in market values and processes through the involvement of the profit-making private sector. McGimpsey (2013) has argued that youth services have entered a new phase, characterised by a focus on measureable returns on investment. Enterprise has become the key word for the provision of public services:

> How do we make this country a really brilliant place for setting up a new charity, a new social enterprise, for opening up the provision of public services? ... It's actually enterprise, it's entrepreneurship that is going to make this agenda work. (Cameron, 2011)

The message seems to be that it does not matter who runs services as long as they are entrepreneurial! And this message does not come only from central government; a very similar language is employed by local authorities, including those run by the centre-left Labour Party:

> Are you an entrepreneurial, commercially-minded service provider who understands young people and is interested in working with them to create exciting, new and innovative out-of-school opportunities to support their journey through adolescence and into successful adult life? Are you able to re-imagine the use of high quality, inspirational youth buildings for other commercial purposes...? ... The council will make available leases on its flagship buildings and will make available initial revenue funding for the provision of an offer for young people. (Islington Council, 2014)

The language of entrepreneurialism is becoming hegemonic in discussions of youth services. There is little contestation around the commodification of youth work, although it is challenged by the campaign network In Defence of Youth Work, the trade unions, the Choose Youth campaign, and local struggles. In contrast, most national youth work bodies seem to have embraced the market (Davies, 2013). For example, the National Council for Voluntary Youth Services (NCVYS), an umbrella body for voluntary sector youth organisations, is coordinating efforts to establish a social finance retailer to pilot evidence-based social investment (Davies, 2014). More prosaically, NCVYS's allegiances are shown in the contents of its regular funding updates sent out to members: for example, one bulletin chosen at random included information about bidding for a contract to run a prison, and details on funding from Starbucks and Virgin (NCVYS, 2014). Other youth organisations openly celebrate their relationships with Barclays (Taylor, 2012) and Microsoft (Puffett, 2012a).

The marketisation of youth work reinforces inequalities and removes young people's access to spaces, opportunities, and supportive, caring adults. Youth clubs and street-based youth work are most often located in disadvantaged neighbourhoods, used and staffed predominantly by working-class and black and minority ethnic workers (Pidd, 2013; Lepper, 2015). In many places these clubs have gone, leaving only a short and over-priced National Citizen Service summer programme for school leavers, and a range of social intervention projects run by private sector providers and 'empire-building national voluntary organisations' (Davies, 2013, p 14). These changes are underpinned by an individualising discourse of enterprise, crudely illustrated by the government's partnership with Virgin Money, which encourages primary school children to start their own business with a £5 loan (BIS, 2014). Current youth policy exhorts young people and youth workers to be ambitious, to take risks, and to overlook structural inequalities and social context. However powerful the dominant discourse, however, it can never entirely capture people's thoughts and actions, as will be demonstrated throughout the second half of this chapter.

Navigating the youth work market

If we are interested in how policy is played out in real life settings, it is important to explore how youth workers experience the marketisation of youth work at the level of everyday practice. Many of the youth workers I interviewed were well aware of market influences, speaking critically about their organisations behaving like businesses, embodying business values, and treating young people as money or numbers. One youth worker, for example, commented on the appearance and 'feeling' of the place he worked in:

'I'm in a very corporate environment ... It's young people-friendly in terms of jazzy colours on the walls ... but it still is a corporate building. You still walk past a receptionist to come in. ... It is not accessible after five if you don't have a fob. There's no intercom to the office so you have to have someone on the door, you know what I mean, it doesn't function as a youth club; it couldn't function as a youth club, so it's in an office environment which is – it's not the best, really.' (Mark)

Mark calls up the idea of a 'youth club', an environment he has experienced both as a young person and (in the past) as a practitioner, and contrasts this with the corporate nature of his current working environment. In various ways, the marketised direction of youth policy was tangible in the diverse settings I visited, heard about and worked in during the study. Whether or not we are critical of such changes, we are both involved and implicated:

> We are 'reformed' by neo-liberalism, made into different kinds of educational workers ... At its most visceral and intimate, neo-liberalism involves the transformation of social relations into calculabilities and exchanges, that is into the market form, and thus the commodification of educational practice ... Neo-liberal technologies work on us to produce 'docile and productive'... bodies, and responsible and enterprising ... selves. (Ball, 2012, p 29)

This does not mean that policy implementation is always successful or that it goes unchallenged, as Ball himself argues elsewhere (Ball and Olmedo, 2013). The workers in my study could be described as 'reluctantly implicated in the market' (Gewirtz, 2002:56); most of them overtly questioned the commodification of their work and of young people:

Mickie: Young people have a monetary value, and it's like, 'how much can we stop them causing us to pay for things, so how much can we get a better return on our investment in these young people?'

Arimas: It's a transaction, a business transaction.

Nicola: ... Even youth workers are doing it though; they're writing books going, 'It will cost you £750 a year, for one person, in this [youth] service, or £2,000 in prison.' Do you know what I mean? We're making them horrible comparisons!

Over the next pages I will explore some of the positions grassroots youth workers take up in this context – protesting, enterprising, working precariously and volunteering – to explore how youth workers navigate the youth work market, and to understand how neoliberalism is created, experienced and resisted in local situations.

Protesting

During the course of my research, young people and youth workers came together with inspiring energy to oppose youth service cuts and closures, both locally and nationally (Taylor, 2010; Nicholls, 2012). However, organised protest was not a focus of this study and I did not set out deliberately to interview youth work activists. Only a small number of the workers I interviewed had been involved in protest, the most active probably being Louise, a street-based and youth club volunteer who took part in a campaign to save her local youth service from closure.

As a volunteer, Louise felt she had more freedom to protest than her paid colleagues, who had been warned by management not to take part, or even to inform young people about the threat to their youth clubs:

> 'In my head I think, well I don't have a contract and you're not paying me, so really I could possibly bend the rules and it doesn't really matter. And at the moment there are a lot of things people are saying you shouldn't do, like protesting for example: "You shouldn't do this because you're a council employee." And therefore they have been told if they are caught protesting in work time ... then it can be classed as a disciplinary. ... So they've been told not to. They've also been told not to tell the young people. ... Not get them involved in any of the protests, because a lot of the young people have been coming to the protests. One youth club had leaflets, anti-cuts leaflets, in their youth centre, and a manager came and told them they had to take the leaflets away.'

Louise's colleagues were not allowed in the council chamber when the cuts were debated, and were ordered not to get involved in the campaign or speak to the media, even outside of work time. If this is representative of other youth services (and anecdotal evidence suggests that it probably is), Louise's account helps to explain why protests against youth service cuts have been limited:

> 'They all had serious talkings to and, because everyone's fighting for their jobs, it's kind of like, well, it's like blackmail isn't it? ... It got people scared I think.'

On launching his Big Society agenda, Cameron (2010) said, 'We need to create communities with oomph – neighbourhoods who are in charge of their own destiny, who feel if they club together and get involved they can shape the world around them.' This seems inconsistent with threatening workers with disciplinary action if they attempt to be 'in charge of their own destiny', and especially with preventing them from giving young people information which might enable them to 'shape the world around them'. Perhaps aspirations for 'communities with oomph' are aimed at *certain kinds* of neighbourhoods, and *particular forms* of community involvement. Louise told me about a nearby village where the situation was very different, and youth workers were *not* prevented from telling young people about the cuts:

> 'There's a lot of important people that live in [village] that've got money, so they've got backing so they're lucky. Whereas other places like [social housing estate], well there's no funding, there's no rich people that live in [the estate] that are gonna say, "Here's a big pot of money." ... [The council] knew that there's people there with money that would sort it out and that the village will run it themselves; they knew that would happen and that's exactly what's happened.'

Here, the wealthy village behaved as an exemplary Big Society community, fundraising and finding volunteers to keep their youth club open. In the nearby poor and ethnically diverse social housing estate, young people and residents were *prevented* from taking action through a lack of information and threats from management. It is hardly surprising, perhaps, that an audit concluded that 'the Big Society is healthiest in affluent and rural communities' (Civil Exchange, 2013, p 8). Fundraising and volunteering are presented as the only legitimate responses to cuts, whereas potential protestors are intimidated, as this blogger reported:

> I gather from local youth and community workers today that the protest outside Cameron's Witney office on Dec 10th is organised through a facebook group set up by a 12yr old young man who wanted to get his mates to support him in protesting peacefully about the closure of the youth club in his area ... I'm told that police officers visited the young man this week at his school ... They warned him that he would be held responsible if there was any trouble at the event and that the protest must not cause any obstruction. They said that he should be aware that if Cameron attended he would have armed guards with him. The young man was apparently (and not surprisingly) very shaken by this experience. (Steph, comment on blog post at IDYW, 2010)

Like the *North Devon Journal* article quoted at the beginning of this chapter, which documents young people being prevented from speaking at a council meeting, this is an example of 'governance by exclusion' (Lipman, 2013). It is not only that 'some communities will be better placed than others to make the Big Society vision a reality' (Commission on Big Society, 2011, p 6), it is that policy versions of local action seem to preclude long-standing traditions of campaigning and protesting for one's own community. Those workers who protest are threatened and isolated, and this is a particular problem when work – and even volunteering – is highly precarious. For this reason, and others, there has sometimes appeared to be a lack of visible opposition to the closure of youth services:

> 'In [city] the youth service just got absolutely disestablished, just ripped apart; you wouldn't even have known it really. I was going to marches in London, and saying "How many people are coming?" "Oh, I can't be arsed with that." No one done it, no one comes together. We say it, but no one actually does it.' (Mark)

Market processes act to diminish the effectiveness of strikes, protests and the refusal of dubious funding sources, as competition for diminishing pots of money undermines unity and solidarity between organisations:

> 'I think we've got to be more hopeful ... make a stand, and make other people make a stand ... I just think ... someone's gonna break it. They're doing the whole divide and rule thing ... We're voluntary, we're a charity, we're small and

we're doing this. And then Catch 22 [a large national youth charity] are there and they've got a million young people and they've got centres everywhere and they're always gonna be the ones that break it. But you've got to find enough people that will stand with you.' (Nicola)

Politically motivated youth workers fear that their potential action will be undermined by colleagues who are too scared or too pessimistic to act, especially in a context where larger organisations are always ready to swoop in and gain contracts. My own experience of protesting against youth service cuts seemed to bear out these concerns:

> Today we demonstrated against the 'reorganisation' of a local youth service which will see youth clubs shut, half of all posts deleted, and remaining employees moved to generic caseworker posts. We had feared the demonstration would be small but the turn-out is still disappointing – around 25 of us. We stood with our banners outside the town hall, feeling somewhat downhearted. No other youth workers turned up – not even the ones who had helped plan this demonstration! – and nobody who works for the youth service is here. Perhaps they have been warned not to come, or perhaps (understandably) they might be worried that they would be even more likely to lose their jobs if they are seen as trouble-makers. (Research diary, 2011)

Louise's story proves that resistance is possible, although it also shows that the possibilities are constrained – particularly for workers employed by local authorities. Most of the workers I interviewed had not been involved in a sustained campaign against youth service cuts. Despite this, however, nearly all of the interviewees were critical of the direction that youth work seemed to be going in.

Enterprising

While protesting is squeezed out, enterprise is celebrated. However, these are not necessarily polar opposites, and Sarah's story illustrates some of the tensions involved in entrepreneurial youth work. She began her working life in administration and became a youth worker through a university access course, but struggled to find a job where she could develop work that was based on young people's needs rather than on funding priorities. Her first significant youth work role was with a social housing provider where she said she found the work 'too structured, too curriculum based and everything's got to fit into a box'. She then moved on to a charity that ran youth clubs on behalf of the local authority, but the charity seemed to be moving in a similar direction:

> 'They started going for all the government contracts ... It was basically accredited training, bums on seats, let's get paid for numbers. And I just couldn't do it. I really, I just felt really bad for the young people. I felt I wasn't doing what I was trained to do, what I wanted to do, what I felt passionate about. So that's why I left and started the business.'

Sarah and her colleague went independent, setting up a youth work business in the borough where Sarah had grown up. This ostensible entrepreneurialism was far from being a move in favour of market values; instead it was a way of gaining autonomy and moving away from the income-oriented approaches that have come to dominate youth work (IDYW, 2011; Davies, 2013). However, there is an inevitable paradox of using a business model to challenge the marketised direction of youth work, and this tension was clearly apparent to Sarah:

> 'I started it with a business partner. I hate the word business partner because like I said before, there's no room for business in youth work, but yeah, we kind of had this idea, "Let's go back to basics, have a community group, meet the needs of the young people we work with, great ideas, let's do this!" ... We moved into a centre for start-up organisations, and the local small business centre jumped on board and went, "Yep, we'll help you with business plan, market strategy and financial strategies," and we was like [uncertainly] "Okaaay, great" [laughs]. So we kind of fell into it. And then we got the local recognition, we got the business awards. But at the back of my mind it was niggling me that we're going down a business route, we're going down a business route; we're losing our grassroots. And like, if I wore a suit the young people would say to me, "Who's in court today? Who are you going to court with?" And I'd be like, "Well no, I'm going to a networking meeting" [laughs]. And they were kind of like, "Huh? Why haven't you got your tracksuit on? You look different."'

Contrasting the ideas of community and grassroots with those of business and market, Sarah is clearly ambivalent about her new entrepreneurial identity, and this ambivalence is embodied in how she presents herself, even in the clothes she wears. Her 'business self' sits reasonably comfortably with her base in an enterprise centre, her business awards and her business suit; however, she also needs to maintain her tracksuit-wearing youth worker identity, for her own sake and to continue to relate well to young people. At different times in our conversation Sarah spoke about the visceral, material and linguistic juggling that was required and how she drew on her past experience as a business administrator:

> 'I'm glad I did have that working business sense because it's helped me to do what I do, and it's helped me with the admin side of doing what I do. It's helped me to be able to throw on a suit, go to a meeting, and articulate what I want to do in the way that they need to hear it and in the way that I'll get the funding. So even though [with] young people I'll talk slang [laughs] but when it comes to being able to achieve my goals I can kind of switch heads and step into different shoes to meet what I need to do, basically. But it is hard to juggle the two.'

Sarah's 'working business sense' informs her conception of business that is about hard work rather than profit. This seems to link to her background as a local person of working class and dual heritage, which not only helps her to 'empathise with young people', but also contributes to her ability to juggle the ethics and identities of business and youth work:

> 'I didn't have the best of the best; I didn't have a silver spoon. It was kind of, come from a single-parent family, make ends meet, was working from age 13; besides having my children I have worked all my life, from 13, all my life.'

Sarah is an accomplished social entrepreneur. She left a stable job to start an exciting and risky new venture, and has achieved recognition and success in the business world. And yet, she also challenges the neoliberal version of the entrepreneurial ideal. Her approach is based on open democratic youth work rather than targeted work with monetised outcomes, and she constantly questions business values and language. She has created a governing board made up entirely of young people and set up a youth forum that campaigns against housing policy. Some of this more overtly political work is enabled by the independent nature of her organisation, although funding is inevitably hard to find:

> 'I think the pros are that we're not governed by red tape. If we want to do something, we'll do it [laughs]. Obviously we have to make sure it's safe and [pause] we have to kind of have some kind of structure to be known, "Right, this is a formal group; we're not just messing around, we are actually, we're in it for the long haul." So the pros are kind of that we can do what we want to do. The cons are funding. You *need* money to be able to do a lot of the things that you want to do. And especially if you're gonna go into kind of political challenges, nobody wants to fund political stuff; nobody wants to get involved with that. If you're challenging a lot of the local authority services, they're not gonna fund you to do that.'

While there is a valid argument against the incursion of private companies into public services, it is important to differentiate between grassroots enterprises like Sarah's and multimillion pound companies like Serco. Sarah's story demonstrates that those who choose to follow a business route are not necessarily willing neoliberal entrepreneurs; forming a social enterprise with a critical agenda can be seen as an act of resistance. It is questionable whether social enterprises are intrinsically less ethical than charities or local government, which themselves are increasingly configured as if they were businesses. And yet, the normalisation of business in the wider youth work field is partly brought about through the 'acceptable' face of social enterprise, which perhaps pushes youth work further and faster in the direction of commodification, normalising privatisation.

However idealistic they might be, grassroots social enterprises are no panacea. Their work with young people is funded according to the logic of profit; distasteful compromises may need to be made in order to buy the space for open access youth work; and youth workers bear the risk, receiving ever lower wages on insecure or non-existent contracts. For example, Sarah's business pays her only for 17 hours a week on minimum wage, and she works much longer hours for no additional pay. However, these disadvantages – insecurity, precarious and low paid employment, dilemmas around funding and contracts, worries about role and identity – are by no means unique to social enterprises.

Working precariously

A survey of nearly three thousand community and voluntary sector workers found that 5% have more than four jobs at a time, 9% are on zero-hour contracts and 24% do not receive the living wage, identified by poverty groups as the minimum income needed to cover basic living costs (Unison, 2014a). Nationally negotiated Joint Negotiating Committee (JNC) pay scales for youth workers have been falling in real terms for many years (CYWU, 2013, p 6) and seem to be increasingly under threat. Many of the part-time workers I interviewed were not employed on these recommended terms and conditions in any case. Instead, organisations are relying increasingly on volunteers and unpaid interns, filling the gaps with employment agency workers classified as 'self-employed'.

The term 'precarious labour' refers to 'all possible shapes of unsure, not guaranteed, flexible exploitation: from illegalised, seasonal and temporary employment to homework, flex- and temp-work to subcontractors, freelancers or so-called self-employed persons' (Neilson and Rossiter, 2005). The workers and volunteers who took part in my research could be seen as working in precarious situations: those who were paid could not rely on the longevity of their jobs, while organisations had less capacity to take on and support volunteers, and voluntary work was becoming less likely to lead to a paid job. For decades, part-time youth workers have patched together several different jobs to make ends meet (Bolger and Scott, 1984), and yet stable part-time jobs were previously available in local authorities and (to some extent) in the voluntary sector. Today conditions are becoming ever more challenging and exploitative. Precarious labour is an equality issue, given that part-time youth workers disproportionately come from socially disadvantaged groups (Mellor and McDonnell, 2010). It is also a serious challenge to the idea of youth work as a long-term career in its own right.

This section focuses on the situations of three part-time workers who seemed to be facing particularly insecure employment conditions. Research participants Zandra (black working class), Keiron (black working class) and Diana (white working class) all came across as particularly enthusiastic, caring and thoughtful youth workers, each with several years of youth work experience, and all relying on youth work for their entire income. Their low income and lack of job security is problematic for them as individuals and for their families; it is also highly problematic for the young people they work with, who cannot rely on these workers being there for them in the long term.

Zandra is a self-employed youth worker – not through choice, but because neither of the two organisations she works for employs her on a formal contract, requiring her instead to manage her own expenses, tax and National Insurance. Zandra has little of the flexibility usually associated with self-employment, and yet suffers all of its disadvantages: insecurity, unpredictable income, and lack of holiday or sick pay. One of her contracts involves working five hours per week running a youth club for a local charity. It is questionable whether this work constitutes genuine self-employed work; it involves running a regular youth work session, and Zandra cannot (for example) contract out the session to be run by somebody else. Despite working there regularly for two years, during which time her youth club achieved some of the highest attendance figures in the organisation, she feels she is shown little goodwill:

> 'I was meant to attend a first aid workshop on Monday, but then [manager] emailed me to say, "Sorry we don't pay sessional workers for training," even though it's mandatory training. ... I said to [manager], "You can't expect me to attend training and not get paid. You don't pay my sick leave, you don't pay my holiday. But training, mandatory training, you should pay me to do."'

Zandra also works 20 hours a week for a friend who is herself registered as a sole trader, supporting young people who are not in training, education or employment. The income for this work comes from a single source, a charity that wins contracts from colleges, national government and European schemes, and then subcontracts to smaller local providers. The local providers (such as Zandra's friend) are paid in arrears and only after they meet demanding performance targets. Such 'payment by results' arrangements are becoming more common in public services; instead of being funded for the work they do, providers are only paid for outcomes they can evidence (Sheil and Breidenbach-Roe, 2014). Research has shown that such contracts are particularly disadvantageous to smaller organisations, which are less insulated from the financial risk (Crowe et al, 2014); they are also particularly risky for self-employed youth workers. When contracts change or targets cannot be evidenced – for example, if a young person forgets to bring in proof of their new job or college course – neither Zandra nor her friend will be paid. This leaves Zandra as a single parent struggling to pay her bills:

'We've been cutting our hours down ... We managed to pay ourselves last week for May ... We're getting paid shit [laughs]. Rubbish. ... I probably get paid about 800 a month. ... I've gone back to basics, that's what I've done. ... My children are going through that stage though ... They want the things, I suppose.'

The problems of self-employment and 'payment by results' contracts were not unique in my research, and neither were they the only manifestations of precarious labour. In a different city, I interviewed Keiron and Diana who are studying together for a part-time youth work qualification. Both are working for a number of organisations in a variety of paid and unpaid capacities. Diana is employed as a youth worker by a charity on behalf of the local authority. The local authority has closed its youth service and no longer employs youth workers, but Diana works in a local authority building and is funded by them. She works on a six-month contract for 10 hours per week, which is inconveniently arranged as four short evening sessions. A single parent with no other income at present, Diana somehow survives on the £125 per week she is paid for this job, minus the £25 it costs her to get there.

Keiron works three evenings each week at a large youth centre (part of a chain of modern facilities set up and sponsored by a large regional company). A recent drop in numbers of young people and staff has made him feel his post may be insecure: the centre is now advertising for play workers rather than youth workers on a lower pay grade of £7.50 per hour.[1]

Keiron: A lot of people are disheartened about the playworker advertising because it's saying basically that we don't need youth workers.
Diana: Yeah. And I've applied like an idiot.
Tania: Why've you applied?
Diana: Only because of my hours and money and my social situation; you know, I have two children and I have 10 hours' work, so, I can't claim any kind of benefit on 10 hours ... And it's just a necessity ... it went against everything I believe in.

Play work is often as skilled a job as youth work, and yet has historically suffered lower wages; Keiron's employer appeared to be cutting corners by renaming job titles. In addition, overtime was no longer available for planning and preparation, and he was now required to do this work during session times while young people were present. Diana and Keiron felt that the management did not understand the impact on practice. Their managers were 'more middle class' and often had little (if any) youth work experience.

Diana: Well, to me the managers get paid far too much ...
Keiron: It's never fair, is it? We do a lot more.
Diana: More. And we're empathetic in what we do and we're passionate about it and enthusiastic. And not too bothered about money. But then it makes you frustrated because you need money to live ... People with salaries, with massive salaries and you see it's a job role and it's like the higher up you get, the less your role is but the more money you get. It doesn't make any sense. None whatsoever.
Keiron: Yeah that's true. ... They work hard to work their way up and when they do they relax. They have a nice salary now.
Diana: But *have* they worked hard to work their way up? ... I can't think of one that's been doing youth work for many, many years.

Here, Diana and Keiron challenge the idea that success (or senior roles) are necessarily the result of either experience or hard work. In contrast, they themselves were working very hard, combining several paid and voluntary roles. As if their working lives were not already precarious enough, Diana and Keiron had also worked recently for a small private company where they were promised wages that never materialised. The organisation failed to reimburse their travel expenses and did not provide adequate money for food for young people during projects and trips. The business they had worked for claimed to be non-profit, but as Diana said, 'It's definitely for profit for someone!'

> 'The professionals think ... that this is an amazing organisation, cos it's branded that way. But I don't. For me myself it's gone from being like a bad organisation to maybe being a little bit dodgy because it's like the funding that's been applied for, [projects] which we've not done ... and there's not been one pound spent on the organisation ... No drinks, no food, no nothing, no petrol money ...' (Diana)

Despite their negative experiences, Keiron and Diana remained idealistic and passionate about youth work and had been meeting with an 'innovations advisor' at a local business school, planning to start up their own company. This was motivated by their love of working with young people and their frustration with the existing youth work organisations in their area:

'Because we see these things all the time and we see so much bad practice ... we want to show that there can be a good organisation there that really cares about young people. We're not all about, you know, money and targets, like other organisations are.' (Keiron)

Echoing Sarah's motivation for setting up her social enterprise, Keiron and Diana hope to use the business model to oppose youth work oriented around money and targets.

Volunteering

Volunteers have always made up the majority of the youth workforce and continue to do so today (Davies, 1999a; Mellor and McDonnell, 2010). However, the Big Society agenda was based on the more ambitious idea that volunteers would take over and manage complex services formerly run by the state (for example, parents setting up schools, and local residents managing libraries). In youth work, this has meant that volunteers are increasingly expected to take the place of professionally trained workers in managerial as well as face-to-face roles, often without the support of professionally trained colleagues (Davies, 2013). This section presents Billie's story. Billie volunteers as a project manager and youth worker, helping to run a youth club in her local neighbourhood in a northern city. Here she outlines her role:

'I'm project managing the partnership. So Sheila, who's the head of the community association, she's the partnership manager, so she's the schmoozer; she's the one that's sort of keeping all the contacts, trying to find us a more permanent base. And I'm sort of looking out for more funding opportunities and ensuring that [the local authority monitoring database] is updated, all the monitoring's being done, paying the bills [laughs], checking CRBs,[2] checking all our volunteers are all registered.' (Billie)

From the way Billie describes her own and her colleague Sheila's roles here, they could easily be taken as professional managers in the voluntary or social enterprise sectors. They have official-sounding job titles within a stratified hierarchy, and are involved in the full range of tasks that are expected of youth work managers today. The only difference is that they are unpaid. Alongside this voluntary work, Billie works full-time for a social housing group. She is understandably tired from her dual roles, saying cheerfully, 'I'm probably going to fall asleep at my desk if I don't step back a bit.' Although she was enjoying her voluntary work, its pressure was exacerbated by the constant round of administrative activity required in relation to acquiring funding. Billie told me how the organisation had recently tendered for a contract in the local authority's commissioning process, the outcome of which was funding for their youth club for only one year. This meant that the following year's funding round was already beginning:

> 'I'm going to a consultation this afternoon ... where we're gonna discuss the upcoming commissioning funding, which is crazy because we've only just really got off the ground, and I'm already looking at next year's funding.'

Although Billie might be portrayed as a good citizen of the Big Society who wanted to do something for the young people in her area, she was also motivated by the closure of her city's youth service and was clearly no supporter of the Coalition government:

> 'The last 18 months I've just seen what a difficult time young people are having, and personally I just think they're having a shitty time to be honest and they're really marginalised ..., they've been really severely affected by the spending cuts. Seeing the end of the youth service was really sad.'

The closure of the city's youth service provided the impetus for Billie and her colleagues to start a local youth club where one had not previously existed. Unfortunately, the support and training that had previously been offered by the youth service to local voluntary youth groups were now absent:

> 'The commissioning thing has been really difficult ... Once you get the funding there's no support there, no advice. ... It's very much just, "Right, there's your money, off you go."'

This highlights the ripple effects when a local youth service is closed. The effects are felt beyond the walls of boarded-up youth clubs; there is also a dissipation of institutional knowledge, experience and resources built up over many decades. Provision becomes atomised and voluntary sector groups become competitors, bidding against each other for contracts. Those fulfilling their roles as good entrepreneurial citizens in the Big Society are unlikely to receive the support they need. This means that new opportunities are available mainly to those with existing skills and wide social networks:

> While government discourse on openness implies a level playing field, responsibilisation brings into the process of access people's differential capacity to mobilise expertise, resources and entrepreneurialism. (Higham, 2014, p 125)

These differential opportunities can be seen, to some extent, in Billie's story. According to census data published by the council, the ward in which Billie lives and volunteers ranks among the least deprived in her city. Billie herself has relatively high levels of social and cultural capital, drawn from her professional employment and university education. However, the reality is more complicated than this characterisation might suggest. The ward may be better off than some others in the city but is far from prosperous, and the youth club members are predominantly Eastern European Roma, a group that is particularly stigmatised and often excluded from services. Neither is Billie's volunteering a form of outsider middle-class do-gooding: she comes from a working-class background, has a local accent, and comes across as humble and down-to-earth.

As commissioning rounds and funding mechanisms become more complex, volunteers need to develop managerial skills and professional networks if they are to 'succeed' even in sustaining relatively small neighbourhood clubs. My own involvement in setting up a local youth workers' co-operative seems to confirm this: as a tiny and mainly volunteer-run organisation we still juggle several funding applications at any time while having to provide a variety of monitoring information for existing funders, some of which give us only a few hundred pounds a year. All of this unpaid entrepreneurial activity has clear implications for equality at a time when youth services are being closed.

For all their faults, youth services once had the infrastructure and experience to support and train local people, of whom many were working class, black and disabled, to employ them on appropriate professional salaries, and to support them through local qualifications and university. This infrastructure has been replaced by a fuzzy notion of enterprise, which seems to transfer the risk and responsibility from

49

elected state bodies to individuals and communities. In entrepreneurial times, 'successful' small youth organisations might only employ one or two part-time youth workers on minimum wage (such as in Sarah's story), or sustain an organisation on voluntary labour (as in Billie's story), while any substantial funding is most likely to go to large private or charitable organisations. This shift has implications for the resourcing of services, and for the exploitation of women and working-class people:

> Public responsibilities have been shifted onto the informal sector, under the argument that the government can no longer afford the expense of such a service... it is largely the unpaid labor of women in the family and in the local communities that will be exploited to deal with the state's shedding of its previous responsibilities. (Apple, 2006, pp 24–5)

The marketisation of youth services entrenches inequalities by limiting *who* has the resources to set up a youth club and *where*, and perhaps by creating conditions where it will be difficult to survive: 'How poorly social entrepreneurs or community representatives will fare in a social market when pitted against hedge fund backed for-profit providers is predictable' (Corbett and Walker, 2013, p 461).

Conclusion

A few weeks later...

Ricky and Jo are chatting with a couple of young women by the swings, when Danny comes by and says bluntly to Ricky, 'I've been looking for you.' Jo nods and says hi but stays with the girls while Ricky walks with Danny towards the pond. Danny seems angry. 'Where've you been? You're never around anymore. We've been coming to youth club all this time and now you're working with random girls instead!' Slightly surprised, Ricky says, 'You know we can't only work with you guys; we're here for all the young people in the area.' Danny looks away, scuffing his shoes on the ground. Ricky thinks for a while and adds, 'You're right though, I know the youth club's been shut a lot and we haven't been out in the area so much. We're short staffed; it's the cuts. What's up anyway?' Danny says he's left college. He never really wanted to go and he didn't get on with his tutors. 'It's not fair,' he says, 'I've gone for about a hundred jobs and they don't even write back. Even if I got an interview I haven't got the right clothes and

I've got no money. Anyway, my face won't fit. The careers office has shut down, and now they won't take me back at college.'

Ricky sympathises; he's been looking for work too since his hours were cut, but he doesn't say anything about that now. Instead they talk through some of Danny's options and arrange to visit a job centre together. They chat about Danny's girlfriend and his football team until he starts to seem more cheerful or at least less angry. As they say 'bye, later, see ya', Ricky thinks back to what Danny said last time they met: 'If someone's not a success in life it's their own fault.' That's what the government wants us to believe, he thinks. As if there's no unemployment, no cuts, no inequalities, no poverty, no racism. Those old ideas of the deserving and undeserving poor haven't gone anywhere. He decides to talk to Jo later about whether there's something they can do other than just picking up the pieces. The trouble is they're busy, demoralised and worried about their own jobs, and it's hard just to keep going. He sighs, watching the ducks for a while before turning back towards the swings.

The rhetoric of the 'entrepreneurial, passionate self' (Kelly et al, 2013, p 11) tells us that if we fail to find a job, or if our services shut down, we only have ourselves to blame. When government ministers are calling unemployed people 'skivers', and telling youth workers that their services were 'crap' and deserved to be closed, this indicates that the government is pushing the blame for the economic failure of neoliberalism onto working class and ethnically diverse communities. Like the current Conservative government, the Coalition government traded on pre-existing sexist, racist and classist suspicions in relation to the beneficiaries and workers of the welfare state, and sold neoliberalism as a form of common sense (Hall and O'Shea, 2013).

The stories of the youth workers in this chapter echo the argument of Stephen Ball (2012) that we are all implicated in, and changed by, neoliberalism, partly through the seductions of entrepreneurialism and a resurgence in voluntary activity, which seem to offer us some hope for a 'different' way of doing things. However, these stories also suggest that neoliberal policy implementation is not only a process of 'freedom' or government by consent; it is important to recognise the elements of coercion. The majority of cuts and closures are imposed on the poorest communities, and 'it is not necessary to obtain their consent except to the extent that their resistance necessitates concessions' (Lipman, 2013, p 12).

Neoliberal governmentality involves 'the governing of populations through the production of "willing", "self-governing", entrepreneurial selves' (Ball, 2012, p 3). If the 'skiver' is the villain in the austerity tale, the social entrepreneur is the hero, whose narrative tells us that we can be creative, take risks, help our communities and pay our bills in the process. Those of us who want to change things, who want to make things better in our communities, are sold the dream that we can all 'do something incredible', in Billie's words. And perhaps we can! Some of the workers and volunteers in this chapter are attempting to use neoliberal freedoms while also critiquing them; a longer-term study would be needed to see how effective these attempts can be.

Is it possible to be a critical entrepreneur? Many of us want to believe that this juggling act is possible; that (like Sarah) we can change between the business suit and the tracksuit, or (like Diana and Keiron) that we can 'show that there can be a good organisation there that really cares about young people'. I use the word 'we' deliberately; my colleagues and I also had this dream, and set up our own small youth workers' co-operative in the face of cuts and in opposition to the outcomes agenda (see Chapter Six). Little wonder that youth workers' response to neoliberal policy is contradictory: even as we challenge the commodification of our relationships with young people, we are almost wholly entangled in these processes. However, it is important to continue to challenge, and critical engagement with entrepreneurialism is very different to a wholesale and uncritical acceptance of business values and methods in youth work.

Alternative definitions of social entrepreneurship distinguish themselves from the idea of imitating business methods and principles: 'Entrepreneurial processes are about identifying, challenging and breaking institutional patterns, to temporarily depart from norms and values in society' (Lindgren and Packendorff, 2007, p 29; translated in Bjerke and Ramo, 2011, p 23). However, such definitions of social enterprise can be problematic because they soften the harder edges of the market: 'commerce is described as art and as revolution and huge corporations are portrayed as agents of the counterculture' (Solnit, 2014, p 34). Using the tools of neoliberalism to challenge its power is inevitably a compromised form of resistance, and it will be interesting to see how today's new grassroots youth work organisations will fare over the longer term, and whether they can retain their idealistic visions.

It seems likely that youth work organisations (whether constituted as charities or businesses) will be divided by the market into two types: small, grassroots and mostly unpaid; or larger, more business-like, and run by well-paid chief executives and managers, with a cast of sessional workers on insecure contracts. What options will there be in these contexts for thoughtful and critical youth workers? One important role is to discuss such dilemmas with young people:

'I think because they're on the receiving end of services, they understand that these services are there to make money, and these [other] services are there to help me. And it's nice that should they start their own stuff in the future, they will have that understanding of, "Am I business orientated, or am I kind of sticking to my grassroots true values and principles?"... Although they all want money, they all want the latest trainers and the iPads and the iPods and whatever, but at the same time they understand that it's good to help each other, and you don't necessarily get paid for helping each other.' (Sarah)

We cannot escape the dilemmas and contradictions of the entrepreneurial society, but critical conversation can keep alive the idea of an alternative to the commodification of everything. There is an important role for thoughtful political discussion with young people and with each other: 'It is nigh impossible to exaggerate the need to be collective in the face of a neo liberal ideology that seeks to undermine the slightest hint of oppositional solidarity' (IDYW, 2014a). Collective discussion is necessary if we are to think about and act on some vital practical questions. If we accept that we are both implicated in, and critical of, the market, what does this mean for our everyday work? How can we know which compromise is a step too far? How might we resist? As Ricky wondered in the fictional passage above, can we go beyond picking up the pieces?

Such questions will be raised throughout this book – not to propose prescriptive answers, but to provide space to reflect on the experiences, thoughts and actions of part-time and volunteer youth workers who are particularly affected by worsening pay and employment conditions, and whose voices are rarely heard. Like the adult educators in Sanguinetti's (1999, pp 157–8) study, grassroots youth workers often appear:

as ethical, professional subjects who are exercising their agency in ways which at once resist, engage with and produce anew the discourse, reconstituting it in order to find new spaces to develop their own 'good practice', within and against it.

The following chapters draw on more youth workers' stories to explore further how neoliberal approaches to youth work reinforce inequalities and domination, while also considering some of the ways that youth workers resist and subvert the dominant policy environment: by prioritising love and care over financial and bureaucratic rationalities, by avoiding and challenging performative targets and outcomes, by refusing to collude in surveillance and social control, and by setting up idealistic and utopian youth organisations.

Notes

[1] Play work is a strong tradition in its own right, which overlaps to some extent with youth work. Play work tends to be aimed at children aged around 5–16 and emphasises the need for child-centred creative play, whereas youth work is generally targeted at a higher age range, around 8–19, and is usually defined as informal education. Play work has attracted even less policy recognition and funding than youth work over the years, and levels of qualification and pay rates have tended to be substantially lower.

[2] CRB (Criminal Records Bureau, now DBS – Disclosure and Barring Service) certificates show an individual's criminal record. Youth organisations are required to ensure their workers and volunteers have had these checks.

THREE

Passionate practice

> **Not just a job (1)**
>
> The sudden burst of music wakes Danny. He disentangles himself from the duvet and reaches for his phone. The voice on the other end is familiar and cheerful. 'Alright, where are you? Did I wake you up?' Danny yawns and smiles, mumbling to youth worker Ricky that he's just coming. He stretches and thinks about getting out of bed. Going to the job centre is never fun but it'll be much better to have Ricky there. Ricky's different. You can tell that being a youth worker's not just a job for him – Ricky actually cares. It might be a good day, for once.
>
> A couple of miles away, Ricky puts his phone in his pocket and eyes up the cafe opposite the job centre. Danny sounded half asleep and his 'just coming' sounded unrealistic. Never mind, he could do with a coffee anyway. Really he should be doing his own job search now they've cut his hours down, but Jo's right – he finds it easier to help young people than to help himself. He's giving up his own time to meet Danny, now that they're only paying him for his evening sessions. But he doesn't mind; this is the kind of thing that makes the job feel worthwhile, and it was a big thing when Danny accepted his offer of help. He likes him; he's a great lad. Ricky orders a coffee. His phone buzzes: a text saying, 'I'll be there in 10 mins.' He smiles and takes a seat, looking forward to the rest of the morning.

In a context where youth work is under threat from spending cuts and marketisation, it is striking that part-timers and volunteers continue to express love, passion and enjoyment for their work, and a genuine care for young people that goes beyond 'just doing their job'. Rather than taking these feelings as self-evident, this chapter explores workplace emotions in more depth – particularly those that are experienced by youth workers as positive, although some attention will also be given to more difficult or ambivalent emotions, both here and elsewhere in the book.

Passionate grassroots youth work can be seen as a desirable expression of care, vocation or calling (Jeffs, 2006), an antidote to marketised and commodified youth work. However, passion is becoming more common as a requirement or expectation in a variety of workplaces (Lazzarato, 1997). Job adverts in shop windows require applicants to demonstrate their 'passion for coffee', 'love of fashion' or 'obsession with sandwiches', and the internet is full of blogs with titles such as 'Ten ways to inspire passion in the workplace' or 'You too can turn regular employees into passionate workers'. As education and welfare work is increasingly organised on market principles, managers in reconfigured services find inspiration in 'management guru' literature that emphasises passion as a form of individual expression and profitable creativity. Passion is a valued commodity, claimed to bolster company profits and boost individuals' career prospects. This does not necessarily mean, however, that genuine passion and care can be wholly commodified or reduced to a market value.

This chapter will explore passionate practice as an intrinsic good for young people and for workers themselves, while also exploring the potential for emotional commitment to be commodified and exploited. The first section draws on interviews with grassroots youth workers where they talk about feelings of love, passion, enjoyment and care. This is followed by a discussion of theories of emotional labour and emotion management, looking at how these relate to grassroots youth workers. Finally, the chapter discusses whether and how passion might play a role in resisting current threats to youth work.

Love and passion

Tania: What do you like about it [youth work]?
Alan: [Pause] I just, I dunno, I feel comfortable with; I just really love it. I don't know. I just love it! [Laughing, shouting] I LOVE IT!

'What do I like about youth work? I just love youth work!' (Bridget)

When I asked part-time and volunteer youth workers what they liked about their work, they often answered with the word 'love'. Their accounts were suffused with displays of passion for and enjoyment of youth work, emotions that seemed strong and genuinely held, expressed not only through their words but also through the excitement in their voices and eyes. While it is important to ask critical and theoretical questions about love and passion in youth work, this chapter will first spend some time discussing emotional commitment on its own terms.

Becoming a youth worker

For many of the part-timers and volunteers in this research, their passionate commitment to work with young people is rooted in their early experiences of youth work and their motivations to become involved in this work. Some had taken part in youth projects as young people, while others felt they would have benefited from such support:

> 'I think I've always wanted to help people, and through experiences of being a young carer mainly, getting involved with young carers' support projects and a project for young people under stress ... experiencing that and seeing the kind of progress *I* made from getting involved as a young person in youth work, it just kind of firmed up that that's what I wanted to do.' (Mickie)

> 'I hated teenage years, and I wish I'd had someone there, or like a club that I went to ... I think teenage years was a really, really hard time ... and I'd really like to be good and support people going through that as well.' (Lucy)

Workers expressed their wish to make a genuine difference to young people's lives; this was not presented as coming from an outside 'do-gooder' position but as rooted in personal experience, or in a political or ethical desire to be part of something positive. Some were motivated by very difficult experiences in their own lives:

> 'I started doing voluntary work round my local area. What really got me into it was one of my best friends, they got killed ... And then it just kind of hit me, you know what? There's too many young people out here that this is happening to ... I wanted young people to have the same choices that I had – and more.' (Forde)

> 'I went to prison for a spate of time and whilst in prison took a good long look at myself and at my inner self and thought that this is just not for me and I'd like to give something back to the community. On coming out of prison I had a really, really good probation officer. And she noticed the rapport that I had with young people... She really encouraged me and pushed me forward, going into mentoring, and done a rites of passage course. Which then

spurred me into thinking, wow, maybe I can be a youth worker and a good role model for the community.' (Bridget)

This 'wow' moment was experienced by others as they started to think that they could become youth workers. Mahad met some detached (street-based) youth workers at a community event that his brother and nephew were involved in. Initially he had been reluctant to go along, but he was impressed by these workers, whom he quickly identified as being 'different':

'I just thought, let me just get this done and over with, I know they're gonna be blah, blah, blah, and I'll just leave afterwards. I went there really with that mentality and I just came back with a wow factor because they had the ideas, and the detached youth workers were really supportive, encouraging; they were giving them information on what to do, what not to do, that sort of thing, and they were just listening to them and they were taking their ideas on board. And I thought, wow, that was quite different compared to other services ... I gained a lot of motivation, a lot of passion for youth work ... I particularly liked the detached youth work, and having that different environment and different agendas every day, it just really made me passionate to take part and maybe become a detached youth worker one day.' (Mahad)

Many of the workers in this study became youth workers either through continued engagement with youth projects they had attended as young people, or as a result of almost chance encounters such as Mahad's. Laura came across youth work even more randomly, through a detached youth worker she got chatting to in a pub. Once again, the word 'wow' is prominent in this account, emphasising the positive surprise with which these individuals embraced the idea of becoming a youth worker:

'I thought it sounded fantastic. It was amazing that you actually have a profession, you actually get paid for walking around on the street, talking to the young people on their terms, on their territory; I just loved the idea of it. And I was like, how is it possible that in this society that exists? It went counter to what I think of this society or this world. And I was, wow!' (Laura)

Most of the participants in this study had been youth workers for several years by the time they were interviewed, and yet they remembered their early motivations with vivid enthusiasm. However, this should not suggest that they all enjoyed youth work immediately or felt a natural affinity with teenagers. Louise's and Lucy's first volunteering experiences were in youth clubs:

'I was sworn at *a lot*. And I cried *a lot*. My mum would always say, "Why do you keep going back there?" and I was like, "The positive weighs out the negative," and I just loved it. And in the end they go from swearing to actually being really nice to you and it was just the thing that I had to go through. So it *was* hard but I did love it.' (Louise)

'I was petrified the first time I walked through the door. Mine was at [my local youth club] and it's a bit of a rough area and I thought, oh my god, I don't know what I'm doing here. After the first day I thought, I'm not coming back, it's awful; young people are horrible. Then afterwards I was like, no, it's fun.' (Lucy)

These quotations are a reminder that youth work is not easy, and that a love for youth work is not automatic or immediate. Emotions are ambivalent and fluid: Louise and Lucy speak here of crying and being petrified, and yet very quickly move on to talk about coming to love the work and finding it fun. Emotions commonly seen as 'negative' and 'positive' are not necessarily experienced as opposites, and it could be that the transformation and challenge involved in building positive relationships from unpromising beginnings can bring particular satisfaction and enjoyment.

Care and love for young people

When workers talked about loving youth work, they also spoke with infectious emotional attachment in relation to the young people themselves. While showing awareness of the need for professional boundaries, many expressed liking and love for the young people they worked with, even for young people in general:

'I've known some of them for three years now and the way you see them grow and the way the relationship is, and I can be myself and they can be their self. I just think young people are fantastic; they're clever and they're switched on and they're fun.' (Lucy)

'I *love* working with teenagers! Love it. That's the age group that I'm most comfortable with.' (Rachel)

Several seemed particularly to enjoy working with young people who others might see as problematic:

'I like working with the challenging ones ... You get more out of it, don't you?' (Lorenzo)

'I love all my young people, even when they're all complete and utter little swear words! They're all still lovely.' (Callie)

The volunteers and part-timers in this study often emphasised what they experienced as the *genuine* and *authentic* nature of working with young people. Workers often spoke of their relationships with young people as *real*; they were not the same as friendships, but neither could they be reduced to client–professional relations:

'There's a lot of the genuineness of the relationships. I find sometimes that they're more genuine than the relationships I have with adults, or with my friends. You know, like, although that doesn't mean that I'd then be mates with the young people ... After my dad died ... I found it really difficult being around adults, but I loved being around the kids, because I knew exactly where I stood, and they knew where they stood ... there wasn't all of this constant thinking about things too much, or judging people, or analysing; it was just like, you just get on with it, you know, and I just love that.' (Alan)

Notably, the youth workers in this study never spoke of young people as clients, instead referring to them simply as 'young people', 'teenagers' or 'kids'. By making this linguistic choice they emphasise a relationship that is fundamentally human and perhaps less formal than most relationships between young people and professionals.

Beyond monetary rewards

One of the ways in which volunteers and workers articulated their commitment to youth work was by contrasting it with jobs that are done solely for financial reward. Some had given up better paid jobs to commit to youth work on a voluntary or low-paid basis:

> 'Outsiders think I'm mad. And part of it is because they don't understand why you'd go from earning money to not earning money and money isn't important to me but it is to a lot of my friends, so they don't understand that bit.' (Louise)

Several of the paid part-timers discussed their willingness to be flexible with their time and to work additional hours:

> 'If something's fun I find it quite hard to count it in my hours, so like we did the community day on Saturday, and that's supposed to be in my hours ... I probably should be claiming it back in TOIL [Time Off In Lieu] or putting in for overtime for it and I just, I, realistically I won't ... It's like, I've taken it on, I'm doing it out of choice almost.' (Alan)

> 'I come in on my days off. Because that's the only time that that meeting, or meeting that young person, could be done ... I can't on any conceivable concept say, "I need money for coming in on my day off."' (Quincie)

> 'When you've got passion for something you don't continuously look at the time or how much you're getting paid; you just get into it.' (Mahad)

These workers did not see themselves as exploited; they 'gave extra' through choice and as a result of their commitment to the work, the young people and their colleagues:

> 'I get paid for 17 hours ... And I probably put in about a fifty-hour week. So it is, it is hard. Exhausting. But I wouldn't change it.' (Sarah)

The workers' flexibility around their use of time and their expected rewards contributed to a sense of commitment, passion and enjoyment that seemed to form part of their youth work identities. At times these identities were formed in direct contrast to people in less satisfying jobs:

> 'I was seeing people that I didn't want to end up like ... just miserable old men doing the same job, day in, day out, not getting any job satisfaction ... They used to say "Nobody likes their job"... I thought, well, somebody must do. So I started looking back into youth work.' (Lorenzo)

Understanding passionate grassroots youth work

So far this chapter has included a relatively large amount of interview data to build up a picture of the passion with which grassroots youth workers discuss their work. Their positive emotions are demonstrative of a principled and value-based commitment to young people that goes beyond straightforward job satisfaction, and can perhaps be seen as a 'political ethic of care' (Taggart, 2011, p 86). This is not to suggest that emotional experiences of youth work are unstintingly positive. Emotions wavered and were often ambivalent and contradictory. The workers also talked about negative emotions, sometimes associated with challenging or upsetting situations with young people. Overwhelmingly, however, their face-to-face work with young people was expressed as enjoyable and satisfying, even when it was difficult. Dissatisfaction, anger and stress were most often expressed in relation to factors such as target cultures, spending cuts, surveillance systems and hierarchical management.

It cannot be assumed that *all* youth workers love their work. Perhaps the emphasis placed on enjoyment by those interviewed in the research might be related to their particular position as volunteers and part-timers; most of them had other interests and commitments and had *chosen* to be youth workers, so any difficulties might perhaps be more easily tolerated. They spent a greater proportion of their time directly working with young people than their managers did, and relatively less time on tedious bureaucratic tasks or stressful managerial work. In addition, it is likely that these interviewees had a stronger commitment than the average part-timer; after all, they volunteered to be interviewed about their work for no personal gain.

Despite these caveats, youth workers' passion for their work is significant. Since transcribing the interviews for this study, I have become more attuned to expressions of passion, love and enjoyment among colleagues and other youth workers, noticing that it is incredibly common for face-to-face workers to refer to youth work in these terms. Before undertaking this research I had come to take these deep positive feelings for granted, seeing the more negative aspects – the things that get in the way of youth work – as more 'interesting' for research. It is important, however, for critical researchers and practitioners to acknowledge love and passion, perhaps particularly in the present difficult circumstances. Youth workers are by no means the only welfare and education professionals who love their work in spite of inherent challenges and encroaching managerialism (see, for example, Day, 2004; Taggart, 2011), and later this chapter will ask whether passionate workplace commitment might contribute to workers' ability to resist target cultures and hierarchical management practices. First, however, it is useful for youth workers to consider how theories of emotion in the workplace – particularly emotional labour and emotion management – can help us to consider the exploitative potential of passionate youth work.

Exploited emotions?

The concept of emotional labour was first introduced by Arlie Hochschild (2003) in *The managed heart*. Originally published in 1983, this book uses ethnographic and interview material from flight attendants (airline cabin crew) to argue that service sector workers' emotions are often tightly controlled and exploited by employers. Building on Marx's analysis of how factory workers are alienated from their manual labour when it is turned into profit, Hochschild argues that service sector workers can become alienated from their emotional labour. The flight attendants in Hochschild's study were taught to boost future flight sales by smiling, being friendly and generally creating a positive emotional experience for passengers. They were trained in staying cheerful when dealing with demanding passengers and their success was closely monitored through customer feedback. Building on Goffman's (1959) analysis of how people present themselves to maintain social norms, Hochschild vividly contrasts the 'emotion work' undertaken in everyday personal life with that which is required in service sector workplaces. Her contention is that emotional work becomes exploitative once it is prescribed and controlled by an employer rather than by the individual themselves:

> Emotion work is no longer a private act, but a public act, bought on the one hand and sold on the other. Those who direct emotion work are no longer the individuals

themselves but are instead paid stage managers who select, train and supervise others. (Hochschild, 2003, pp 118–19)

Hochschild argues that emotional work in both personal and work spheres can be seen as either surface acting or deep acting. Surface acting means feeling one emotion while displaying another. This might take the form of a false 'have a nice day!' at a supermarket checkout, or insincere friendliness at a party. Deep acting means calling up a real feeling in order to act more convincingly. To use the same examples, this would mean actually *wanting* the customer to have a nice day, or being *genuinely* friendly at the party. Wearing a 'painted-on smile' at work was not seen as good enough by the airline managers in Hochschild's study. Customers and managers demanded *genuine* good humour, so that 'seeming to "love the job" becomes part of the job; and actually trying to love it, and to enjoy the customers, helps the worker in this effort' (Hochschild, 2003, p 6).

Emotional labour is a gendered concept, and has been most widely developed and adapted in the study of female-dominated service work and the caring professions. Whether in private or in public, women's emotional work is under-valued because it is perceived as 'coming naturally' (Steinberg and Figart, 1999). This can be seen in particular in Smith's (2012) studies of the emotional labour of student nurses, which found that complex caring and emotional skills are insufficiently recognised in training and pay structures. Clearly, emotional labour does not operate in the same way across different spheres: in contrast to flight attendants whose emotional work is rigidly controlled and monitored, the emotions of relatively professionalised occupations like nursing and youth work tend to be less tightly prescribed. As boundaries between public and private break down, however, the experiences of service sector and professional workers are moving closer together. For example, nurses' care skills have been distilled into a 'compassion index' which monitors their emotional work (Smith, 2012), while airline crews negotiate an increasingly complex set of emotional demands that encompass safety responsibilities and care for ill passengers (Bolton and Boyd, 2003).

Passion and emotional engagement seems to have become a feature of all modern workplaces, and some theorists and activists argue that we have entered a new phase in which labour is increasingly 'immaterial', oriented around relationships and technology rather than producing material products (Lazzarato, 1997). Workers across sectors are now expected to engage emotionally and mentally in what they do, and the boundaries between work and non-work are breaking down – not only as a function of communications technology but also because of the emphasis on workplace relationships. While youth workers' passion for their work reflects their genuine commitment and particular workplace cultures, it is also characteristic of modern capitalism, which:

> seeks to involve even the worker's personality and subjectivity within the production of value ... The worker is responsible for his or her own control and motivation within the work group without a foreman needing to intervene, and the foreman's role is redefined into that of facilitator ... Today's management thinking takes workers' subjectivity into consideration only in order to codify it in line with the requirements of production. And once again this phase of transformation succeeds in concealing the fact that the individual and collective interests of workers and those of the company are not identical. (Lazzarato, 1997)

In an era where workers are required to be passionate and engaged with their work, and yet are also expected to negotiate bureaucracy and target cultures that seem to undermine the importance of human relationships, the concept of emotional labour has renewed relevance as well as increased complexity for caring professionals. Public and voluntary sector workplaces increasingly use business methods and workers 'find themselves having to present the calm and caring face of the public sector professional while also having to present a smiling face to clients who now behave as demanding customers' (Bolton, 2005, p 128).

Youth work as emotion work

Caring engagement with young people is intrinsic to the youth work role. When young people demand genuine rather than false or contrived emotional engagement from their youth workers they are expressing a reasonable human desire rather than acting as demanding customers. Nevertheless, youth workers' emotional work can still be exploited, particularly when profit is involved. The previous chapter discussed how private companies have entered the youth work field, commodified systems such as 'payment by results' have become more common, and youth workers are increasingly employed in precarious and poorly paid conditions. In this marketised context, the survival and success of youth work organisations are heavily reliant on the often poorly paid labour of grassroots youth workers. Youth work organisations profit from the emotional labour of workers, particularly volunteers, part-timers and sessional workers, who do most of the face-to-face work and yet are least rewarded, and often seen as more disposable or replaceable than senior managers and administrators.

Recognising the complexity of emotions in diverse work settings, Sharon Bolton (2005) builds on Hochschild's work to develop a theory of emotion management that can be usefully applied to youth work. Bolton agrees with Hochschild that there is potential for exploitation and control of workers' emotions, and yet emphasises that workers must be understood 'as knowledgeable agents who are able to consent, comply or resist and who also have the potential to collectively alter the balance of power' (Bolton, 2005, p 87). This model is based on four overlapping types of emotion management (shown in Table 1), and is useful in emphasising how workers manage their emotions in complex ways and for different purposes.

Table 1: Emotion management in organisations

Pecuniary	Emotional work that is harnessed for profit (similar to Hochschild's emotional labour)
Prescriptive	Emotional work that is required by organisational or professional norms
Presentational	Everyday emotional interactions, particularly with colleagues, which tend to follow social norms
Philanthropic	Emotional work as a 'gift' to customers, clients or colleagues

(Based on Bolton, 2005)

Hochschild's emotional labour or Bolton's 'pecuniary' emotion management can be seen in some of the examples discussed in the previous chapter. For example, Keiron and Diana worked for a small private company that promised to pay them but failed even to provide essential travel and food expenses. Their other employers sought to keep labour costs to an absolute minimum, employing workers for very short sessions, not paying for preparation time, and replacing youth workers with play workers on lower rates. Similarly, Zandra and her colleagues are exploited by their funding body, which profits from their close and caring relationships with young people who might be seen as 'hard to reach'. This funder, a charity, only pays them if targets have been met, irrespective of how much time the workers have spent with the young people. These are good youth workers with the ability to form relationships with young people in complex and challenging situations, partly because the young people can tell that the workers *genuinely* care about them. Without these caring and genuine relationships, the organisations will not meet their targets or maintain a good reputation. In this way, organisations can be understood as directly profiting from youth workers' emotional labour.

Bolton's 'prescriptive' form of emotion management refers to emotions that are prescribed or required by professional or organisational rules or norms. This understanding emphasises the professional aspects of workplace emotions in an era when love and passion might almost be seen as *required* – or at least expected – rather than being remarkable. This expectation is not new for youth workers, who were said half a century ago to need a 'burning love of humanity' (Brew, 1957, p 112; see also Orpin, 2011). Emotional commitment continues to be seen as almost mandatory; for example, one popular youth work text argues that anybody who doesn't enjoy the work 'should find another job' (Robertson, 2005, p 47). It would be seen as counterintuitive, and perhaps socially unacceptable, to work with challenging and often vulnerable young people and say, 'It's only a job – I don't really care about it.' This is not to say that youth workers' passion is contrived or inauthentic, only that it could be seen as fulfilling professional expectations.

Similarly, Bolton's 'presentational' emotion management emphasises the emotional work involved in fulfilling social norms at work, particularly in relation to colleagues. 'Philanthropic' emotional work goes beyond these expectations, and is conceived of as a gift. As such, it might perhaps be thought of as an alternative or in opposition to the commodification of public and voluntary work. This chapter will return to 'presentational' and 'philanthropic' emotion work later, when discussing passionate youth work as resistance.

The demands of passionate youth work

Theories of emotional labour, immaterial labour and emotion management illuminate how emotional work involves great effort and complexity and seeps into every aspect of workers' lives. And yet, it is under-rewarded and too often seen as something that comes naturally, particularly to women. Although emotional commitment was reflected among both women and men in the research, the caring side of youth work might traditionally be understood as women's work, while the more practical and disciplinary aspects could stereotypically be seen as the role of men. In the following quote, Quincie expresses some of the intense effort and deep reflection involved in working with her emotions:

'I'm such a massive character, such a massive personality, sometimes even within youth work it's overbearing, it's overcrowding, it's too much, it's too inviting, it's too open, it's, oh my goodness! ... You have to self-reflect; everything that is required of you in terms of your work with young people you have to first be able to do it yourself, be completely honest with yourself ... You have to honestly ask yourself, if that happens, how would I react? And if this happens? And then depending on what you get back will determine the kind of work or how far you engross yourself within your role ... Youth work throws a lot up about yourself, you know?' (Quincie)

Here, Quincie expresses clearly and passionately how she uses her personality and emotions in a sophisticated approach that goes beyond an instinctive use of self and requires deep reflection. Aware that she can be 'too much', she reflects on how she might be perceived and what she might do in different situations. This encompasses being honest with herself and reflecting on how to use her personality most effectively. Several of the participants in this study spoke about their development as youth workers in terms of the deep emotional work involved. In the following quotation, Ox illustrates that being 'natural' or genuine is not straightforward or automatic, but involves him in the hard work of reflection, which itself relies on an organisational commitment to making time available for meaningful staff debriefing sessions:

'My persona now has changed ... It has to do with my shyness. I'm coming out of myself a bit more; I'm being more confident, just being able to communicate better ... One of the things that I really like about youth work is the debrief sessions that we have, where you're able to actually reflect on practice ... I'm a lot more laid back, a lot more relaxed ... I'm slowly being more confident, being more natural.' (Ox)

The level of reflection engaged in by Quincie and Ox constitutes skilled, intensive and challenging work. For many of the workers in this study, their care and concern for young people inevitably remains with them beyond their working hours:

'In the last few months round here there's been like three stabbings, on one estate. And that's just on their doorstep, where they live, and so it is – it's difficult ... It's always hard not to get too stressful with them and bring *your* personal feelings into things.' (Forde)

'A lot of the time I struggle that I can't live their life for them. So I have to accept that they might do something that I would love them not to do.' (Laura)

'... it's never fully done, is it? ... And I never stop thinking, oh, I could have done more; I've met that young person for a coffee today and that's been really nice but [pause] how much – if I'd had more time I could have done more.' (Tracey)

As Hochschild (2003) and Smith (2012) argue, work based on care tends to be underpaid and under-recognised, partly because it is associated with women's work and seen as being naturally feminine. In addition, it could be noted that there are other types of emotion work, alongside care, that are necessary for effective youth work, and that these are often seen as 'natural' for black and working class workers. Some of the work that youth workers seem to do as a matter of course involves complex emotional skills built up over years: 'getting on with' young people who others see as 'difficult' or 'challenging', reaching those who are labelled 'hard to reach', coaxing a smile or a laugh from a teenager who is having a really bad day, remaining calm but assertive when pool cues are thrown, dealing with a smashed window or averting a fight. These skills are necessary and highly valued in youth work settings. A part-timer who is said to be 'a natural' in these situations will very often be black and/or working class. When emotional skill is associated with groups that have less power and status in the workplace, the level of skill is rarely reflected in the pay structure. It is managerial and administrative skill (associated most closely with middle class and white workers) that is most generously rewarded. Those who cannot cope with extensive administration (however emotionally skilled they might be) may have difficulty finding a stable youth work job.

For the workers in this study, the recognition they wanted was not only related to pay. They wanted to feel involved in decisions made about their work, and to know that they were listened to and treated as skilled and knowledgeable. This was not always the case, particularly for volunteers:

'Being a volunteer is quite liberating in the way that you are just able to kind of go in, do your thing, focus on the young people [pause]. But at the same time I'm frustrated with it because I've not got the opportunity to say, "We should do this, we should take this forward, and we should try this". (Nicola)

Many of the workers in this study felt marginalised, not only informally but also through their practical exclusion from the places where decisions were made and policies discussed (de St Croix, 2013). This was starkly experienced by Bridget when her voluntary sector employer reduced her hours and changed her contract:

'When I went onto a sessional contract I wasn't allowed at meetings any more; I wasn't allowed at the away day any more. Because [colleague]'s a volunteer she isn't allowed at meetings. Now [different colleague]'s part-time, oh, *she's* not allowed any more.' (Bridget)

As well as being excluded from meetings, several part-timers lacked access to other vital communication systems and training:

'Part-time staff didn't have access to any of the computers so we couldn't log on, didn't have an email address, couldn't access the intranet ... I thought part-time and full-time staff had to be given equal rights but we never had any of that.' (Rachel)

'Because I'm a sessional worker ... I am not considered as anybody, so no, my input's not really needed ... It's things that have happened since I started with them as a volunteer. Not being involved in team meetings, not seeing me as someone worth paying me to do a certain amount of training, and that's what they're still doing now.' (Zandra)

'My initial training in youth work was very, very bad ... I had no previous experience, and I found out, like, two or three years later that you're supposed to actually do an induction, which I didn't do ... I had no training behind me so ... I was more like a, when I look back, more like a bodyguard.' (Ox)

These youth workers were highly committed and engaged in immensely challenging emotional work, and yet many were marginalised in their organisations. This marginalisation is based on a history of hierarchical staffing structures and reproduced inequalities, in which it is assumed that volunteers and part-timers turn up and hang out with young people, while full-timers hold the keys, the money and the information (Bolger and Scott, 1984). Ox felt he had acted as something like a bodyguard when first working in a challenging youth club; this echoes a history of black male youth workers being employed to 'deal with' and discipline young black men (Williams, 1988).

This picture was not reflected among every worker I interviewed, and several participants did feel appreciated, respected and listened to at work. However, an overall pattern of marginalisation seems to reinforce long-standing social and structural inequalities. Broadly, it could be argued that the youth industry relies on the complex and under-rewarded emotional, physical and mental labour of a largely working class, female and black workforce. Money is made for organisations through the exploitation of this labour. As Zandra starkly expressed it: 'They just see me as someone who can get their work done but someone they can also save money with.'

Emotions in a changing policy context

This discussion relates closely to the marketisation of youth work outlined in the previous chapter. Emotion work is affected by multiple and changing influences, including personal, organisational and professional norms (Bolton, 2005). As accountability and monitoring mechanisms are increasingly required in marketised systems of measurement and comparison, some of the interviewees experienced stress and frustration around these obstacles:

> 'There's a *lot* of politics involved; it's always those kinds of things, lots of obstacles involved in terms of information sharing and all those bureaucracy and politics that's involved. Sometimes it is emotionally draining and that's the downside to it to be honest. Cos one minute you can be really great and emotionally, you know, on a positive, and the next minute you can be really negative.' (Mahad)

> 'At the back of all our minds was always these targets. As much as we tried to do really good youth work for what

young people wanted, at the back of our minds it was always
there ... And the young people even feel that.' (Laura).

Hochschild's (2003) theory of alienated emotional labour has renewed
relevance as youth work is influenced by the principles of the market
and enterprise. Alongside direct private sector encroachments into
youth work, organisations in the public and voluntary sectors are
increasingly run on business lines (Davies, 2013, 2014). Young people
benefit from the emotional labour of grassroots youth workers, and
yet so (in many cases) do directors, senior managers, organisations and
funding bodies: the income of organisations is partially reliant on the
continuing emotional work of low-paid and unpaid workers such as
those who took part in the study.

In making use of theories developed in different contexts, the
similarities between youth work and more commercial sectors should
not be overstated. Organisational requirements for monitoring and
targets clearly influence youth workers' emotions, but this cannot be
equated with airline companies micro-managing the feeling displays of
their workers. Unlike flight attendants, youth workers are not (yet) told
exactly when and how to smile! However, we might wonder whether
this is so far-fetched; some youth programmes are now measured
using happiness indicators and wellbeing indexes (McGimpsey, 2013),
and there has been a growth in methods such as neurolinguistic
programming, which teaches specific techniques for building rapport,
such as the mirroring of body language.

There is a clear tension between the need for youth workers to
care about and like young people, the stress that this caring can cause,
and the potential for exploitation and marginalisation. This particular
situation needs to be understood in a wider context, in which shifts in
capitalism have resulted in both a homogenisation of work processes and
a growing emphasis on emotional capacities (Lazzarato, 1997; Gill and
Pratt, 2008). There will always be the possibility for organisations to
exploit and profit from the emotional labour of frontline youth workers,
particularly in an increasingly marketised system, but what should
workers themselves do about this? It is clearly a good thing for young
people to have youth workers who like them and find it enjoyable
and satisfying to work with them, so withdrawing emotional labour is
unlikely to be an ethical form of action. This chapter will now discuss
whether grassroots workers' commitment can itself be a challenge to
commodified and profit-oriented ways of valuing youth work.

Passionate resistance

Is passionate youth work liberatory and subversive, and if so, how? Traditional critical scholarship defines resistance in broadly Marxist terms, as conscious class-based struggle that takes such forms as strikes, occupations and street protest. This kind of resistance is present in youth work, and in recent years has tended to focus on defending youth facilities and services against cuts (as in Louise's story in Chapter Two). In recent decades, feminist and poststructuralist theorists have understood resistance more broadly as encompassing everyday forms of action that challenge the status quo. The approach throughout this book is to draw on both of these understandings – to value both 'organised' and 'everyday' forms of action that oppose the dominant neoliberal interpretations of youth work policy – partly because:

> ... if we limit our gaze to that which is public and open, then we are doing just that: limiting our own vision, and with it the impact of our dignities. We are in fact reproducing the capitalist distinction between public and private, whereas our aim is to cut through that distinction. (Holloway, 2010, p 76)

When the workers in this study discussed negative emotions in relation to youth work, they distinguished between the challenges of direct work with young people and the stress of managerial and organisational demands. Rachel had recently left her job, and reflected on the contrast between these different kinds of challenge:

> 'I didn't ever not enjoy working with young people. Even when they were being difficult, I've never found I didn't enjoy that, because that is challenging, but it's still interesting; it's still working out how you're gonna work with them and overcome things [pause]. Towards the end I really stopped enjoying a lot of the things with my managers. That was really difficult.' (Rachel)

Alan echoes this account, discussing the prevalent lack of trust in part-time workers:

> 'I think the job's actually on the one hand incredibly complex and on the other hand quite simple ... it's all of this constant analysing and managing that pisses me off.

It's like, look, we turn up, we do our job, we do it well. Trust us. And there's not much trust in part-time workers at all ... which then leads to resentment and then people *become* untrustworthy, because they're like, "Well, I can't be bothered." We never get any praise for anything; we never get any thanks for anything. We're the ones doing the bloody job.' (Alan)

Youth workers tend to be critical of things that get in the way of their passion for youth work: intrusive monitoring procedures, hierarchical management, intensified time pressures, funding cuts, redundancies and inappropriate performance targets. How might their passion for working with young people form part of an alternative to these potentially dehumanising systems?

Putting relationships first

At this point it is helpful to return to Bolton's (2005) theory of workplace emotions, particularly 'presentational' and 'philanthropic' emotion management, which can provide spaces for being human and for resistance. 'Presentational' emotion management draws on Goffman's (1959) work on social interaction to argue that workers present themselves in ways that uphold or disrupt social and emotional norms. For example, they might engage in humour and play that can be seen as disruptive of efficiency in ways that contribute to positive friendly relationships. 'Philanthropic' emotion management refers to the possibility of giving 'a little extra' out of kindness and care. Bolton argues that there are unmanaged spaces in every organisation where workers are not necessarily governed by explicit guidelines, policies or managerial directives:

> Many forms of activity take place in these various spaces according to social feeling rules and people in organisations use them to create and maintain familial bonds, to relieve anger and anxiety, to register their resistance to demands made of them by management and to take time to offer extra emotion work as a gift to colleagues or customers and clients. (Bolton, 2005, p 135)

This analysis resonates with the accounts of grassroots youth workers. As their work becomes more regulated in many organisations, there is a sense that even a hug can become a form of resistance:

'You know what I like? Somewhere in [employer's] protocol is that you mustn't be physical with young people. You know what I love? Young people come and they're like, *"Bridget!"* and I get big hugs!' (Bridget)

In the space between an organisation's policy and the practical enactment of a relationship with a young person, a youth worker will often put the young person first. If a young person decides to hug her, Bridget joins in – and enjoys it! Similarly, she maintains relationships with young people who are over the age limit or have moved away, and are no longer in her funded remit:

'I break the rules. If [young woman] called me tomorrow, I'm gone. And she now lives in [a different borough] and I'm not supposed to work with her any more. If she calls me I'm sorry, I'm going. And I've done it before.'

In using the phrase 'I break the rules', Bridget is clear that her decision to put young people first is a form of resistance. Her actions are consistent with understanding relationships as *central* to youth work rather than as a means to an end. While she is aware of requirements for professional conduct and is concerned to act sensitively and ethically, Bridget enjoys the fluidity and often familial nature of her role:

'One day I'm a counsellor, then I'm a nurse, then I'm a teacher, then I'm a mother, then I'm an auntie, you know; it's amazing, the amount of different hats you have to wear doing [the employment project]. I love it.'

Bridget follows emotional demands that are not encompassed by her organisation's policies. Her approach could be defined according to Bolton's (2005) typology as 'presentational' emotion management: the human requirement to maintain bonds and follow social norms rather than refusing a hug or breaking off a relationship for funding-related reasons. It could also be seen as 'philanthropic' emotion management because her relationships with young people are generous. They involve her in extra work (working with young people who do not 'count' against her targets) and encompass genuine enjoyment of young people's company as well as care for their welfare.

It is clear that passionate youth work is not only restrictive and exploitative. Even in highly regulated workplaces, workers can undertake autonomous emotional action that 'serves to liberate them from management's control of their emotions and thereby alleviates some of their sense of estrangement' (Tolich, 1993, p 362). When Bridget told of breaking the rules in these ways, she spoke with pride and satisfaction. In public and voluntary service work, such autonomous actions can be seen as enactments of personal and professional ethical integrity (Cribb, 2011). As Banks (2011, p 6) argues, a deep and genuine concern for human relationships 'mitigates against treating people as cases, consumers or numbers'.

Making space and time

Putting relationships first is not merely a rhetorical aspiration; it involves creating spaces where young people feel welcome and included, and making time for them. Although this might be assumed to be intrinsic to the youth work role, the growth of bureaucratic demands and pressure on resources means that both time and space are squeezed (Fusco et al, 2013). Despite these challenges, some of the participants in this study work in places where space and time remain priorities. Mickie works in a project for young people who are lesbian, gay, bi, trans or queer (LGBT); the project is particularly valued by this group, who are excluded from many other spaces:

> 'It's not unusual for people to say it's a kind of home from home, or a home where, you know, where they feel most safe, really. Cos a lot of our young people come here and they may not be out to friends and family. A lot of young people travel a fair distance ... People do come and join in and get involved with planning what we do, you know, so that's really important. Young people form it. And we've had a lot of progression from young people being young people to volunteers ... People stick with it ... they stay here, or they dip in and out.' (Mickie)

This idea of a 'home from home' calls up a place that is qualitatively and emotionally different to spaces typically found in the provision of more formal services for young people – and when I visited Mickie's centre the feel of homeliness was visible and palpable. Such spaces can be more difficult to achieve for workers in more traditional youth organisations, where institutional systems might be valued over feelings of homeliness. However, Alan, a part-timer working at a local authority youth club, was particularly assertive about creating as much space and time as possible for face-to-face practice with young people. Although his role included administrative responsibilities, he made a principled decision to direct his energies towards face-to-face work with young people rather than peripheral tasks. Historically, the youth clubs in his borough had been open only for specific sessions in the evenings, but along with his colleagues he had argued to adopt a more flexible approach where young people could drop in and use the space in the daytimes when he was officially doing admin:

> 'We have kids in here like all the time – there'll probably be someone knocking on the door in a minute ... we have parents coming in chatting ... We won't say "Well, we're not open, you'll have to come back at such and such a time." ... It's been happening for years, but it's been kind of like against the grain. And it's been, kind of, people have frowned upon it. And now it's becoming, people are just so much more confident and saying, "Actually this is good youth work."' (Alan)

Like Bridget, Alan is clear that his commitment to working with young people might be seen as rebellious in an organisational culture where bureaucracy often takes time away from direct work with young people. He is critical of full-time colleagues who do not allow young people into buildings because they have too much work to do; he keeps his own admin to a minimum, and if he needs to work on something he lets young people in the building anyway to use the computers, keeping an eye on them while he gets on with whatever he needs to do. He is not resisting management pressures in this case, but rather acting against prevalent working cultures which prioritise bureaucratic tasks:

> 'It's like, this is our job; the job is we work with young people ... in the youth service the amount of hours worked face to face ... would probably be about 15%. And it's like, it should be at least eighty. What else can you be doing? What else is there to do? That's the job!'

For the volunteers in the study, an emphasis on face-to-face work was particularly important. Those who were relatively free of administrative demands were able to spend most or all of their time working directly with young people.

> 'There was someone who used to come to see me and I'd spend eight or nine hours with her, all day. We'd go

shopping together and I'd be with her all the time. She'd
always phone and see where I was and come and see me ...
[Manager] always used to say to me, "But what you're doing
is exactly what she needs ... You're being there for her" ...
If you were to say that to your manager, how would he be
able to record that you had actually achieved something just
by spending all that time? I don't know.' (Louise)

It seemed initially puzzling to Louise that she had been encouraged
to spend so much time with one young person, and this is certainly
unusual. But why should it be seen as a luxury? If the young person
needed someone to spend time with and Louise was available,
particularly as she was a volunteer, should this be seen as a problem?
Clearly there are possibilities of over-dependency on the part of the
young person or burnout on the part of the youth worker, but a short-
term investment of intensive time and energy might have been just
what this young person needed (as Louise's manager recognised). It is
almost as if the rationing of time and space has become so endemic
among youth workers that we impose it on ourselves.

Where youth workers insist on creating caring and welcoming
spaces for young people, and are willing to spend the time it takes in
working with them, they are using their passion to resist profit-oriented
ways of working. Clearly, understanding the potential for passion
in resistance does not remove the exploitative aspects of emotional
labour, particularly if the complexity and skill involved is unsupported
and unrecognised. It remains important for workers' organisations,
including trade unions, to campaign for better recognition of emotional
labour, but also to develop more understanding of the liberatory
potential of resistance.

Conclusion

Not just a job (2)

'Hey Ricky, there's a job for you in here!' They've finished in the job centre and
are back at the cafe. Danny hands the local paper over to his youth worker, who
reads out loud: 'Youth hub operations manager. Must have extensive experience of
negotiating contracts, liaising with key stakeholders, implementing a sustainable
financial strategy and ...' He breaks off, laughing. 'Danny, can you really see me
getting that job?' Danny shrugs and says, 'I don't even know what half of it means.'
'Neither do I!' says Ricky, 'But that's the way things are going now, that's the
kind of person they want. Not someone like me. I hate paperwork, I'm dyslexic,

I hate sitting in front of a computer.' He hands the newspaper back. 'Thanks for thinking of me though, that's kind of you.'

Danny says, 'That's good. I don't want you to leave us anyway. I wouldn't go to youth club if you weren't there.' Ricky feels flattered, but a bit embarrassed too. He says, 'I'll try not to leave, if they don't sack me! Anyway, we need to get going and see if we can find some money to buy you a smart shirt for your interview. Or shall we have another cuppa first?'

Although the research did not set out to explore grassroots youth workers' love and passion for their work, emotional commitment was a strong theme that linked directly to workers' critiques of dehumanising systems and policy frameworks. This was apparent in their everyday resistance and (for some) in their involvement in campaigns. As Callie said, 'Because we love youth work we stand up for it.' Callie had been running a youth club in a village hall that was threatened with closure.

> 'When I'm arguing with the council about why they should keep the youth club open, if they can see that I care about this, then, they are still human, there might be a little bit more chance ... they'll be like, "Well, there's something she's seeing that we're not seeing.". And they might not agree with me in the end but at least they know that I've cared enough to try and fight for it.' (Callie)

That is not to suggest that passion is *always* or *only* a form of resistance. Being a passionate youth worker might mean conforming to the role of caregiver in a welfare workplace, of obedient employee in a hierarchical structure, and of dynamic entrepreneur in a youth work market. Passion could even be seen as an inhibitor of resistance, for example, if strike-breaking was done in the name of care: 'It's not fair on the young people to shut the youth club for the night.' This chapter does not intend to deny these tensions or argue that passion is inherently revolutionary, only to argue that it is as important to explore passion's role in resistance as it is to think about the exploitative and conformist aspects of emotional labour.

As welfare and education settings are infused with market principles and managerial practices, there is a growing potential for employers to exploit the emotional commitments of workers in the pursuit of profit. Hochschild (2003) explains how emotional labour might alienate workers from their emotions and complicate their feelings of love and passion for their work. By itself, however, this theory does not help workers decide what to do in practice. Young people need adults who genuinely care about them, and most employees want work that is fulfilling and enjoyable. Whatever the complex consequences for exploitation and resistance, it must also be emphasised that youth workers' love for their work is important, satisfying and enriching in its own right.

Interviewed at a time of serious threat to both the nature and funding of their work, the workers in this study feel that youth work brings its own rewards for themselves and for young people. They express an authentic love of youth work that calls into question or at least complicates the arguments of those who worry that there is little space for care and commitment in the current policy context. Nobody is likely to feel passionate all of the time, and there will undoubtedly be some youth workers who do not feel passionate at all. However, the passion, care and commitment of those who took part in this research was striking, and to honour its importance, the chapter closes with some final quotations:

> 'I would love to continue to do youth work because I want to give back something to the community and to the young people and hopefully continue 'til the day that I haven't got the passion.' (Mahad)

> 'I love every minute of the job that I do ... I've met so many young people and met all the parents and you know, communities; it's a brilliant job! [Laughs].' (John)

Tania: Thank you so much ... Is there anything else you want to say about anything?
Callie: No. I love my job!

FOUR

Target cultures and performativity

Paperwork (1)

Jo looks out of the club window at the splashing puddles. Apart from keeping us all dry, she thinks, this evening's been a waste of everyone's time. She'd organised a debate on the legalisation of drugs, something the young people have always discussed before without any encouragement, and hoped to get them a quick certificate in time for the quarterly deadline. But hardly anybody turned up and those who did just wanted to play pool as usual, and only joined in with the debate for five minutes. Now she's trying to persuade them to fill out the paperwork for the certificate, which feels a bit fake. Jenna and Shay have only got as far as writing their names, and now they're whispering and laughing, looking over at Danny and Femi, who have somehow got juice and crumbs all over their table and haven't made a start. Sadiq said he was going to the shop half an hour ago and hasn't come back.

Jo glances over at her colleague Ricky for support but he's as bored as the young people, checking his phone, distancing himself from her and from the whole thing – as if his job, like hers, didn't depend on getting these targets met. She knows she'll pretty much have to fill in the sheets herself; it's just a question of whether to do it now, with the token involvement of the young people, or later when they've gone. She feels a sharp irritation: at their manager for harassing them over their targets, at Ricky for doing nothing, at these young people for making things difficult, at the other young people for not being here, and at herself for going along with the whole charade. She breathes in slowly and gathers her energy for a final attempt: 'Come on then, do you want these certificates or not? Let's get this thing done and dusted!' She hears herself say too loud and falsely cheerful, bounding across the room to tease, humour and cajole them all into getting it over with so they can all escape into the dark wet night.

In recent decades, monitoring and outcomes-based systems have transformed the nature of youth work practice. They have become an everyday reality for youth workers to the extent that targets and outcomes are now accepted as part of the job. This chapter will show that, despite this normalisation, target cultures are widely questioned and criticised by grassroots workers as an impediment to the quality and authenticity of their work with young people.

Target cultures and systematic monitoring technologies arrived in English youth work around the turn of the century during a time of increased investment under the New Labour government and particularly in the wake of the policy document *Transforming youth work* (DfES, 2002). By then, targets were already well embedded in schools, youth offending teams, social work and healthcare, adapted from the private sector as a key element of public sector managerialism (Power, 1994; Gewirtz, 2002; Mooney and Law, 2007; Towers, 2011). These audit cultures were renewed and reinvented under the Coalition government, contributing to centre-right privatisation of the welfare state by enabling comparison between providers and thus making services 'legible for the market and private appropriation' (Lipman, 2013, p 2).

Youth work writers have argued compellingly that quantitative performance management and a focus on pre-planned outcomes are *particularly* inappropriate to youth work, which primarily draws on informal, open, person-centred and context-dependent methodologies (Brent, 2004; Jeffs and Smith, 2008; Fusco, 2013; Taylor and Taylor, 2013; Ord, 2014; Davies, 2015). Targets and outcome measures are justified by their supporters on the grounds of quality and accountability, but research suggests that youth workers and young people are critical of these procedures (Crimmens et al, 2004; Spence and Devanney, 2006; Tiffany, 2007; Davies and Merton, 2009, 2010). Such views are reflected by the grassroots youth workers in this study, who spoke with anger, frustration or resignation about tick-boxes, monitoring, targets, bureaucracy and admin: words used as shorthand for a wide range of performance management procedures.

This chapter aims to contribute to and extend these discussions by focusing on the everyday experiences, feelings and resistance of part-time and volunteer youth workers in relation to audit and target cultures, drawing on theories of performativity. In critical education policy sociology, performativity refers to how performance management technologies change not only *what we do* but also *who we are*, our workplace identities and emotions. In his 2003 article, 'The teacher's soul and the terrors of performativity', Stephen Ball argues that systems of regulation employ judgements and comparisons as a means of control and change. In these systems, employees are required to monitor and improve their own performances and those of the people they work with. Performative systems in youth work often obstruct the building of mutual and trusting relationships that start from young people's interests, experiences and wishes, and indirectly encourage workers to favour those young people who are most compliant in relation to fulfilling the requirements of the audit (Tiffany, 2007). They can also change more subtly *what it feels like* to be a youth worker, engendering a sense of dislocation and inner conflict.

It is these everyday experiential and emotional aspects that are the focus of this chapter, rather than the more abstract policy debates about the need for accountability. I do not deny the importance of youth workers and organisations being held to account, and I recognise the existence of poor practice that needs to be challenged. However, the negative consequences of accountability mechanisms based on top-down edicts, surveillance and routine paperwork are harming rather than improving grassroots practice.

This chapter has three sections. In the first I will explore how targets, outcomes and excessive bureaucracy are coming to saturate the everyday lives of grassroots youth workers, drawing on material from my study alongside theoretical work on performativity as it has been developed by Ball and other education scholars. Targets, tick boxes and paperwork were seen by many interviewees as obstructive and demeaning of authentic relationship-based work with young people. Measurement systems do not seem to reflect 'real' youth work, and this creates a clash that challenges how grassroots workers see themselves; this is the focus of the second section. For some, the clash seemed to augur a sense of shame – both when they complied with inappropriate systems, and when they failed to meet their targets. In reflecting on shame and authenticity, I continue to draw on Stephen Ball's work as well as on an earlier strand of performativity theory from feminist, queer and gender studies, particularly in the work of Judith Butler and Eve Kosofsky Sedgwick.

In both its education policy and gender interpretations, performativity is primarily conceived of as restricting and limiting the diverse expressions of self. As in other chapters, here I am interested in exploring restrictions while also thinking about elements of contestation. Resistance is particularly challenging in a context where cuts, commissioning and 'payment by results' mean that refusal or avoidance of performance technologies can risk the loss of jobs and projects, sometimes even the closure of entire organisations. In the third section I consider whether claims for authentic, open and informal youth work constitute counter discourses in neoliberal times, as well as reflecting on how some youth workers create spaces and times that – while never entirely free of performative mechanisms – are somewhat less governed by them.

Youth work and performativity

When I asked part-time youth worker Forde whether she saw herself as a professional, she replied:

> 'Yeah! I do. ... I have standards. When I'm at work, I'm not Forde from home, I'm not Forde that has my home hat on. I'm Forde that comes to work, that yes, unfortunately we have to comply to standards, figures, numbers, that's what we are. We're numbers, we've got to reach a target; that is what we do. Unfortunately. If for a month we got 10 young people but then two of those young people went through to start college, or started an apprenticeship, that still wouldn't be good enough sometimes. It needs to have all 10 of them. And it is figures; it's just targets. You've got to hit targets. So I do see myself as a professional in the sense that I come here, and you know, I wear the face of [borough] I guess.' (Forde)

Forde spoke with equanimity about the need to 'comply'; she did not seem to be complaining, but rather accepting targets as unfortunate but inevitable. She explains her professionalism as an embodied shift from her 'home hat' to a 'local authority face'; once she has put on this face, targets become both what she does and who she is: 'standards, figures, numbers, *that's what we are*. We're numbers, we've got to reach a target; *that is what we do*' (emphasis added). This is a particularly clear articulation of performativity, the intersection between performance management and workers' understandings of themselves.

Cultures of performativity create the conditions for what grassroots youth workers do and what they cannot do, who they are and who they cannot be. Drawing on work by Lyotard and Foucault, Stephen Ball (2001, 2003, 2008b, 2013) identifies performativity as a policy technology that both relies on and creates the self-governing worker, compelled and incited by systems of control and comparison. In youth work, these systems come in such forms as targets, outcomes measures, inspections and marketing materials. These create information about the performance of workers and organisations that is then used to measure, compare and judge their work. In this way, the technologies are an effect of hierarchical and marketised power relations, while also reinforcing and reproducing these relations. In performative systems it is not the production of adequate models of understanding that 'count', but the production of new work and fresh ideas, the maximisation of productivity (Lyotard, 1984). Change does not flow unproblematically from practice to representation because 'rendering something auditable shapes the processes that are to be audited' (Rose, 1996, p 351) and thus practice begins to be oriented towards the demands of target cultures. This is not to say that accountability mechanisms are always damaging; for example, young people's spoken or written evaluations can give workers ideas for improving their practice in line with what participants want, and show young people that their views are important. Unfortunately, however, the use of high-stakes quantitative targets has more often reorientated practice towards individualised and surveillant technologies that fail to encompass the perspectives and experiences of young people and grassroots workers.

Target cultures mandate the grounds on which practitioners are judged; and 'since performativity increases the ability to produce proof, it also increases the ability to be right' (Lyotard, 1984, p 46). If the database says a worker has not met their target, they are presumed to be in the wrong. Where monitoring systems represent the worth of an individual or organisation, a crucial issue is who controls the field of judgement (Ball, 2001). Apple (2006) emphasises the role here of the professional and managerial middle class, who may be politically liberal but provide the technical expertise that enables the proliferation of audit systems. Unequal systems of judgement and comparison have long been a feature of organisational life, but continuous audit places more value on displays of competence, which tend to be classed, gendered and racialised (Lumby, 2009). People for whom performance, audit and appraisal are familiar and 'natural' are most able to demonstrate competence through successful, almost effortless performances, and certain ways of working (predominantly occupied by middle class white men) become the norm by which everybody is judged (Apple, 2006). Grassroots youth workers are more likely than their managers to be working class, female, dyslexic and/or black (Mellor and McDonnell, 2010); they might be less likely to find audit systems natural and familiar, and perhaps less likely to be perceived as competent in relation to these systems (Lumby, 2009).

Youth work targets

Audit and target cultures were introduced into English youth work through various local and national policy and funding mechanisms, the most significant of which was the New Labour policy document *Transforming youth work: Resourcing excellent youth services* (DfES, 2002). This policy required the use of performance indicators, known colloquially as the 'REYS' outcomes, as compulsory targets for English local authorities (Smith, 2002; Lehal, 2010). Targets and outcomes quickly became normalised as measures of the quality and competence of youth services and workers. Local authorities bought in computer software to monitor the performance of individuals and teams (see Chapter Five), and qualitative evaluation was swept away as workers struggled to keep up with the growing weight of administration. The 'REYS' outcomes – reach, participation, recorded outcomes and accredited outcomes – became non-mandatory in 2009 and yet remained a high-stakes performance mechanism in many local authorities when I interviewed workers between 2011 and 2013. They are referred to by workers throughout this chapter so are explained here in Table 2.

Table 2: REYS (Resourcing Excellent Youth Services) outcomes

Reach	Proportion of local 13–19 year olds in contact with youth services.
Participation	Percentage of that age group who participate regularly in youth services.
Recorded outcomes	Number of participants who achieve an outcome through their participation in youth services that is recognised by a youth worker and the young person themselves. The aim is to record subjective changes such as improvements in confidence or behaviour. In practice, the target is often met by a young person and/or youth worker filling in a form to state that the young person has participated in an activity or demonstrated a skill.
Accredited outcomes	Number of participants who achieve an accredited qualification such as a first aid certificate, the Duke of Edinburgh's Award, a Youth Achievement Award and (most commonly) an AQA basic skills certificate.

Sources: DfES, 2002; Smith, 2002; Lehal, 2010; as well as interviews and personal experience

The above benchmarks remain significant in the lives of many youth workers employed or funded by local authorities, whereas voluntary organisations are encouraged to buy in 'bespoke' tools such as New Philanthropy Capital's Well-being Measure (NPC, 2012; McGimpsey, 2013). Smaller organisations that cannot afford such technologies (or do not want to use them) are nevertheless affected by the assumption that youth work's value must be 'proven'. The workers' cooperative that I am involved in, Voice of Youth, was set up partly to avoid funding that involves surveillant and time-consuming monitoring procedures; however, funders are increasingly unwilling to hand over even relatively small amounts of money on trust:

> One of our funders gives us £1,500 per year towards our insurance, refreshments for the young people and travel expenses for volunteers. In the past this has been granted on a relationship built up over years, and we have reciprocated with regular contact and an annual report. Now they have told us that we need to enter the personal details of all young people we work with on a database to provide 'evidence' of who we are working with. This does not seem a good use of our time as volunteers, and we are concerned about confidentiality. We are engaged in discussions between ourselves, with young people and with the funder. Our instinct is to say no, but we are worried we will lose this funding as a result, money that we rely on for our core costs and that would be difficult to replace. (Research diary, April 2014)

The burden of monitoring can fall on volunteers and part-timers in small organisations, whereas meeting targets in larger organisations and youth services is usually the responsibility of managers and senior administrators who are increasingly required to perform a complex set of procedures. As a result, employers value high-level administrative skills over youth work experience when recruiting senior staff. Many grassroots workers understandably resent having managers who do not understand youth work and yet appear to be highly rewarded.

Diana: The managers at the [youth centre], none of them have come from a youth work background. ...
Keiron: We had the CEO who was a graduate in fashion. ... it was like she didn't know what she was doing.
Diana: Yep, was she on sixty-odd grand?
Keiron: Yeah, the wage, yeah.
Diana: I remember, and she used to come into work dressed in like tight shirts and tight pencil skirts, to a youth club, to a session on an evening ...
Keiron: Never spoke to young people, never spoke to young people.

Where organisations employ business-oriented managers it is difficult for part-timers and volunteers to relate to them or learn from them, let alone to imagine attaining a senior role themselves. Even where managers are from youth work backgrounds, as is more often the case in local authorities, their heavy administrative workloads remove them from the practice arena:

'A full-time worker said to me, "There might be some sessions whereby I will be stuck in the office, I won't be able to be out with the young people in the session." I'm thinking to myself, you can't lock yourself in an office, at a computer, really. ... I thought, being a full-time worker, surely you should be able to engage with young people, otherwise you're just an administrator then, aren't you?' (John)

While managers make well-meaning attempts 'to protect the part-time staff from paperwork in order to maximise the time they can spend with young people' (Spence and Devanney, 2006, p 111), part-timers are often disappointed when their experienced colleagues do not have time to work alongside them, and the pressures tend to trickle down to grassroots level in any case:

'Here they *do* have a *lot* of targets. ... You don't really sort of get a huge disciplinary over it or anything like that. ... But we kind of face the pressures of it as part-time workers cos the full-timers come and go, "Right, we got our targets: we have to meet 400 young people this year." ... I had a supervision last week and the full-time worker said, "We have this many, we have this target of young people." I think it was like a thousand accreditations to meet within a year.' (John)

Like many grassroots workers, John respects his managers and wants to support them, even though he finds the targets questionable and unrealistic. As part of the placement for his university youth work degree he was given the task of filling in the local authority monitoring database, and despite criticising its surveillance aspects he seemed proud to do this; it was a symbol that he was trusted and perceived as competent. In this way, the completion of performative tasks becomes (for some) a matter of satisfaction (Ball, 2003). Not only does it feed into the entrepreneurial project of the self (Rose, 1996), it is also rewarded with recognition for the worker's project, and potentially protects resources for young people.

Mobile bus youth worker Callie is a relatively new worker hoping to broaden her own skills and experience and make a career in youth work. Like John, she was given the responsibility of entering young people's details and achievements on her local authority's monitoring database. She did this at home after work in her own time, and seemed invested in the achievements of her own team in relation to – and perhaps in competition with – the local youth centres.

Callie: They've got [youth centre] targets, we've got the mobile team target. ... Contact and participation we don't worry about, because on the bus we smash [youth centre A] and [youth centre B]. ...

Tania: What do *you* think about targets?

Callie: I hate targets! With a vengeance. Because there's some things that you can't measure in targets.

It is symptomatic of the peculiar allure of targets and outcome measurements that we can recognise their inappropriateness while at the same time finding them strangely satisfying. Callie is proud when the youth bus 'smashes' the contact numbers of the local youth centres and yet she hates targets 'with a vengeance'; she expresses both pride and disgust in relation to these systems and her role in them. Workers' pride and sense of achievement helps to instil and reinforce unpopular target cultures because:

> Performativity works best when it is inside our heads and our souls. That is, when we do it to ourselves, when we take responsibility for working harder, faster and better as part of our sense of personal worth and the worth of others. And it is important to recognise that it also offers us the possibility of being better than we were or even being the best – better than others. (Ball, 2008b, p 52)

Performativity in these accounts is not outside of us. It becomes part of us even as we criticise it, even if we tell ourselves that we do not care. I use the word 'us' here because I cannot place myself outside of these paradoxical feelings of pride and shame in relation to monitoring mechanisms. The following research diary extract is from a time when I worked in a voluntary sector organisation funded by the local authority:

> Today's session was inspected by the local council (who fund us) with a few hours' notice. I am too stubborn to adapt the session plan (what is the point of them inspecting an atypical session?) and I guess it went ok despite this, but I felt flat afterwards. There was nothing useful or helpful in the feedback, and little recognition of the good and difficult work we are doing. I do not care what they think. Or maybe

> I do care. I care, I suppose, that we only got 'satisfactory' for equal opportunities, when I feel that anti-oppressive practice is one of our strengths. I am irritated that our only 'outstanding' was for 'young people's attainment', presumably because I handed out some almost worthless AQA[1] certificates that had arrived that morning in the post. I am annoyed with myself for wasting emotional energy thinking about any of this, embarrassed that some part of me wants to succeed according to criteria I disagree with. I seem to want to be a rebel and to be outstanding: a maverick who does not care about inspections but does well in them anyway. (Research diary, July 2011)

Being a youth worker today means working with young people on a genuine level, while also creating moments of inspection and systems of monitoring that rely on a different regime of judgement. Perhaps we can hardly complain if we are not judged as excellent in systems that are not congruent with our beliefs; we cannot expect recognition from others if our aim is to be true to ourselves (Ball and Olmedo, 2013). We might criticise target cultures and find ways around their requirements, but it is difficult – perhaps impossible – to avoid the meanings they impose.

Playing the game

Youth workers are not wholly captured by the discourse of target cultures. Interviewees in the study spoke articulately about young people and groups who had developed, achieved and changed through their involvement in youth work – 'real' changes that were difficult to translate into the monitoring systems used by their employers or funders. And yet, they could not ignore the audit mechanisms that shaped their work:

> 'Things that I don't so much enjoy, is the kind of numbers game of having to tick boxes.' (Mickie)

> 'All the projects went out the windows, and it was basically accredited training, bums on seats, let's get paid for numbers.' (Sarah)

These specific phrases – 'numbers game', 'tick box', and 'bums on seats' – were used consistently as a shorthand for a wide range of administrative, performative and bureaucratic activity. Perhaps workers employ this language as a means of downplaying tasks that feel unreal, inappropriate, damaging or demeaning. 'Numbers game' seems particularly apposite, emphasising both the quantitative nature of monitoring mechanisms and their inauthenticity:

> Fabrications are versions of an organisation (or person) which does not exist – they are not 'outside the truth' but neither do they render simply true or direct accounts – they are produced purposefully in order to be accountable. Truthfulness is not the point – the point is their effectiveness ... their transformational and disciplinary impact. (Ball, 2003, p 224)

Part of the 'game' is knowing which fabrications are desirable and which are unacceptable. Workers are kept guessing: how far should the truth be pushed and made to bend? Should we prepare a special session when the inspectors are due? Should we add a young person's name to the attendance list if they only popped in for a moment? Should we share our doubts and false starts when we attend a neighbourhood meeting, or focus only on our achievements? Knowing which compromises are acceptable and which are straying too far from the truth requires a deep and habitual familiarity with systems of judgement. These games are complicated; cheating is frowned upon, but providing wholly honest versions will not make the grade.

In repeated accounts, workers had been told by colleagues and managers that targets *must* be met, or jobs and projects would be at risk. They are incited through fear, competition and the possibility of self-fulfilment to 'be creative', even when this means implementing systems of measurement that detract from genuinely developmental relationships with young people. Since the introduction of targets for accredited outcomes (see Table 2) the certificate for boiling a kettle or making a cup of tea has been widely discussed among youth workers. I had wrongly assumed such stories were apocryphal, but volunteer Louise told me that these certificates actually exist:

Louise: In the youth clubs though they want you to accredit the kids for everything ... We did a first aid course and that's amazing, that's a really good useful thing to do, and the cooking thing's good. But accrediting them for boiling the kettle I don't.

Tania: Is that serious or are you joking?

Louise: No, no, no, no, that's not me joking, that's serious, you
            can. There's a huge database of all the different things you
            can accredit and that's one of them.
Tania: And have you ever accredited someone for boiling a kettle?
Louise: I haven't but I know other people have [but] if I worked
            in a centre and the centre was going to be closed or not if
            you did these things then I guess I probably would ... then
            you probably would do anything you could, and picking
            the easiest accreditations are probably better, so I guess that's
            why they do it. But yeah, I do think some of them are just
            stupid and pointless. And it's just a tick box exercise and
            isn't actually youth work.

Few of the youth workers who took part in the study opposed
accreditation outright, but most questioned its suitability for settings
that aim to be informal, fun and attended by young people who have
already been at school or college all day. Louise and others mentioned
first aid as an accredited course that carries genuine value, but it is
also costly, requires specialised tutors and can only be 'counted' once
for each young person. Few workers could meet their targets only
through courses they saw as worthwhile, hence the widespread and
often reluctant use of AQA unit awards in a variety of subject areas.[2]
Even though making a cup of tea is a useful life skill, and teaching it
may be appropriate in some cases (for example, in a disabled young
people's group), the actual skill seems diminished by its accreditation.
It is possible to imagine a young person saying proudly that they'd
learned at youth club how to make a good cuppa, but providing a
certificate seems condescending. The 'cup of tea' AQA has become the
epitome of the tick box exercise, seen by workers and young people as
inappropriate, worthless and demeaning of more notable achievements,
as explained by one worker in relation to his LGBT youth group:

   'My line manager had said to me, "Lorne, you're not
   meeting, you need to get more recorded and accredited
   outcomes down ... without the numbers you won't be
   able to keep your job,", basically. ... I did a lot of resisting
   and then I didn't do so much resisting, and I thought, OK,
   I'd better do some numbers. ... And she goes, "You know
   there's a recorded outcome for making a cup of tea?" I said,
   "You're having a laugh, aren't you?" ... I was so shocked
   that I printed it out and stuck it to my wall, and I was like,
   this is the ludicrous-y that we're working in, that there's an

accredited outcome for making a cup of tea. ... I mean the lunacy of all of this, right, the absolute ridiculousness, is that this pressure from them is alongside me reaching record numbers in that youth project of young people attending, of making national links with organisations and doing projects of a national scale ... My young people stood on the stage in front of government ministers and the head of the education authority ... and they're going, "You need to get them doing cups of tea accreditations."' (Lorne)

Lorne's work could be seen as highly successful according to its impact and attendance figures, but he was falling behind on targets and thus required to engage with practices he saw as ludicrous. In this way, performative systems seem to undermine grassroots youth workers' feelings of authenticity. Meanwhile, those who call for accountability in the form of targets, outcomes and payment by results insist that youth work must prove its effectiveness, and even its existence.

I do not mean to argue that there is no need for accountability of any kind. Most youth workers will know a small number of colleagues who are not sufficiently accountable to young people, their colleagues, the community or the field of youth work. The spectre of the 'bad youth worker' is often exaggerated, but it casts shame on the youth work identity and sometimes wins grassroots support for reform. Quincie's youth service employer was being restructured when I interviewed her, and she expressed enthusiastic support for this change even though it would lead to cuts in services and threatened her own job:

'The informality of youth work, I think the resistance, and the informality in youth work, resides in the laziness, and I firmly believe this, resides in the laziness of the worker. Does not want to work, essentially. ... Within youth work now you've got your support staff, who do have their day jobs and they're tired, they're knackered and they're just sitting in the corner and don't youth work ... You've just come in for a pay cheque [laughs] you know, essentially. So what's happening with youth work now eliminates all those people; basically what it is doing is shaking all the weeds off and that's what they've done. Youth work is a dusty old rickety thing that they've clawed out of the closet ... and this is the dusting off process, literally, and everything that's falling off [pause], urgh, it's what's falling off.' (Quincie)

Quincie spoke with eloquent disgust when she equated old-fashioned youth work with lazy 'support staff' (her fellow part-timers) who only come in for a pay cheque. If such cases are true, they may themselves be a legacy of long-term disinvestment and neglect; it is not the aim of this chapter to think about what should be done in these situations, but it does aim to question the assumption that time-consuming and surveillant monitoring systems are a suitable response. The alleged 'ineffectiveness' of the minority is used to justify a 'dusting-off process' of performance-related cuts and redundancies in which workers and teams are found wanting, removed and never replaced. Sometimes this is a way of removing 'ineffective' staff without having to go through disciplinary procedures, yet 'good' workers are lost in the same processes, and those who remain are fearful and insecure. Organisational restructuring has become a periodic feature of life in nearly all youth work bodies; austerity and the cry of 'value for money' reinforce the demand for further performative measures.

Those who escape this year's round of cuts may breathe a cautious sigh of relief and return to work with renewed incentive to be obedient and play the game. And yet, there is a shame and guilt in remaining when others have gone, as well as in performing according to criteria that feel 'fake', in betraying the ideals of youth work. The next section explores issues of identity, recognition, authenticity and shame, continuing to work with performativity as it is discussed in education policy sociology while also drawing on ideas from theorisations of gender performativity.

Authenticity and the youth worker identity

> 'The amount of times that admin and shit like that, excuse my language but it's *shit*, gets in the way of detached [street-based youth work]. Like when me and Bridget do it, because we both have so much admin, and a lot of times it's, I just need to finish this, oh no it's a dash, we need to go out!' (Laura)

Laura spoke with anger and frustration as she articulated the practical time and effort of the heavy administrative burden that she experiences as 'shit' work. This specific word, alongside 'crap' and 'bullshit', was frequently used by workers in relation to monitoring and administrative procedures. These slang words for animal waste suggest something that is dirty and perhaps disgusting, evoking palpable disdain for the monitoring procedures used in youth work. Recorded and accredited outcomes (see Table 2) came under particular criticism. Accredited outcomes have already been discussed in relation to the AQA in making a cup of tea. Recorded outcomes were designed to complement accreditation and recognise qualitative changes in young people's lives that might not lead to a certificate. Although introduced as an attempt to capture subtle outcomes, they were operationalised on a local level as a standardised form to be filled out and signed by youth worker and young person. High targets for recorded outcomes required tactical practices:

Alan: I did [a recorded outcome] yesterday in rap vocals for someone who's blatantly been able to rap for ages, but apparently he's done it in this session! Even though you've already done that one last year. ...

Tania: So do you always, you do sort of tend to record something actual?

Alan: I do actually do it, yeah, yeah. ... Otherwise you're just gonna be making stuff up, and it's all made up anyway but it's like, well, where do you stop? So I prefer to actually do it so it's meaningful, slightly. Even if that means I, we, we don't even get 50% of our targets on [recorded] outcomes. We hit everything else, by a mile. But we know that we don't get them because they're bullshit. Kids don't want them. And they're not aimed for the sort of work that we do. ... You sit down with a kid and you have a really meaningful conversation with them and you're like, 'Now can you fill in this sheet and tell me,' it's like it completely undermines everything that you've just done. ... 'You've only just had that conversation with me about my life and the different issues I've got at the moment so you can record it? So it looks like you're a decent youth worker? Is that it?' It's, yeah, bullshit.

This conversation is rich with references to the real ('actual', 'meaningful', 'blatant') and the unreal ('made up', 'looks like', 'bullshit'). Alan understandably prefers to write up an outcome that is 'meaningful, slightly' (something that really happened, even if it did not necessarily demonstrate new development) rather than risk a relationship by producing a piece of paper at the wrong moment. Even when the actual outcome is genuine, filling in a form can turn a 'meaningful conversation' into a commodity to be counted, which makes the encounter *less* authentic in the young person's eyes. Alan suggests that forms cannot adequately describe or represent the good work that he is *actually* doing. In this account, what is meaningful and what is made up seem to become intermingled – this is particularly uncomfortable for grassroots youth workers, who tend to attribute great value to being genuine and honest:

> 'I love youth workers. I think they're a special breed. ... There's something, like, genuine about a lot of youth workers.' (Laura)

> 'We are just genuine grassroots people who want to work with young people and have got that passion, and we're not ones for bragging. And I just think that's the nature of us.' (Leo)

Performing authenticity

To think more about the role of authenticity in the youth work identity, it is useful to return to theory, and to think about performativity from a different angle as it has been developed in relation to gender and sexuality, particularly by Judith Butler and Eve Kosofsky Sedgwick. Sedgwick (2003) explains how the concept of performativity derives from the work of J.L. Austin (1976). A philosopher of language, Austin proposed categories of spoken language in which performative utterances *do* an action rather than describing or referring to that action; examples of this are sentences including the words 'I apologise', 'I dare you' or 'I promise'. Later in his career, Austin argued against categorising language as either performative or descriptive, because every speech act contains elements of both (Sedgwick, 2003). Sedgwick (2003) traces the development of Austin's concept of performativity, through Derrida (whose work we do not have space to focus on here) to Butler, who emphasises that performativity is at its *most* effective when it is *least* explicit. Although it has a different emphasis, this is consistent with the interpretation of performativity already discussed: as form-filling becomes intrinsic to youth work, the worker and young person might begin to recognise themselves in (or as) what can be counted, written down, compared and ticked off – even as they say and feel that this is not the case.

Butler initially outlines her theory of performativity in *Gender trouble* (1990) and continues to clarify and develop it in subsequent work (1997, 2004, 2006). She argues that gender, sex, desire and subjectivity are created and restricted by iterative acts, discourses (both words and action) which regulate how it is possible to be. In this sense boundaries are created around what we can and cannot be, placing us in relation to a 'norm'. Our performances are never entirely freely chosen, and even by identifying and acting against gender norms (for example, as gay, trans, queer or bi) we still exist in relation to what is seen and created as 'normal' (Butler, 1997). Butler uses this argument to challenge gender and sex essentialism, arguing that performance is all:

> There is no gender identity behind the expressions of gender; that identity is performatively constituted by the very 'expressions' that are said to be its results. (Butler, 2006, p 34)

If we can replace 'gender' with 'youth work' in this sentence (and I will discuss in a moment whether we can) it might be important to question whether there is such a thing as a genuine youth work identity, which would blossom if only these inauthentic monitoring systems would go away. Passionate and caring attachments to youth work – as discussed in the previous chapter – are *also* performances that we create and recreate, perhaps by imitating other youth workers, or in response to our own past experiences of encountering professionals who do and do not seem to 'really' care. The accounts that youth workers gave me – and the accounts I give myself – are performances, even when they make claims on what is and is not real.

> 'You know the kind of youth work community meetings where everybody sits together with what they're doing with young people and so on, I just thought, this is a farce! It's just going round and round and especially when you're part-time, the frustration is, I can either be a youth worker, or I can attend meetings. And I can't attend your meetings because they're rubbish. And it's just a voice of you telling us everything's going brilliantly and that's not *real*.' (Tracey)

When Tracey talks here about meetings, she is at the same time giving an account of herself – her claims to what is and is not 'real' are performative. I am not arguing that claims to authenticity are meaningless or wrong; I recognise what Tracey is talking about here, and I agree with her. However, it seems useful to remind myself – especially as somebody who uses authenticity claims and is attracted to them – that these, too, should be subjected to scrutiny. Reading about performativity as a policy technology, my intuitive interpretation was that target and audit cultures undermine and remove the 'true' nature of youth work based on relationships and centred on young people's everyday lives. As well as romanticising what existed before the era of the audit, this understanding might diminish the effort involved in creating whatever we (collectively) choose to name as 'real' education, or 'real' youth work. Authentic youth work does not emerge on its own in the absence of oppressive systems of measurement or farcical community meetings. It is not automatic; rather, it needs to be performed, created and struggled over in its own right.

Workplace identity

Before going further I will pause here to think about whether the above is an appropriate use of theory, given that Butler and Sedgwick are writing about gender rather than workplace identity (see also McGimpsey, 2013 for further discussion on the use of feminist and queer theory in relation to youth policy). Performativity in Butler and Sedgwick's usage draws on psychoanalytic theory which emphasises the disavowal, mourning and denial of same-sex love and desire from infancy, the splitting of desire and identification, and the shame that derives from being rejected or being different from what is seen as normal (Butler, 1997; Layton, 2002; Sedgwick, 2003). Humans in most societies are conditioned to experience gender identity as if it is natural, as if it is something we *are* rather than something we *perform*. Only a minority of us might feel that we *are* our workplace identity in a similar way, or that our work identity is natural, unquestionable and unchangeable. In language terms, gender just *is*, whereas work is explicitly referred to as a 'role', an 'act', something we *do*; this is borne out in the language of the workplace: 'taking on a new role', 'performing well' or 'acting manager'.

Even though workplace identities tend not to be seen as 'fixed' in the way that gender and sex often are, perhaps they are not so very different. When a child is born people tend to ask, 'Is it a girl or a boy?' To place an adult in a category it is customary to ask them about their work: 'What do you do?' This is gendered, of course, and women are as likely to be asked, 'Do you have children?' Some people have a strong sense of vocation and calling in relation to their work; many of the participants in this research became youth workers by accident or chance and yet passionately claim 'youth worker' as a *central* aspect of their identity:

'I'm a community person, community worker, a youth worker, in my core.' (Lorne)

'I'm not into labels because then it defines how you work with someone or how you treat someone ... the only kind of definition I would say, "Yep, that's me," is a youth worker.' (Sarah)

Feelings of work identity can ebb and flow, particularly in an age of flexibility and precarious employment, and it remains more socially acceptable in neoliberal and conservative times to have a fluid work identity than a fluid gender identity. Nevertheless, work *can* sometimes feel like an expression of genuine or authentic self: perhaps if we have been doing a job for a long time, if we find work particularly enjoyable or fulfilling, if it overlaps with or subsumes other parts of our lives, or if it feels particularly congruent with our values or beliefs. Identifying ourselves with our work is consistent with an expansion in emotional and immaterial labour, as discussed in Chapter Three.

What does it mean to identify so strongly and passionately with a work role, particularly when this role is untaken part-time or on an unpaid basis, and particularly when it is as marginal and misunderstood as youth work? What does it mean if 'youth worker' feels like a core aspect of our identity and yet is being threatened from all angles? It is hardly surprising if we feel estranged or confused when we encounter clashes, inconsistencies and challenges within our work identities. As Judith Butler writes:

I am always constituted by norms that are not of my making ... norms work their way into what feels most properly to belong to me ... I am other to myself precisely at the place where I expect to be myself. (Butler, 2004, p 15)

For the youth workers in my study, audit and monitoring systems played a significant role in estranging the worker from their sense of self:

'It's not as much my organisation being able to say, "Yeah that's really good work and actually this is quality work," it's a numbers game, and we have to meet what the funders' expectations are. ... I'm conflicted about it because I think whilst I always try and make sure my work is, um, young people have ownership of it and they have options and they choose things, sometimes that isn't the case. And I'm aware of that.' (Mickie)

Authenticity becomes an arena of struggle. It is vitally important to assert a professional or personal identity that values honesty and rejects the false, the fake, the demeaning and the distracting. And yet, youth workers in this research did not seem able to escape audit and measurement systems that they experienced as dehumanising.

The role of shame

Grassroots youth workers are compelled to take part in systems of measurement, and usually attempt to succeed according to such systems, even when they see them as damaging, false and demeaning. I experienced this strange paradox myself, long before I heard of theories of performativity. A clash becomes internalised; we are implicated in systems we disagree with and are often unable to reconcile our beliefs and our actions. Reflecting on my own practice, I sometimes feel confused and conflicted, embarrassed and ashamed:

> In my previous job there were a lot of targets. When I did not meet my targets I felt I had failed, that I was not good at my job. This is despite the fact that I opposed and hated them, and perhaps also *because* of this fact. And so, I nearly always managed to succeed, somehow. What was the cost? I am trying to remember and the picture blurs. There were many times I bribed young people with a trip or a pizza in return for filling in paperwork. I remember simplifying the recorded outcomes forms so they were quicker to fill out, turning them into a tokenistic tick-box exercise. Once I agreed to some extra funding which came with so many targets that we ended up doing AQAs almost every week. Young people hated it. I'm on my own as I'm writing this but I am blushing, cringing, looking at the floor, shaking my head. I do not want to think about it. (Research diary, January 2014)

The shame is inescapable in performative systems, whichever way we turn. We feel shame when we do not meet our targets and are judged as failing. Then we also feel shame − perhaps of a slightly different nature − when we engage in practices that we know are antithetical to our work in order to meet our targets. The following is an excerpt from the focus group that met three times during the course of this research to discuss questions its members devised and selected themselves. Here, they reflect on one of their chosen questions: 'Do we need to be driven by outcomes?'

Mark: When I sit here and read that question I feel sick. Because I've done full sessions before that have been an hour, that I've had kids in a queue and I've gone, 'Right, outcome. Right. It was to cook. What did you think about it? Der, der. Sign there.' ... We were driven by the city council. They created these recorded outcomes; you had to have so many done within a certain month. But because I didn't like the system, because I just done youth work with the young people, there comes a point where your manager's like, 'I want your recorded outcomes,' so you're like, 'Kids, work with me.'...

Nicola: Yeah. But you're cheating the system cos you're thinking, this is a load of rubbish. I'm just gonna do it; I'm gonna make it look beautiful, and send it off. ... But what are you teaching them?

Mark: I don't know! I don't know. That's why I said I feel sick! I'm not saying I'm right. ... I'm having one of them moments. I don't know why I done it! I should have just not done 'em, and just got sacked! No, but honestly, the city council recording system was, oh [sighs], it was. You know. You used to get reports from the guy who used to collate the thing saying, 'Oh, you only contacted 10 young people. Why was that this month?' You know, questioning why you only contacted 10.

Arimas: The analyst.

Mark: The analyst. It analysed your data ... If you went out and you'd been on a detached session and you didn't see anyone, 'How did you not see anyone on your detached session?' Cos it was throwing it down and it was the coldest night of the year. 'Oh no, that's not a real, you didn't really go out.' Well, I did!

We might feel satisfaction in 'cheating the system' by meeting our targets in a perfunctory way, but our tactics offend against our sense of authenticity so we might also feel ashamed. Like Mark, I feel sick when I think back on some of the compromises I have made. And yet we continue to meet our targets, perhaps in order to keep our jobs and keep the funding coming in, but also perhaps to prove that we *are* authentic. Because it is not only youth workers who make claims on the real; the real is also the justification and the challenge of the audit. The system (represented in Mark and his colleagues' experience by a person who collates statistics and also by a computer 'analyst') suggests that *we are not real*: that we did not do the work, we were not there, our work did not take place – or that if it did, it was not good enough. Not 'being real' is a serious insult to a youth worker. Our identity is threatened when we do not meet the demands of the audit, and yet by meeting inappropriate targets we fail to live up to our own ideas of how we should be.

Audit systems are strongly coercive. If we do not conform we are threatened on a personal level with disciplinary procedures, with losing our jobs, with having our projects shut down. In times of austerity the stakes are raised to the survival of our entire youth service or voluntary organisation, even of youth work itself. Refusal is not a heroic option: if we fail, we take everybody down with us. The passion we feel for our work is harnessed in a bid to save money and meet targets. We engage in systems we do not agree with to save our projects, our colleagues and ourselves, and we might be embarrassed or ashamed of what we have had to do. These feelings might be hidden, or they might sometimes be shared, 'performed' in conversation with young people or with colleagues we can trust. Performing embarrassment and shame over issues of principle might sometimes be a way of asserting or claiming an authentic, grassroots identity. Perhaps this is what some of the research participants and myself have been doing here when we share our shameful feelings in interviews and research diary excerpts.

The shame of *not* meeting targets is somewhat different; this is a public shame that we do not choose, made publicly visible through systems of 'naming and shaming':

> 'A big thing comes round to all the youth groups to tell you how the other youth centres are getting on. It's like a pecking order. So depending on how many accreditations they've had, all that kind of thing ... it puts you in order of who's had the most and who's had the least and it gets sent round to everybody. ... So then those people get hoicked in the office individually and spoken to about the fact that they either need to get their numbers up or they need to start putting more information on there to be able to do it so they are monitoring it that way.' (Louise)

Software systems play an important role in workplace surveillance and control, and contribute to what Perryman (2006) refers to as panoptic performativity, where workers feel constantly observed. In this process of placing projects in a visible 'pecking order', youth workers become defendants and senior managers act as arbiters and enforcers. Love and passion are repositioned, now imagined in relation to monitoring systems rather than direct work with young people:

> 'They were in love with this data monitoring ... These centre management meetings every Monday mornings and we went round the table and there's all the different projects in [borough] and all the managers sitting there. ... The meetings were so dictatorial, authoritarian ... Basically they went round and they checked with every manager, had they entered their data for this week? And everyone had to say sort of "Yes" and you did feel like you were sitting in the headmaster's office at school while he was wielding a bloody cane or whatever. And I say "he" deliberately.' (Lorne)

Public shaming and comparisons create an atmosphere where non-conformity is almost unthinkable; not to fulfil your targets is to let the side down. Those who cannot adequately account for themselves are isolated and yet, somehow, their embarrassment flows outwards and everybody is implicated because 'shame is both peculiarly contagious and peculiarly individuating' (Sedgwick, 2003, p 36). Lorne's metaphor of the headmaster's office is apposite, as is his emphasis on 'he', implying the gendered nature of a system that is reinforced by the structural gender imbalance between senior managers and practitioners. There is no room at large youth service meetings for reflection on practice or for critical debate; they have become a place where workers are called to account before returning to their neighbourhoods, chastened, with renewed pressure to meet their targets.

Part-timers and volunteers are somewhat shielded from these processes. The downside is that they have little chance to defend, explain or object. In any case, shame seems to multiply and disseminate beyond the individuals who are seen as failing at any particular moment, attaching itself to their teams, the young people they work with, their colleagues, their organisation, and to youth work as a whole. Those who are seen as failing become marginalised, almost out of reach; just as youth work itself is marginal in relation to the school, the youth offending team, the family centre and the clinic. During a recent government inquiry into services for young people, youth work was shamed for its inability to produce quantitative evidence of its effectiveness (House of Commons Education Committee, 2011a). National youth work umbrella groups rushed to support the development of the Young Foundation's new outcomes framework (McNeil et al, 2012) rather than defending and asserting the necessarily unpredictable and highly contextual nature of youth work (Ord, 2014).

Writing in relation to gender, race and class identity, Layton (2002, p 202) argues that 'Non-dominant versions generally carry some shame – shame generated by looking at them through the lens of dominant positions'. Youth work is disproportionately organised for working class, black and minority young people, and staffed predominantly by working class, black and minority workers, often women. What might this mean in terms of how youth work is seen through the lens of monitoring mechanisms that are designed according to middle class professional norms (Apple, 2006, 2013)? Perhaps youth work can be seen as the 'other' in relation to more dominant forms of education and welfare (McGimpsey, 2013). Stubbornly open-ended and indeterminate, youth work has always been difficult to grasp. The 'outcomes' of open youth work may be significant, but do not follow a quarterly timetable and are often difficult to prove. Such a divergent approach becomes almost unintelligible in the era of the audit. In this context, workers can become ill, angry, depressed and isolated:

> 'I burnt out. I left. I was totally exhausted from the council, from not being supported enough, from not having the right staff, changes in the youth service at the time, the pressure being put on me to meet targets that I didn't even understand let alone had I or my colleagues or my young people set. So that was me being like, uhhh, I'm absolutely ill, basically. I felt ill. So I left.' (Lorne)

> 'It gives me a stomach ache every single time I go to those [team] meetings, every time I leave there I'm absolutely exhausted and low because I'm just so angry. I'm just so; I feel so alone ... I just feel really disappointed. I'm like, how can they be a youth work organisation?' (Laura)

Workers are operating in systems that produce bodily shame and exhaustion. Stress, pressure, illness, depression, anger and disappointment tell a sad and difficult story that counterbalances the love and passion discussed in the previous chapter. I want to keep this sadness and difficulty in mind while going on to think more hopefully about some ways in which the youth workers in this study engaged in performances that actively challenged cultures of targets and audit. In both its policy and gender versions, performativity is presented as a restrictive regime of power that it is not possible to escape; and yet there is always a possibility of exercising agency, contestation and resistance:

> If I have any agency, it is opened up by the fact that I am constituted by a social world I never chose. That my agency is riven with paradox does not mean it is impossible. It means only that paradox is the condition of its possibility. (Butler, 2004, p 3)

I do not intend to underestimate the difficulties and dilemmas involved in exercising agency in contexts where jobs are always under threat, nor to suggest that there is a clear solution, rather I will explore the possibilities and the actions that are already taken by grassroots youth workers to defend the authenticity of their work.

Contesting and subverting performativity

Even if youth workers cannot escape performativity by returning to an 'original' authentic identity, they can – and do – challenge the norms of managerialism and audit cultures. Before considering some workers' overtly subversive performances, I want to consider everyday examples of contestation that are commonly performed by passionate youth workers. When Forde was quoted early in this chapter she spoke about standards, figures, numbers and targets as both 'what we are' and 'what we do'. Here, she explains how her own satisfaction depends on outcomes that are less tangible than those represented by the targets she is compelled to meet:

> 'To be honest the target thing, it doesn't really concern me. Because if I reach my target, I reach my target. If I don't reach my target, but I've managed to help young people through the way, and I *know* that they've made progress, that is my greatest thing. To know that that young person, I've met their needs, they've achieved something, they've come out of it well, they're doing something. That is how I feel.' (Forde)

By emphasising the importance of the young person's experience, Forde places value on relational and informal processes that may be 'known' but are not always translatable into measurable outcomes. Her intuitive softening of the importance of targets seems to echo Hill Collins' (1990) articulation of black women's relational and caring 'ways of knowing' that challenge binary and linear forms of understanding. Target systems assume that a young person with the right support will progress from unemployed to employed, from anxious to confident, or from unhappy to happy – and (crucially) that these changes will be observable and measurable. Forde is suggesting that human life is more subtle and complicated, reminding us that what might appear to be small progress (or even no progress) from outside could be of vital importance to a particular young person.

The values expressed to me as an interviewer and fellow grassroots youth worker (especially one who might be guessed or known to oppose target cultures) may not be as easily articulated in the workplace. Nevertheless, some workers make explicit interventions against performative cultures, exploring alternatives to the most inappropriate and damaging monitoring systems. Here, Laura reflects on a meeting with managers and trustees where she attempted to tell them about youth work in ways that went beyond what is easily communicable:

> 'I had to show what opportunities we give young people. I gave a few examples of concrete things we give them, very concrete tangible things. And then I said, "But the most important things are the things you can't touch," and I made a massive emphasis on that because they're so obsessed with bloody targets. So then I sort of made, from the concrete ones, which intangible ones come out of that. And then some comments from the young people.' (Laura)

Like Forde, Laura can be understood to be 'proceeding from a different field of judgement' (Lipman 2013, p 13), countering targets with outcomes that are difficult or even impossible to capture: 'the things you can't touch'. She tells her voluntary sector managers that youth work is not easily captured in language let alone through numbers, as does Alan in his local authority workplace:

> 'People have become much better and more confident in defending the work we do here, because the work here is quite different to anywhere else really, because of the history of the youth club, the history of the estate, the style that we do. There's no targeted stuff at all; it's all completely open, and loose, and so now we're kind of trying to sell this idea

of having a loose kind of relationship to the work, and to opening times, and to relationships with young people and *when* we do stuff and that kind of stuff, and now that's kind of becoming more and more actual like policy or like good practice, whereas before it was just seen as a negative thing. Because we couldn't communicate what we were doing.' (Alan)

Alongside conventional targets for recorded and accredited outcomes, Alan's employer had introduced written storytelling as part of its quarterly monitoring requirements. This was an adaptation of storytelling as an alternative approach to accountability, developed by campaign group In Defence of Youth Work (IDYW) (2011, 2014b). IDYW's storytelling methodology aims to record the effectiveness of youth work in all its complexity. Stories are usually gathered at group workshops in which workers share experiences through collective critical questioning and reflection. In these workshops, the *process* of youth work is considered as important as its outcomes; perhaps a young person might not have found a job yet, but their feelings about themselves right now (and their ability to make their way in the future) might have been radically changed through the youth work process. Workers are encouraged to think about their own role in the story, and how this relates (or does not relate) to the cornerstones of democratic and emancipatory youth work (IDYW, 2009). Young people, volunteers and external agencies have also been involved in the storytelling workshops, and some youth organisations have embedded storytelling practices in their evaluation processes (IDYW, 2014b). This is a form of accountability to young people and the youth work field rather than to funders or government: a form of accountability that is collaborative rather than competitive.

Communicating about youth work in ways that go beyond the quantitative and the specific can be seen as critically subversive – unsettling the hegemonic practice of outcomes-focused work. Despite the development of counter-discourses and alternative evaluation methods, however, audit cultures retain significant power in youth work. Workers might not 'feel' that targets are important, and might find ways to articulate the non-quantifiable and the non-linear benefits of youth work, but they remain subject to high-stakes measurement systems that they are required to comply with. However, this should not be taken to mean that targets and outcomes are non-negotiable or that resistance is futile.

Several workers relayed stories of avoiding targets by working with colleagues and young people to oppose elements of managerial systems they felt were particularly damaging. This involved a tactical 'weighing up' of the relative gains and potential losses of compliance and refusal at different times – in other words, the choosing of battles. Lucy and colleagues refused to fulfil a target that required them to organise a certain number of sessions bringing young people together with the police, after young people objected to the idea (this story is discussed in more detail in Chapter Five). Their ability to refuse this target seemed to be contingent on a form of strategic performativity where they perform as 'good employees' in order to earn a relative degree of autonomy and the right to challenge aspects of their work they are particularly opposed to:

> 'We all work very hard. We don't have sickness. We don't have "can't come into work" dramas. We don't cause any hassle as individual workers. ... If we say we're gonna do something we get it done. We respond to emails. So I think no matter how much they don't like us or we don't totally mesh with them, we're good as youth workers and we're actually quite easy, good employees. We don't have long bouts of sickness. We don't cause them any trouble, really. ... We never cancel sessions. We say we're doing a project, it happens. We do a trip, it happens. ... We give good reports. ... We don't give them any trouble. (Lucy)

This picture does not conform to the image of a maverick or rebellious youth work team; by acting as 'quite easy, good employees' workers are sometimes able to create spaces to work differently, engaging in what we might call 'tactical performativity'. Similarly, Alan worked long hours and went beyond the usual expectations of a part-time worker, which earned him substantial autonomy over how he carried out his work. Louise's team engaged in specific projects to meet their targets in order to protect the core of their informal street-based work with small groups of young people that might not otherwise be seen as cost-effective or time-efficient. These practices of 'earning' the freedom to challenge or refuse the most damaging aspects of performativity echo wider policy discourse; for example, schools or colleges that are judged as 'outstanding' by Ofsted earn greater autonomy in their teaching methods and curriculum (Avis, 2005). It is difficult to assess the effectiveness of tactical performativity, which may partly act to reinscribe norms (Butler, 1997), but such practices also disrupt the assumed truth and necessity of standardised monitoring procedures.

Although workers commonly drew on support from colleagues and asked young people for their views, it was rare for young people and members of the wider community to be involved in direct campaigning against monitoring systems. A notable exception in my research was the LGBT project where Mickie worked, which refused to engage with its local authority's monitoring databases. Information on this database was shared among many agencies, effectively 'outing' the young people attending the LGBT project:

> 'It was brought to the young people and the young people made a campaign and we supported that and they wrote to the head of youth service ... We had parents come in and talk and stuff and public meetings and things, and supported the young people in their campaign to have their privacy respected. ... they were still getting the kind of statistical data, they just weren't getting the names ... it's about an ethos and a principle of respecting young people's details and not seeing their information as currency to get funding.' (Mickie)

The success of this campaign related to the politicised ethos of the project, its workers, and members of the wider LGBT community who were drawn in to support the young people:

> 'I think the staff and volunteers are not threatened, are not gonna be pushed over ... your threatening my job doesn't make my principles, or the principles of this place, any different ... the young people were supported into collectively sharing their voice with the people as well that were the decision makers, so the people of influence really. I think it's partly just because of the kind of the general vibe of the place but also there was a lot of support from a lot of people who were kind of outraged by this kind of stuff and said "no".' (Mickie)

For some workers, setting up their own organisations seemed to be a way of regaining control over their work and making decisions over the forms of monitoring they were involved in. My experience as part of Voice of Youth suggests that working outside of oppressive monitoring systems is possible if it goes alongside a willingness to negotiate, support each other, and turn down funding where necessary (see Chapter Six). Struggles against audit cultures are a challenge to the assumed necessity and normality of measuring outcomes according to prescriptive criteria. They also show young people that their views are important and that top-down requirements can be contested. Negotiations and campaigns can take the struggle over performativity beyond the worker's individual experiences of the clash between the work they believe in and targets they do not, into a more public realm.

Conclusion: breaking the rules?

Paperwork (2)

'Where are they?' asks Shay indignantly, looking up and down the street. 'They usually do their street work on Fridays!' Jenna shrugs and sends a text to find out. They wander into the corner shop and eye up the vodka. Soon, Jenna's phone beeps. 'Huh! Jo says they have too much paperwork to do, they'll see us next week.' Shay sighs, 'Paperwork, again!' A few minutes' bike ride away, a group of young men are sitting on their usual wall. Danny surreptitiously checks that nobody's mum is about, and passes a spliff to Sadiq. 'Youth club is shit,' says Sadiq. 'It's like school, always forms to fill in. We never do anything fun any more.'

It's the last day of the quarter, and the youth workers have a system. Jo is checking the forms are filled out properly and Ricky is battling the photocopier. They moan, grumble and worry their way through the task, bored and strangely satisfied as they create neat piles of paper, stapled and labelled with coloured Post-its. This time they'll miss their target for accreditations (that drugs debate was a waste of effort) but maybe they can catch up by the end of the year. Or maybe, suggests Jo, they should go to their manager and explain again that accreditation isn't working. 'No point, it's a waste of time,' says Ricky.

This research contributes to a growing weight of evidence against the taken-for-granted use of inappropriate audit mechanisms in and beyond youth work. The experiences and emotions expressed by grassroots youth workers in relation to monitoring and target cultures will be recognisable in settings outside youth work – they are likely to be familiar to workers throughout education and the wider public and community sectors. There are also ways in which this analysis is specific to youth work: the things that make youth work special (its informality and responsiveness) also make it *particularly* unsuited to pre-planned outcomes and competitive monitoring technologies (Fusco, 2013; Taylor and Taylor, 2013; Ord, 2014). For youth workers, targets can be distracting and demoralising; for young people they can be tedious and demeaning.

Over the past decade, audit cultures have become a dominant and normalised feature of youth work. Throughout this research, workers consistently emphasised how targets, outcomes and paperwork clashed with what they saw as *real* youth work. Performativity evokes struggles over identity and authenticity; over what it is to have genuine and honest relationships with young people and with colleagues. It is hardly surprising, perhaps, that debates over what is 'real' are prominent in contexts where youth work must be recorded on a database if it is seen to exist at all. If the database does not recognise some of the work they are doing, some youth workers come to the conclusion that good practice means breaking the rules:

Lucy: You find ways around it. ...
Laura: So basically to be a good youth worker we need to break the rules.
Bridget: Yeah.
Lucy: We need to be creative with the way you meet your targets.

Some spend time and energy being 'creative', or explaining the difficulties with monitoring systems to their managers and funders. A few openly rebel, refusing to aim for 'excellence' according to systems they oppose (Ball and Olmedo, 2013). Some act collectively with colleagues, young people and the community to challenge monitoring procedures, such as Mickie's organisation's rejection of database monitoring, and In Defence of Youth Work's development of storytelling as an alternative approach to accountability (IDYW, 2014b). Overt challenge may be rare, and arguing or breaking the rules is stressful and risky. Where it occurs, though, dissent questions the normalisation of targets and keeps the debate alive.

Workers' attempts to think and act differently constitute meaningful political action, even when they seem like private rebellions – Forde's refusal to take targets as a measure of success, or Laura's emphasis on 'the things you can't touch'. Such challenges can be seen as seeking or opening up cracks and fissures in the dominant power structures: it is possible that 'tiny, subterranean revolts may be far more radical in their potential than the noisiest demonstration' (Holloway, 2010, p 78). Youth workers are rarely able to escape target cultures, and the neoliberal ideology that lies behind systems of surveillance and competition seem to survive any form of challenge. However, small acts of subversion may change the world in ways that are difficult to predict, as Judith Butler writes:

> It's as if one says, 'You think that's subversion, and you think that's criticism? Actually, it's nothing other than an extension of an existing power regime – end of story.' Now, what I want to be able to say is, 'Sure, we are extending the contemporary power regime by our ostensible subversion, but there's extending the power regime and there's extending the power regime.' Extending it does not mean extending it always in the same form; it could mean reiterating it in new forms. Extending is not a mechanical process. We need to understand power as something that produces unanticipated effects, that we can certainly extend power but that we can extend it into an unknown future. (Butler, in Olson and Worsham, 2000, p 740)

Targets, outcomes, databases and bureaucratic requirements herald disillusion, frustration, anger and even illness among grassroots youth workers; they also lead to creativity and rebellion. There were numerous signs of contestation among the participants in this research, from widespread counter-discourses to local negotiations and attempts to build more collective forms of resistance. However, for most youth workers, most of the time, it is barely possible to avoid or resist targets or outcomes-based monitoring, particularly in a context of cuts and precarity. The resulting heavy administrative workloads and feelings of inauthenticity can drive youth workers away from what they are good at, while monitoring systems tend to distort the work that takes place. They also create an insidious culture of distrust and pathologisation, where young people are tracked by surveillant technology with which youth workers – however unwillingly – collude. It is this focus on surveillance and how it positions young people in relation to youth workers that is explored in the next chapter.

Notes

[1] AQA is an awarding body offering basic skills awards that it claims are used by hundreds of youth services (AQA, 2014).

[2] Awarding body AQA offers over 23,000 unit awards, including AQA unit 83,522: 'Making tea or coffee' (validated 1999).

FIVE

Surveillance on the street

Something to hide? (1)

Squeezed in with the buggies on the bus, Jenna feels someone looking at her. She turns around quickly, ready for anything, screwing up her eyes so they look small and mean, but nobody is looking her way. It's been a bad day, and she hopes Shay will have money for vodka. All day at school she was in the unit again, where the teachers ignore you unless they want to get something out of you. They're all snitches anyway, asking about her mum. As if they care. They'll go straight to social services if she tells them anything, so she doesn't trust them. She jumps off the bus by the youth club and sees Jo across the road, and they both smile and wave, shouting, 'Hiya!' They're meeting up later to organise a trip to a theme park. Jenna's never been. It's going to be amazing.

The siren gets louder, and Danny pulls his hood up. Then sucks his teeth, wondering why he's acting as if he's got something to hide. Like at school where he was always the one pulled out of line, even when he'd not been doing anything wrong. It was like a prison there. 'Line up, no touching, stand against the wall, hands where we can see them.' Cameras everywhere but it's not the ones you can see that you need to worry about, it's the ones they've hidden and the secret microphones in the walls. The bully van passes slowly, siren off now but lights still flashing. He expects them to get out and stop him: 'We are looking for someone of your description' – yeah, black boy in a hoody. Surprise, surprise. 'You're detained for the purposes of a search, let's get this over with "mate". Arms up, anything sharp in your pockets?' Blah blah bullshit. But the van drives on into the estate. He messages his mates to warn them, just in case, and then sees Jo walking his way. He looks away but it's too late, she smiles at him, so Danny has to mumble 'Alright.' He's not in the mood for talking. Jo just says 'Hi' and keeps walking. She's OK. Hopefully she'll be out with Ricky later. Ricky's always good for a laugh.

At home, at school and on the streets, young people are habituated to networks of surveillance that are designed to watch, control and protect. Some young people may experience this surveillance as hostile, particularly those who are already marginalised and discriminated against. This is partly because, as Introna (2003, p 212) argues, 'Surveillance is not just a general "staring" at the world; it is always with a purpose, i.e. to make some judgement about the one being monitored.' Surveillance produces data that justifies its own expansion, becoming a cause as well as an effect of information gathering and social control (Hier, 2003).

What is the role of youth workers in – and against – the surveillance of young people? This chapter will discuss this question, focusing in particular on detached youth work. Detached work is a form of practice in which workers aim to build relationships with young people on their own terms and in their territory. They mainly work on the streets and in public spaces, settings that give a particular character to their relationships with young people. Detached youth work is particularly interesting in relation to surveillance, because it has a somewhat romantic reputation as a space where maverick youth workers and marginalised young people can stay out of sight of some of the controlling mechanisms that govern most public and voluntary sector work. My contention is that detached work can no longer sustain such claims of distance and independence – if it ever could – but that detached workers nevertheless have an important role to play in creating qualitatively different spaces and relationships, where surveillance can be critiqued and discussed with young people.

There is a well-established tension between youth work for social control and youth work for social change, and this tension is particularly salient in relation to detached work. Of those research participants who were involved in detached work, many expressed discomfort – and explicit opposition – in relation to some of the things they have been asked to do. They were particularly critical of policies that brought them into the realm of the 'establishment' in their own or young people's eyes, such as requirements to work alongside the police, and systems that required them to gather information on young people they met on the street. They rarely used the word surveillance; however, it is a useful concept in understanding youth workers' street-level dilemmas, particularly around who they work with and how they share information.

Bronwyn Davies writes here about surveillance in higher education; despite this being written in relation to a context that is rather different from youth work, her point about the role of surveillance in neoliberal cultures of individual responsibility is highly pertinent:

> Surveillance becomes a key element of neoliberal systems, necessitated by the heightened emphasis on the individual's responsibility and the de-emphasising of inner values and commitment to the social good. Trust is no longer

realistic or relevant. Each person no longer trusts the other to work properly, and each becomes one of the multiple eyes spying on each other. Further, reporting mechanisms for monitoring and producing appropriate behaviour are mandated. These mechanisms are, in turn, very costly and devour an enormous proportion of shrinking funds, thus requiring an increase in the amount of work each worker is expected to do. (Davies, Bronwyn, 2005, p 10)

Many youth workers will recognise this analysis. Surveillance, like the performativity discussed in the previous chapter, is not only something that is 'done to' or 'done by' workers, it is something that we are implicated in, that we do to ourselves and to others (our colleagues and young people), whether we like to or not. Such an analysis draws on Foucault's theory of governmentality in which he employs the metaphor of the panopticon, an eighteenth-century design for a circular prison with a central viewing tower (Foucault, 1977; Bentham, 1995). In a panopticon, prisoners are situated in individual cells around the periphery and can be monitored by the guards at any time, but they cannot see into the viewing tower. They do not know whether or when they are being watched so they monitor their own behaviour in case they can be seen. In Foucault's view, this is a metaphor for how modern societies are governed: pervasive surveillance means that we may be observed at any time, and we act to regulate our own behaviour according to what is and is not acceptable or allowable.

Surveillance systems, then, are not primarily deployed to 'catch' those who break the rules; more importantly, they are a disciplinary mechanism to encourage certain modes of behaviour and discourage others among the wider populace. This had clearly been felt by young people interviewed for a piece of Australian research into young people's views on surveillance:

'Me and my mates we're always getting some look from the security guard, or you know, security cameras. We're not trying to be bad, we're not starting any trouble, we're not doing anything wrong. But it's the mentality.' (Young person quoted in Wilson et al, 2010, p 27)

Like Danny in the vignette, young people know when they are categorised as potential trouble-makers. Even if they have done nothing wrong, certain groups are treated as suspects because of how they look and their perceived age, class, ethnicity, sexuality and/or gender. The security guard feels that he or she is preventing crime or nuisance by watching these young people, and there might well be substantial public support for the removal or policing of young people 'hanging around', but this cannot be understood separately from the wider demonisation of young people in general, and working class, black and Muslim young people in particular. Those groups who are already disadvantaged are most likely to be the target of surveillance, and this weakens notions of a public sphere where everybody feels included and respected. Marxist theorists have pointed out that urban surveillance operates against marginalised groups in the interests of capital, and rarely targets serious corporate or environmental crime (Coleman et al, 2005). Profit becomes the justification for the targeting of young people on the streets, as was borne out by the same Australian research:

> 'Just want us away from their areas because apparently we make their business look bad or whatever like. But that's not the case; it's just that we don't have our own place to f★★king chill.' (Young person quoted in Wilson et al, 2010, p 27)

Like homeless people and working class pensioners, teenagers have limited economic value. These groups are designated as undesirable in the entrepreneurial city, so that 'it is often merely their visibility alone and not their behaviour that is deemed problematic' (Coleman, 2005, p 141). Shiny privatised malls and gated residential areas create an illusion of security and pleasure for those who can afford to live there, leaving no space for young people to 'hang out'; they are instead 'designed out' through heightened surveillance and security measures, the removal of benches and the privatisation of previously public space. New urban spaces become 'visualised spectacles that promote ways of seeing urban space as benign, "people-centred" and celebratory' (Coleman, 2005, p 132), and black and ethnic minority communities are often displaced (Lipman, 2011, 2013). This was exemplified in artists' impressions of a redesigned shopping area in a gentrifying area of East London, which:

> revealed Hackney's transformation into a borough inhabited almost entirely by young white people. The diversity of the borough has almost completely disappeared and the different communities, cultures and people of all ages and abilities have been replaced with white children and cyclists. (Ngoma Bishop, in Loeb, 2013)

Towards the end of this chapter I will discuss how youth workers and young people might reimagine the street quite differently – not as a money-making arena for the privileged, but as a diverse and contested space to be claimed and shaped by those who inhabit it. First, the chapter focuses on detached youth workers' responses to policy that involves them in the direct or indirect surveillance of young people on the streets. Drawing on stories of collusion and resistance told by detached workers involved in my research, the chapter begins by looking at how practitioners make claims of distance from systems of control. I will then explore how policy has drawn these same workers into surveillance roles, particularly through working with the police, and sharing young people's details on electronic databases.

Youth work on the streets

Detached youth workers build relationships with young people in places where they spend time, such as street corners, bus stops, squares, shopping centres, cafes, beaches and amusement arcades. They aim to reach young people who are disengaged from mainstream services and work with them on their own territory rather than necessarily bringing them into organised clubs or centres. Detached work's origin as a distinctive approach began in the 1950s, building on earlier histories of neighbourhood play and youth work, as well as on street work with gangs in the US and elsewhere. From its beginnings it was intended to be different from other forms of work with young people, 'detached' from institutions that young people identified as hostile or irrelevant (Morse, 1965; Goetschius and Tash, 1967).

Initially an experimental practice, detached youth work has become well established over time; in the UK it has formed its own independent organisation, the Federation for Detached Youth Work, and built a body of literature (see, for example, Wild, 1982; Kaufman, 2001; Tiffany, 2007; Whelan, 2010). The detached workers in my study saw their practice as qualitatively different to other approaches, and distinguished themselves from other agencies that worked on the streets. Here, Rachel talks about starting out as a part-time detached worker in her southern town:

> 'At the time in [town] there were a lot of agencies working with young people in their own settings but most of them were there to move young people on or to stop the behaviour that they were exhibiting whereas obviously we were coming at it from an entirely different point of view.

... We were there to advocate with them, work with them where they were, not expect them to go to a youth club, not to expect them to go home or move on ... we came at it from such a different perspective than other agencies.' (Rachel)

Rachel talks here about what detached work *is not* as well as what it is, challenging assumptions about what a professional is likely to be doing with young people on the streets and disputing the idea that young people should be moved *off* the streets. In contrast, Rachel views it as normal and reasonable for young people to spend time on the streets and even to take risks:

'It is their own time, and they have chosen to meet their friends and they don't necessarily want adults involved or any organised activity ... I can totally understand why they would want to meet outside away from people and not be hassled, you know, and even if it is to kind of drink and smoke, to go through the normal rites of passage, you know, meeting people, I can totally understand why they want to do that.'

While many detached workers maintain a positive view of young people on the streets, this contrasts with the terms under which they are often funded and employed: public and political concerns over young people's presence on the streets. This entrenched 'moral panic' is echoed in everyday language, where the street is a metaphor for trouble. If someone is 'on the streets' they might be taken to be homeless; if 'working the streets' they are assumed to be sex workers. In urban slang, if someone is 'on road' it implies they are involved in gangs. Young people who spend time on the streets with their friends are spoken of as 'youths', 'vandals', 'sluts', 'hoodies', 'drug dealers' or 'binge drinkers'; whatever they are *actually* doing, they are said to be 'hanging around', 'up to no good'. The detached workers interviewed for this study were generally critical of these stereotypes, but held a spectrum of attitudes that perhaps reflects their differing organisational and professional cultures as well as their individual perspectives. In contrast with Rachel's view of young people, here is a passage from my interview with Olly, a centre-based, outreach and detached worker who works in a rural area:

'What we tend to base the detached work on, again it would tend to be perceived problems around town ... they'll tend to have their picnics and get up and go and they'll just leave a ring of litter, and it really upsets the residents ... People hanging out late at night in places that are sort of dry and a little bit lit, and we've got bus shelters, um, outside of supermarkets, um, kids' playgrounds, and you know, there's questions of alcohol, and cannabis use. Um. That really upsets the public and is a perceived problem. Um. Older lads hanging around places like the skate park in the old days, um, and seeing that just as a good place to, you know, polish off a few bottles of beer and suchlike, and then you might get smashed glass. That sort of thing. So we're told of these sort of problems and we'll go out and just explain to people sort of, um, look, you know, this is the perceived problem, this is why we're on the streets, what's their take on it?' (Olly)

In this passage, Olly draws on a local policy discourse that identifies young people on the street as problematic, and positions detached youth work as a possible solution. Here 'the residents' and 'the public' are set against young people who are associated with 'problems' including leaving litter and smashed glass, hanging out late at night, drinking alcohol, using cannabis and upsetting people. However, Olly does not seem comfortable with this discourse, speaking more hesitantly than he usually does, and going some way to challenging it. Of the four times he uses the word 'problem' here, three times he precedes it with 'perceived'. He avoids using negative labels for the young people, calling them 'people' and 'lads', and although he approaches them on the basis of an externally identified problem, he asks them for 'their take on it'.

Detached workers have for many years been under growing pressure to tackle 'hotspots' of youth crime or antisocial behaviour, and the differing accounts of Rachel and Olly echo the divergent perspectives of detached youth workers in earlier research (Crimmens et al, 2004; Tiffany, 2007). What most detached workers have in common is a commitment to building voluntary relationships and taking young people's views seriously:

'For me, detached work is about building relations, just talking to young people, finding out where they're at, what's pissing them off, what they enjoy, but letting them know that actually you're, you're not the police, you're not an authority so to speak, but you can work with those people and hopefully have some stuff going in. We always take sort of suggestions back with us.' (Olly)

Of all the workers interviewed, Olly was probably the most enthusiastic about working with the police, as will be discussed below. However, he clearly differentiates himself, telling young people he's 'not the police ... not an authority', echoing Rachel's emphasis on what detached work is not. It was common among the detached workers in my research to speak about their work as 'different' – more community based, more free, more flexible and less target orientated:

> 'On detached you've got more freedom, I feel, you can go out and do more with the community.' (John)

> 'Things can come out of detached work but you're not advertising something ... And I think it's the only space in youth work where I think they can lead and it's not too target focused.' (Lucy)

> 'When you're on the streets you're like, you're not in that position of power.' (Tracey)

This latter point from Tracey is interesting in relation to control and surveillance. The point here is not that detached workers have no power: they have structural power as adults and workers, as well as access to personal information that could be used or misused. It is how they exercise this power that is crucial: by treating the streets as young people's space and respecting their time and what they want to talk about, detached youth workers have a more equitable dynamic with young people than is possible for most professionals:

> 'Literally you're just approaching a group of young people on the streets, in their own environment, in their own social space, in their own social time.' (Quincie)

> 'You're on their turf at that time, and it's not that it's hostile, it's just that if actually they want to get on with what they're doing at that time and without you, that's something to respect ... you start getting into a conversation and then they suddenly feel it's uncomfortable and they don't want to go any further, that's the end of that.' (Olly)

One of the ways in which detached workers show their respect for young people is to take time to build relationships on their terms, often slowly and painstakingly:

'If we move to a new area we always start our work through reconnaissance and slowly develop reconnaissance through the area, through the community members, through where young people hang around, through the parks and everything and open spaces and slowly build that, and if we see young people slowly build that relationship, say hi and bye and that sort of thing, greet members of the community and just slowly, slowly do that ... that sort of open approach and taking it easy.' (Mahad)

'You slowly get to know them on the street. You slowly start seeing them to begin with. You hardly say hello because that's intrusive, unless they want to. They start seeing your face. Then eventually you start saying hello, you start chatting for a bit, randomly about anything. They start seeing, OK this person's around here. All of a sudden you start having really deep conversations about something really important to them. And this all just from slowly seeing them around there, on their terms, you know?' (Laura)

These workers emphasise being friendly and open, taking it easy, avoiding intrusive questions, chatting, sticking around. It is notable that the word 'slowly' appears eight times in these two short passages from Mahad and Laura, showing a respect for the pace of real human relations that do not always fit in with external targets and time pressures (Colley et al, 2012). Because of its working methods, the time it takes, and its spatial positioning away from the office, detached work has historically been less monitored than other forms of youth work:

'We have a freer rein than youth centres do ... The management and that don't really tend to come and see what we're up to or make sure we're in or whatever. Whereas at youth centres I know they often, when you arrive at the youth centre there might be a manager there to see if you've arrived on time ... They have been checking up on a lot of people but they haven't been checking up on us as far as I'm aware, not yet anyway [laughs].' (Louise)

None of this is to suggest that detached youth work is a panacea, and perhaps it is rarely as free, open and equal as its practitioners claim (Siurala, 2014). Detached work has not been immune to the changes affecting youth work over the past decades, including the spending cuts, marketisation and target cultures that are discussed throughout this book. It has been particularly vulnerable to requirements to take part in the formal surveillance of young people on the streets, including through joint work with the police and the use of electronic database tracking systems. These requirements have been introduced through national and local government strategies, funding priorities and the actions of managers and practitioners on the ground.

As policy is decentralised and dispersed, it is formed through networks of governmental, private and charitable organisations and enacted at the level of practice (Ball, 2012; Ball et al, 2012). At times, decentralisation enables flexibility and negotiation at a local level for practitioners as well as policy makers, and we will see that youth workers are sometimes successful in challenging local manifestations of policy. On the other hand, decentralised processes tend to mystify and obscure the ideological forces that lie behind policy developments which are played out differently in each local context, and this can make collective resistance more difficult.

As in other chapters, my analysis here relies on an understanding of policy as a process of struggle and contestation (Ozga, 2000; Ball, 2008a). Practitioners do not simply implement policies, they change, develop, avoid and contest them, as well as being influenced and shaped by them (Ball et al, 2012). In this context it is useful to look at the experiences of a small number of part-time and volunteer detached youth workers from different organisations, both local authority and voluntary sector, and in different urban and rural areas in England. The following section will explore these workers' experiences of policy that involves them in the surveillance of young people – first working with the police, and then electronic tracking – and discuss how their work is affected, how they collude and how they resist.

Working – and not working – with the police

'A lot of young people don't trust youth workers because they expect us to work with the police.' (Laura)

When I entered youth work in the 1990s, it was impressed on us that police officers were not to be allowed into a youth club without a warrant. One of my past employers, Manchester Youth Service, even had a written policy at one time that prevented police officers from volunteering in youth clubs. The distance placed between youth work and the police, at least in urban areas, was formed in the context of widespread police harassment of black, working class and subcultural groups of young people, particularly in the wake of inner-city riots in the early 1980s. Institutional racism in the police force was confirmed in 1999 by the Macpherson Report on the inquiry into the murder of black teenager Stephen Lawrence. Today's force is more aware of the need at least to appear to uphold equality, although this position is called into question by the continuing disproportionately high rates of stop and search of black young men (Bowling and Phillips, 2007; EHRC, 2010), and the over-representation of black and minority ethnic community members in deaths in or following police custody (INQUEST, 2015). Young people in many areas have an understandable distrust of the police, as do many youth workers, who are often from the same communities as the young people they work with.

Other youth workers have more positive views of the police and there is a long tradition of informal working relationships and events such as football matches between police and young people, aimed at building relationships:

> 'It's good to build bridges between people they might not necessarily associate with, certainly on the police side. And actually see underneath the uniform they're real people. And it's also I think quite good for the police to see, you know, these kids have got some sort of potential and just because they spend an awful lot of time in the sort of bus stops and such like, doesn't mean they're actually bad people. Just not got much direction.' (Olly)

Olly finds it satisfying and rewarding to bring police and young people together, arguing that it makes a difference to attitudes on both sides, although he emphasised that he always asks young people for their views and would not bring the police to a session without young people's agreement. John, a younger and newer detached and centre-based worker, spoke with similar optimism about improving relations:

> 'On detached I've done a lot more with communities, and I've been involved with PACT [Partners and Communities Together] meetings ... it's open to everybody just to come along, and talk about any issues that are sort of within their community and you also get the police come along as

well. So, the young people ... get to know the police well in a positive way within these meetings ... With [county] police there's the ... Independent Advisory Group. It's a group that's set outside of the police; it's independent, um, and they advise the police on how to do their job ... everybody's involved, the youth service, the police, social services, churches, er, young people, politicians, the whole sort of shebang, just all sort of group together and sort of, "Well, what shall we talk about?" You know, "What's going on and what can we do to improve?"' (John)

John enjoys the opportunity these meetings give him for involvement with the wider community and different agencies. Like Olly, John has positive reasons for wanting to work with the police, and finds that this work brings certain satisfactions. However, police involvement in community meetings and youth clubs can be seen as a means of intelligence gathering and legitimisation, examples of Foucault's governmentality: 'the deliberations, strategies, tactics and devices employed by authorities for making up and acting upon a population and its constituents to ensure good and avert ill' (Rose, 1996, p 328). There *are* real people underneath the uniform, as Olly says, but it is important to recognise that the uniform is meaningful: it stands for an institution that has exerted and misused its structural power in relation to young people (Macpherson, 1999; Bowling and Phillips, 2007; MPA, 2008; EHRC, 2010; Lepper, 2013a, 2013b; INQUEST, 2015).

While there is a worthwhile debate to be had about whether youth workers should facilitate the improvement of relations between police and young people, and whether this does more harm or good, youth workers I interviewed were primarily concerned about policies that *required* them to work alongside the police, rather than being able to make this complex judgement together with young people and colleagues. The Crime and Disorder Act (1998) was significant in requiring public bodies to publish crime and disorder strategies, as well as introducing a raft of legislation aimed at youth crime (including antisocial behaviour orders, child curfews and the removal of truants off the streets to their homes or to 'designated premises'). As part of these changes, detached workers were brought into closer partnerships with the police through schemes such as Operation Staysafe, where police officers worked with other agencies to remove young people from the streets at night and take them to a 'place of safety' (Home Office, 2009). In my research, some workers objected that such arrangements would exploit their relationships with young people and co-opt youth work into policing and surveillance roles.

Some youth workers in the study refused to work with the police despite policy requirements to do so, engaging in overt rebellion that represents more straightforward examples of refusal than much of the 'everyday resistance' discussed in the book so far. Here we will look at two examples.

'You do not control us' (Tracey's story)

Tracey is the part-time coordinator of a small Christian youth charity that had received local authority funding for some years, with slightly different stipulations each year. As part of one year's contract, Tracey was informed that she would be required to work with the police on Friday and Saturday nights, confiscating alcohol from groups of young people and encouraging them to 'move on'. This was a sudden change in direction that seemed to undermine the independence and experience of her organisation:

> 'It was like, "We're doing this, we fund you, you need to do it like this." And of course immediately your back gets up. Cos you're like, well, no actually, I'm not so sure as I want to walk around with the police. Because I'm not so sure this is gonna help our relationships with young people and how they see us.'

Tracey's misgivings were grounded in a local knowledge of young people built up over many years, rather than a principled opposition to working with the police per se. In fact, she already had a positive working relationship with a police community support officer,[1] although they did not walk the streets together. Tracey has always felt that it was important to keep the roles separate, and knew that young people would otherwise feel uncomfortable:

> 'They're gonna get so confused ... because we've not worked with the police before, and while we've got relationships with the community support officers that are amazing and really lovely in [town], most of them anyway ... now all of a sudden the police are *with* us.'

Nevertheless, the new funding contract required that Tracey started working with the police, so she reluctantly went along with it for the first few weeks. As she had expected, she disliked confiscating alcohol and telling young people to go home, which she felt were outside of the youth work role. In addition, she found it problematic working with different colleagues every week and felt that her own experience built up over many years was not respected. Weighing up these issues, Tracey and her manager (the chairman of trustees of the charity) decided that they could not continue with the project as it went against the ethos of their organisation. They attempted to negotiate with the local authority, but to no avail:

> 'We stuck to our guns and they said, "Well if you don't do it like this then we won't fund you, you will lose your contracts with us and we won't pay you"... And it was brilliant because my chairman was like, "Well actually, what you're saying to us is you own the purse strings. Well actually, this type of work doesn't fit in with what we think our remit is, our mission statement. And we won't do it." So that was amazing.'

This organisation's refusal to continue working with the police lost them their local authority funding, around £4,000 a year. This was a significant sum for this small organisation, and pulling out was a big decision:

> 'I got so upset over it, I was coming back from the meetings in tears and I was thinking, this is not [pause] this is absolutely not worth it ... The lead, this particular woman one day said to me, "Well you need to do this and you need to do that." And I was like, "You do not control us." And I think from that viewpoint she decided she didn't, she couldn't work with me any more. No, it was really horrible actually.'

Tracey's organisation plugged the funding gap and finished in a position of strength. However, this was not without considerable upset and interpersonal conflict. Similar themes of stress and struggle are echoed in the following story from another group of workers in a different area of the country.

'We were very honest with the young people' (Bridget, Lucy and Laura's story)

Bridget, Lucy and Laura worked together for a medium-sized voluntary sector organisation in a London borough, and I interviewed them together as a group. They were enthusiastic about their work but critical of many of the things they were asked to do, particularly in relation to a detached project funded by the local authority on the basis of crime prevention. The contract included a target for working with young people at risk of getting involved in crime, and another target for organising a certain number of joint events with the police. Although this funding enabled the project to maintain relationships with a particular group of young people they had known for several years, they were deeply unhappy about its conditions:

> 'I think one of the targets that kind of got me was, can you identify how many young people were at risk of crime? ... that horrified me, it absolutely horrified me. Cos I thought, number one, I'm not going to go up to the young people and say, "Right, what category do you think you fit then? Crime?" ... I ran a mile from it. I ran a mile. I actually went to my manager and said, "Hell no, I don't want to do that project no more, take me off."' (Bridget)

As a self-employed youth worker on a sessional contract, Bridget removed herself from this project despite losing some of her earnings as a result. Lucy and Laura, both of whom had permanent part-time contracts, felt obliged to continue working on the project despite their doubts. However, they felt it important to meet up with the young people they knew in the area to discuss dilemmas around the targets:

> 'We were very honest with the young people at the beginning of the project and said, "You know, we do have these targets, but we also consider your views on the targets very important, and if you say downright no we won't go with it." And we said to young people, "Look, we do have a target where police would come to the project." And they said no ... They wouldn't move on that at all. And that's fine and we really respected that ... So in the end we didn't do it. And we just said to our managers, "There's no way we can do that and expect young people to come to the project."

127

... We said we couldn't do it and spoke to the funders and said that this target is never going to happen.' (Lucy)

As a result of talking to the young people, the workers refused to work with the police despite this having been a requirement of funding. They used the pragmatic argument that young people would not come to the project if the police were involved. Their resistance on this point was successful, and they retained their funding, although they remained unhappy about the ethos that required them to categorise young people on the streets as being at risk of involvement in crime. The following excerpt from their discussion illustrates their continuing mixed feelings:

Laura: I have to give us a bit of a pat on the shoulder though. Because I think we as workers ... we were really stressed out about it, but we did do a really good balance all the time ... We sat the young people down, number one. We didn't do the horrible things; we didn't actually brand them as 'at risk' [of involvement in crime], anyone.

Lucy: And we were honest with them as well, I think, from the beginning.

Laura: Yeah we were honest with the young people; we didn't do the police visits ... we haven't compromised the young people's integrity, I think. Which at least is something. So I do think we deserve credit ...

Bridget: It's sad to say, but at the back of all our minds was always these targets. As much as we tried to do really good youth work for what young people wanted, at the back of our minds it was always there.

Laura: Yeah. Exactly.

Lucy: Or how can we find a way around it? Like, can we watch a film that young people have made *about* the police? You know.

Laura: Yeah. Exactly. And the young people even feel that ... And that's what annoys me, that these targets, it's proving them right. They *know* what it's all about.

Taking a stand

Both of the stories shared here demonstrate that part-time grassroots youth workers can take a stand and make a difference on a local level. These workers refused on principle to do what had been required of them. Their projects were not shut down and they did not lose their jobs, but there were costs and risks involved, both financial and emotional. Tracey's organisation lost significant income, Bridget lost personal earnings, and all of these workers found it extremely stressful to challenge their funders. Would their successful resistance embolden them in future, or were they left feeling professionally and emotionally vulnerable? My impression was that they felt both strong and fragile as a result of their resistance, proud of acting on their principles but experiencing residual fatigue, worry and anger. Tracey felt her competence as a youth worker had been called into question, had stopped attending local authority partnership meetings, and when I met her she was planning to leave her job and return to teaching – not necessarily as a direct result of this negative experience, but perhaps it had played a role. Bridget became disillusioned with detached work and focused instead on employment support work, which she felt gave her more autonomy despite also carrying onerous targets. Lucy and Laura worked harder than ever to meet their remaining targets, perhaps in order to justify or mitigate their refusal to work with the police.

It is difficult to know what conclusions can be drawn from these stories, which may be unusual or unrepresentative. Other youth workers (such as Olly and John in my research) work willingly in partnership with the police, at least as long as young people agree. Olly worked in a local authority where diverting young people from crime was seen as the main purpose of detached work, and John was sent to represent his employer at police partnership meetings, where he felt valued and believed that young people's voices would be heard. Both used their roles in these settings to challenge stereotypes of young people as troublesome.

Why might some youth workers risk their funding and even their jobs by refusing to work with the police, while others are relatively happy to do so? The stories here may provide some insights. Both Olly and John worked for local authorities while Tracey, Bridget, Laura and Lucy worked for voluntary sector organisations; the latter may be seen as having more autonomy to turn down or renegotiate funding contracts. Olly and John worked in relatively rural areas and in small towns, whereas Tracey worked in a larger northern town with a significant working class population, and Bridget, Lucy and Laura worked in a disadvantaged London borough. Perhaps youth workers in urban areas see it as more important to differentiate and distance themselves from the police.

It could be that such differences are coincidental. What is clear, however, is that those workers who refused to work with the police were not acting as lone rebels or mavericks. They felt strongly on these issues, and had moral and practical support from their colleagues which enabled them to take a collective (if localised) approach to resistance. Tracey relied on support from her management committee and chairman, reinforced by the Christian ethos of her organisation. Lucy, Laura and Bridget supported each other, and their refusal was consistent with their principles and ethics.

When national policy is decentralised and played out differently in each context, it makes sense that workers respond in different ways to particular local situations. What might be lost, however, in such diversified and localised forms of resistance, is the sense of solidarity and mutual learning from colleagues across different localities and organisations. Those workers who had refused to work with the police were supported by their closest colleagues but were not connected to others taking similar principled actions; whereas those who were happy to work with the police seemed relatively disconnected from debates around whether youth workers should take part in the policing and surveillance of young people.

Tracking and databases

To further explore how youth workers engage in and resist involvement in surveillance mechanisms, the chapter now turns to a second key instance: the use of electronic databases to 'track' young people's participation and outcomes. The steep rise in the use of databases in youth work is partly explained by the growth in audit cultures discussed in Chapter Four. When nationally mandated benchmarks were introduced for youth work under the *Transforming youth work* agenda (DfES, 2002), English local authorities were required to calculate the percentage of the youth population they had contacted, as well as keeping track of how many times each young person had been engaged in youth services and whether they had achieved 'outcomes'.

Up until this time, record keeping in youth work had generally followed the principle that paperwork should be kept to a minimum and shared with as few people as possible. The following advice issued to youth workers in the 1960s remained common practice for many decades:

> Your records are your personal property and primarily for your own use. Keep them in a private place; only you can decide when and how to share them with others. (Goetschius, 1962)

Before *Transforming youth work*, these records included attendance registers, session evaluations, membership details and parental consent forms. Detached workers would tend to keep minimal written information outside of what was legally required, instead building up a working memory of nicknames, networks and places where different groups were to be found. Evaluation recordings have long been integral to good detached youth work practice, but would rarely include young people's personal details (Burgess and Burgess, 2006; FDYW, 2007). Detached workers in recent decades would require parental consent forms for trips which, like session recordings, would not be shared outside of the team. Further sharing of information would only take place in relation to medical emergencies or child protection. The situation today is very different.

Normalising databases

The introduction of 'tracking' databases in the early 2000s marked a significant departure from the established methods of monitoring youth work. Bespoke database systems were purchased by local authorities from private sector software companies, often shared between youth work, youth support, case work, careers advisors and youth justice teams. Under these systems, youth workers have to ensure that every young person they meet is registered on the database, that their personal details are recorded (for example, name, address, date of birth, ethnicity and sexuality), that attendance is logged for each session, and that progress against targets is recorded and evidenced. Voluntary sector projects, if funded by the local authority, are usually required to use these databases too.

It is possible for anyone with access to the database (often many hundreds of people in each local authority area) to look up a young person and find out, for example, where they live, how they define their sexuality, and what youth project they attended on the previous night. Unsurprisingly, the software companies sell their databases on technical and financial grounds while minimising these ethical implications, which are further complicated by the potential for hacking and identity theft. The most commonly used software, Core+ IYSS, is described on its website as allowing services:

> to record youth activities along with plans, aims and objectives, membership lists, dynamic attendance lists and evaluation records. Multiple session records can be associated with any activity record each having an

attendance list for young people, staff and volunteers; as well as a non-attendance list and the ability to create and evaluate outcomes for young people ... While the requirement to produce the best value performance indicators may no longer be in place, our Youth Activity Solution still fully supports the production of this data with Contact, Participant, Recorded and Accredited Outcomes available and much more. (Career Vision, 2015)

This extract underlines the normalisation of database monitoring and the recording of 'Contact, Participant, Recorded and Accredited Outcomes'. As noted here, and discussed in the previous chapter, these indicators are no longer a policy requirement but are still in operation in many services and seen as a key selling point of the market-leading software. While the recording of attendance lists and outcomes may sound relatively benign, this 'youth activity' element is just one part of a wider system which tracks each young person's involvement in multiple health and youth justice services, leading to a plethora of information about each young person. Other popular systems have a similar model, once again presented as a common-sense approach:

One Youth is a single system that effectively supports all the teams that work with young people. It ensures that relevant information available on a young person can be consolidated into a single record. Details entered by one service can be re-used by another where this is appropriate, meaning teams spending less time in front of computers and more time with young people. Maintenance costs are slashed as there is only one system to support and all the statutory reporting requirements for youth teams are taken care of. (Capita One, 2013)

Here, Capita argues its case in terms of cost savings and more time spent with young people rather than in front of a computer; the implication is that such shared databases are a pragmatic and youth-centred solution. It is hardly surprising that privacy and surveillance implications are never mentioned. Such marketing information taps into the widely held view that tracking each young person is a 'good thing', protecting young people by sharing information and concerns about them, while increasing efficiency. However, the move towards computerised information seems to have been experienced by youth workers as increasing the amount of time spent on administration, as discussed in Chapter Four. Computerised systems have enabled an extension in the perceived 'good' of every service being required to share information on young people (whether or not this is in the young person's best interest at the time).

The introduction of databases was initially controversial among detached workers, who have always emphasised the importance of waiting for young people to divulge personal information about themselves at their own pace (de St Croix, 2009a, 2009b). One of the indirect results of the introduction of databases is that young people not recorded on the database no longer 'count' for monitoring purposes. Some local authority employees are not permitted to work with any young person who does not agree to their data being recorded in this way. To participate, a young person must agree to data sharing:

> At the end of a networking meeting of youth organisations in our neighbourhood, we chat about organising a joint trip together. One worker says he can get the funding to pay for it, as long as all of the young people fill out his membership forms so he can enter them on 'the system'. My colleague and I say that we always give young people a choice over whether they are willing to share their details, and some have said no – we are not willing to exclude them from the trip on this basis, but perhaps we can pay for them separately, from our own budget? The manager of another organisation says her forms also give this choice, but 'nobody ever ticks no'. The first youth worker laughs cynically, saying, 'Our young people *can* tick no, but if they do I'm not allowed to work with them!' (Research diary, January 2013)

Questioning surveillance

Although youth service databases may not be the most serious form of surveillance that young people face, they are important partly because they fundamentally change the relationship between youth workers and young people. This is particularly the case in a street-based setting, where workers who could once present themselves as detached from the authorities are now required to gather young people's personal details and place them on shared databases. This development was unpopular with nearly all of the detached workers I spoke to:

'Obviously if someone came up to me, and I don't care how many badges you've got, and they're trying to get my name and address, "*No!*" You've got to know kind of what it is that you're asking of young people. Be respectful of them. So if they do turn round and say no, for me it's not a tick box exercise.' (Quincie)

'It's always good practice never to ask names or anything like that ... Because young people are not stupid, they will think straight away. Being a detached youth worker is a very unique youth work so it *has* been around for many years, but young people still in many areas still think, still see them as undercover police officers.' (Mahad)

It is clearly of vital importance for Quincie and Mahad to distinguish themselves from the police and to respect young people's right to privacy. Their comments are typical among the detached workers interviewed for this study. They also echo the findings of an earlier small study on youth work databases, in which detached workers spoke of their struggles to be allowed to enter anonymous contacts on the system:

'I've already had the argument with my Principal Officer about anonymity and young people that want to remain anonymous, and obviously for my detached workers and my mobile workers I don't want them having to go out and be pressurised into getting names, addresses, postcodes. So we are still arguing with regard to being able to enter people anonymously.'

'It's a nightmare because you can't put in anonymous group contacts or anonymous individual contacts at all, which we used to be able to do but they decided to change it and go with the newer system ... now the firmer line has been brought in that, you must get dates of birth, you must get surnames, you must get addresses.'

'We just put everyone in as anonymous, and they've just got onto us and said, "Who are all these anonymous people?" And we're like, "I don't know!" And they're like, "They can't all be anonymous," and we're like, "They are." So they're kind of a bit not happy with the way we've been

anonymising contacts, so we're sort of in an early fight stage.'
(Detached youth workers, quoted in de St Croix, 2009b)

Several years later, detached workers remain engaged in struggles over young people's right to choose and the need for an option to record anonymous contacts. Mahad and his team successfully campaigned for the ability to make anonymised entries on the database of their inner-city London borough:

'And even though it is a horrible thing to put the stats into the system, you know, we've got really no choice about it, but the good thing that we have is that we can put that young person as anonymous ... We follow young people's feedback ... We've said to management we want that to be recorded as it is.' (Mahad)

John explained that the computer system used in his youth service had previously not enabled the counting of anonymous contacts, but that this had recently changed due to an update in the software:

'With this system we can put in saying we met five males or five females or just five people. So if you don't have their names it doesn't actually sort of matter in a way, because with this system you can just say, "We met this number of young people around this age group." ... It's really handy for detached.' (John)

The ability to enter street-based contacts without providing names, addresses and dates of birth was an important concession won by these grassroots detached workers and their managers. The fact that a leading database provider changed its software to allow this could be seen as a small victory. Nonetheless, detached workers remain uncomfortable with the databases, even as they have begun to see them as 'normal':

'It's easy to use, once you get used to it. Um. I mean, in, in some ways it feels like we're sort of watching the young people.' (John)

'I'm sure a lot of the parents don't know that we've got that sort of information but literally you can just put someone's surname or first name and it tells you everything about them. And it's obviously linked to the other services so it tells you whether they've had a warning by the police and all that stuff and it's all on one database ... And I think it's really wrong.' (Louise)

Detached workers spoke about the data gathering process with considerable unease, often emphasising the element of choice and negotiation with young people, and the disagreement of themselves and their colleagues:

'We always get their first name, um, if they're willing to give us other stuff then that's fine, but we just kind of put whether they're male or female and their name. And then [manager] has a system which he's meant to then enter all their information in and that system's pretty much meant to have all the kids on the education roll in the [county] area so if he puts their name in he should then be able to find them. But we don't tend to do that, because he doesn't agree with having this database because it's meant to be voluntary, and it's meant to be confidential, and so we give them as little detail as possible ... So far we've got away with it.' (Louise)

Louise and her team clearly take a thoughtful and ethically informed approach, and yet it is not entirely clear exactly what it is they 'got away with'. Louise told me that her team is doing well in terms of meeting its targets, and that these are calculated according to what is recorded on the database. They meet most of their targets not through their street-based work but by involving young people in specific projects and one-to-one support. This seemed something of a norm among detached youth workers: a reluctant engagement with the system, a delicate balancing of their desire to give young people choices with an understandable need to perform as competent workers and teams.

'I don't agree with the reason of having those people's details and, yeah, I think it's wrong ... And I know that most youth workers do but then also they don't want to lose their job.' (Louise)

It is difficult to know whether the likelihood of being sacked is overstated, but it seems an entirely reasonable and realistic fear in the context of ongoing cuts, reorganisations and redundancies. It is clear that many detached workers are engaged in some level of negotiation and challenge regarding databases, at least by contesting street-level information gathering. Several detached teams have been successful in winning concessions regarding the ability to enter anonymous contacts onto the system. And yet, the idea of refusing to use the databases altogether – in the way that some workers refuse to work with the police – did not seem to be considered a possibility. Instead, detached workers tended to frame their struggle in terms of an individual young person's right to choose.

Resistance and accommodation

Weitz writes that most people engage in both 'resistance and accommodation' in many aspects of their everyday lives; they 'do not so much choose between the available strategies as balance and alternate them, using whichever seems most useful at a given time' (Weitz, 2001, pp 682–3). Although formulated outside of a workplace context, this theory is useful here, pointing out that accommodating to existing structures can be attractive to marginalised or less powerful groups in particular: it is 'a far more reliable and safer route to power, even if that power is limited' (p 683).

A balance of resistance (challenging and evading the systems) and accommodation (continuing to gather information for the database) may well be the most rational response when jobs and projects are at risk. But is rationality always the 'best' way to make ethical and political decisions? As explored in Chapter Four, performative systems such as monitoring databases encourage workers to act as compliant, self-monitoring subjects (Foucault, 1977; Ball, 2003). Because these databases are the systems on which youth workers are judged, refusals might become unthinkable. Any practitioner wants their work to be recognised; a database that does not demonstrate 'successful' youth work damages the worker's self-image as competent, committed and caring. Refusal might render the work – the work about which we are passionate, the work we love – invisible, non-existent. The database produces spreadsheets and numbers and analyses whether we have met our targets or not; in this system, there is rarely any room to dispute the 'facts' or explain 'failure'.

The views of young people are of vital importance in addressing these dilemmas. Like many of the workers in this study, I have been part of teams that insisted on giving young people a choice over whether their details would be included on a database, and have engaged in prolonged arguments with funders and managers even for this minor concession. The choice seemed to be appreciated by the young people we worked with. Yet, given the suspicions many of these young people had towards authority figures and their discomfort with giving away personal information in general, it was often surprising how few objected to the idea of us sharing their information with the local authority. Perhaps young people are habituated to surveillance: most share sensitive information about themselves on social networks, their mobile phones track every movement they make, and many of their schools use fingerprint technology to charge them for their dinners and monitor their library loans. The databases used by their youth workers might seem to be just more of the same; or perhaps young people feel morally obliged to help their youth workers by complying.

Detached workers' resistance in relation to databases is small in its scale. This does not mean it is pointless or ineffective, and individual struggles in teams have won important concessions that may reverberate more widely when they are discussed among youth workers from other organisations. However, more radical or collectivised action is also possible, as shown by Mickie's story in Chapter Four about her organisation's refusal to use databases to record their work with LGBT young people. Mickie and her colleagues drew on principled political discourses to argue that database monitoring would 'out' young people as members of stigmatised sexual minorities. Young people who spend time on the street can also be seen as constituting a stigmatised group, as emphasised and challenged by the Federation for Detached Youth Work (FDYW) which organises conferences with names such as 'Positive about the street'. It is perhaps a missed opportunity that as detached workers we have not taken more collective action against surveillance ideologies and in favour of young people's right to take part in decisions that affect their lives – not only in relation to privacy, but also in relation to their use of public spaces.

Conclusion

Something to hide? (2)

The shop wouldn't let them buy vodka so the girls make do with bubble gum and lie on the big swing, laughing and pretending to be drunk anyway. They see the youth workers coming through the park gate. Jenna drags her trainers on the ground to stop the swing and Shay leaps off with an ear-splitting screech, both racing to claim the picnic bench where they like to sit.

Ricky empties a carrier bag of paper, juice cartons, pens and biscuits, while Jo looks serious and a bit embarrassed: 'This might sound funny, but is it ok if you fill out

---

these forms? We need to give our manager some details about you. It's just, um, they're really impressed with you, that you're helping us plan the trip, but they keep telling us we need to give them information on who we're working with for our paperwork. It's just to prove we're working with real young people and not making it up. It's up to you. Is it ok? Or what do you think?' 'Yeah whatever,' says Shay, opening the biscuits. Jenna likes Jo and Ricky but she doesn't like giving out information, so she doesn't know what to say. She looks away and sees Danny coming towards them on his bike.

Danny gives a screwed-up piece of paper to Ricky, grabs the biscuits from Shay and tips a couple into his mouth. Ricky smiles and says, 'Maybe see you later?' Danny nods and frowns, 'In a bit,' and is gone, dropping the pack of biscuits onto the table so half of them fall out. The girls grumble, looking to see how many are left and whether they're broken, Shay keeping one impressed eye on Danny who is doing a wheelie as he leaves the park. Ricky uncrumples the sheet of paper. Danny's consent form, at last – it's taken so long to get this back, he must really want to come to the theme park. Ricky scans down the form to check it's correctly filled in. After the question, 'Can we store your details on our database?', he's quite surprised to see that Danny or his mum has ticked 'yes'.

The core of detached work is the building of supportive and educational relationships with young people who are disengaged from other services. Such relationships may be obstructed if detached workers are seen working with the police, or known to share personal information with other agencies. This is not to say that all young people will object to such practices; some will be unconcerned, while others will tolerate them in exchange for relationships with youth workers, participation in groups, or simply for the chance to take part in an exciting trip. In this way, surveillance in youth work is normalised through the (often reluctant) consent of workers and young people.

Grassroots youth workers' involvement in street-based and electronic surveillance can be seen as a product of both resistance and accommodation. Where resistance is present it usually takes place on a local scale, through seemingly tiny decisions about when to ask a young person for their name, or whether to engage in conversation with a police officer. Such everyday actions and inactions are important because they help to preserve an approach to detached youth work that puts vulnerable and marginalised young people at the centre of practice. However, it is questionable how far small actions challenge societal assumptions about young people's use of the street, and the ethics of surveillance. For example, asking young people whether they consent to their information being recorded on a shared database shows respect for rights to privacy and choice that are enshrined in the United Nations Convention on the Rights of the Child. However, this approach might subtly reinforce the idea of individual choice on the technical issue of data sharing, rather than involving young people as a group in considering the implications of the widespread use of databases. Involving young people in deciding whether to work with the police usually requires a more collective approach to decision making, but still might not go beyond a simple expression of opinion. We might wonder why young people said 'no' to Bridget, Lucy and Laura (who were already sceptical of working with the police), and 'yes' to Olly (who was already keen to do so). How much choice do young people really have when they are asked a question of this nature, beyond the choice to self-exclude?

I want to suggest that detached youth workers might think about placing a greater emphasis on critical engagement with young people over the issues that affect them on the streets. Such critical discussion and investigation are already happening in places, of course, but perhaps the emphasis of detached work overall has moved too far away from the idea of taking young people's side, and putting young people at the centre of the work. These older orientations towards detached work are, admittedly, somewhat simplistic – for example, we might want to question whether young people are such a cohesive group that it is possible to 'take their side', or to think about what to do when groups of young people are in conflict, or when some groups of young people express oppressive attitudes or behaviour towards other groups. However, such questions and tensions do not mean that the idea of 'taking sides' is not a useful and productive one for youth workers today.

Youth work theory has long been influenced by the radical Brazilian educator Paulo Freire (1988), who argued that education is never neutral and that educators must support the liberation of oppressed groups through critical reflection on their current situations, on possible futures, and on different ways to take action. Education in this view is about combining critical awareness and active engagement (hooks, 1994), where young people reflect on how they are oppressed as a group and what they might want to do about it. This is difficult work; exploring one's own oppression is complex and risky:

> To name your oppression is an act of courage, where often the language used has been pushed outside of the borders of common courtesy, political acceptability and generalisable truth and into the realm of delegitimised subjectivity, where

personal, political and theoretical marginality are outcomes.
(Khan, 2013, p 16)

As Khan argues, complexity and risk should not prevent youth workers from having difficult conversations with young people, exploring their experiences and perspectives. This is particularly the case in detached work, because much of the discourse that underpins surveillance suggests that young people who spend time on the streets are deviant and must be watched, judged and controlled. Decisions about surveillance cannot be separated from this problematic rationale with its assumption that young people should be 'kept off the streets'. Surveillance mirrors other oppressions, and is aimed disproportionately at groups who are seen as being risky and/or a nuisance: black young people, young Muslims, working class young people, young women who drink and have sex, activists, skateboarders, members of subcultural groups, disabled young people, sexual minorities, homeless young people, and those in local authority care. It is no coincidence that these are the groups that detached youth workers are most often funded to work with. In this context, is it any surprise that detached workers are asked to become watchers, reporters and information gatherers? The challenge is not only what we should do in response to these requirements, it is in the nature of the conversations we have and the space we create for critical thinking and debate.

Challenging surveillance involves a process of critical understanding and action alongside colleagues and young people. Hearing and acting on young people's views is an element of this work; it is also important to stimulate critical dialogue, working alongside young people to think collectively about the situation they are living in and how things might be different. The practitioner networks Federation for Detached Youth Work and In Defence of Youth Work have been critical of surveillance cultures, as have youth workers' trade unions and the girls' and women's network Feminist Webs. These groups and networks might provide spaces for grassroots workers and young people to think about and organise on these issues.

It is also essential to reach beyond youth work, to make links with community and activist groups that are engaging critically around the use of the streets. Can the street be reimagined as a public space for play, chat, debate, fun and creativity by people of all ages? The 'right to the city' movement is useful here as a theoretical concept and practical example. It is a disparate international movement that has ebbed and flowed at different times since the 1970s, and involves local and global visions 'to remake the city and in the process change ourselves and how we live together, to create qualitatively different urban social relationships' (Lipman, 2011, p 160). The right to the city was initially theorised by Lefebvre (1996) who suggested that it had two main elements: a struggle for people's genuine participation in the decisions that affect urban life, and a demand for the right to physically occupy and use the spaces in the city. This is about a radical collective transformation of space:

> It is a right to change ourselves by changing the city. It is, moreover, a common rather than an individual right since this transformation inevitably depends upon the exercise of a collective power to reshape the processes of urbanisation. The freedom to make and remake our cities and ourselves is, I want to argue, one of the most precious yet most neglected of our human rights. (Harvey, 2008)

Such an understanding of 'rights' moves us beyond an individual choice over whether to share information, towards participative and collective forms of decision making, combining critique over the present situation with positive demonstrations of alternatives. In recent years, street-based activist movements such as Occupy and the Turkish Gezi Park protests have opposed the dominance of profit in urban life while simultaneously experimenting with new ways of working and living. For decades, 'Reclaim the Night' marches have involved women in occupying the night-time streets in empowering protests against gender-based violence and intimidation. In the late 1990s, 'Reclaim the Streets' organised street parties in opposition to the dominance of the car and in favour of more liveable places, creating a vivid expression of protest against current conditions while envisioning a different world:

> The street, at best, is a living place of human movement and social intercourse, of freedom and spontaneity ... The logic of this vision implies, not only ending the rule of the car and recreating community, but also the liberation of the streets from the wider rule of hierarchy and domination. From economic, ethnic and gender oppressions. From the consumerism, surveillance, advertising and profit-making that reduces both people and planet to saleable objects ...
>
> This vision, which the street party embodies, is collective imagining in practice ... A utopia defined, not as 'no-place', but as this-place, here and now. (Reclaim the Streets, 1997, pp 7, 10)

I am drawing on activism here for inspiration, rather than necessarily suggesting that youth workers organise marches and occupy the streets (although if young people initiate such ideas it might be appropriate for youth workers to support them, and workers may also be involved in radical political action in their own right). What I want to emphasise here is that youth workers have an important role in supporting young people to become aware of their own situations (collective as well as individual) and how they might work together to change them. This requires a subtly different attitude that emphasises and reclaims the idea of taking young people's side. Perhaps this starts with a willingness to share dilemmas with colleagues and young people, more overtly discussing workplace issues and the satisfactions and risks of resistance. It could be about asking different questions that might include the issues of individual choice that seem already to be on the agenda ('Can we store your details on a database?') as well as more collective and critical forms of reflection ('What do we think these databases are for? In whose interests?').

Critical conversations do not need to be planned and neither do they need to be gloomy; they might involve 'just chatting, having a laugh and a row' (IDYW, 2011, p 27) or as Laura said, 'having really deep conversations about something really important to them'. Claiming and changing the streets might also mean *using* the streets more often – having fun in public spaces, working creatively with and on the streets, as well as in other improvised and non-institutionalised spaces (Batsleer and Hughes, 2013). It might involve challenging the surveillance and oppression of young people on the streets, while also challenging young people themselves on how they see and treat others. It could involve learning about young people's struggles, locally and in other countries, now and in the past. It might mean enabling and encouraging the creative and communal use of the streets by groups of young people together and separately, laughing and playing, chatting and debating.

At a time when youth work is increasingly oriented towards 'risky' groups and predefined outcomes (Tiffany, 2007; Coussée et al, 2009; Davies, 2013), it seems a good idea for those of us involved in detached work to remind ourselves that we can be rebellious and creative on the street, even in the context of persistent surveillance. If detached youth workers are to maintain relationships with young people who are sceptical of authority figures, we need to continue to resist our co-option into systems of surveillance and control. We also need to discuss and reflect on where we *have* been co-opted, so we can remain thoughtful and refuse to accept our role in surveillance. In this chapter I have attempted to celebrate the places where workers are already doing this, while also suggesting a reinvigorated questioning, challenging and resisting attitude in everyday interactions with young people.

Note

1   A police community support officer is a uniformed civilian member of the police force, with fewer powers than full police officers (e.g. no power of arrest).

SIX

Practising differently

Throughout this book, grassroots youth workers' love and passion for their work contrasts with a policy context that is often experienced as harmful, restrictive and constraining. This chapter contributes further to this analysis while marking a departure in focus, style and research material. While the book so far has been informed and inspired by the views of grassroots youth workers from a variety of settings across England, this chapter focuses on a single organisation.

Voice of Youth (VOY) is a youth workers' cooperative in Hackney, East London, which was set up by a group of young people and youth workers aiming to do grassroots youth work differently. VOY opposes and avoids some of the most restrictive forms of funding and aligns itself with values of equality, cooperation and participation. There is no formal hierarchical management structure; instead, decisions are made collectively in small working groups or at cooperative meetings, and all workers are paid the same hourly rate. In contrast to many other organisations, where grassroots workers feel marginalised from decision-making while their managers are distanced from practice (de St Croix, 2013), all of the workers at VOY are part-time and/or volunteers, and all share face-to-face work, organisation and decision-making. Devoting a chapter to this organisation gives space to think about the potential for (and problems with) youth work that starts from radically alternative assumptions.

VOY started in February 2011 when a group of young people and youth workers (including myself) met to discuss setting up a cooperative during a time of threatened cuts to youth work in our area. Rather than replicating existing ways of working, we aimed to create a space for youth work that was based on our shared principles, explicitly questioning and opposing the cultures of competition, targets and surveillance that have become characteristic of youth work in neoliberal times. By July 2011 we had registered as a workers' cooperative, and in January 2012 opened a weekly youth club on a local housing estate in Hackney. Soon we added a detached project on a neighbouring estate and another youth group on a third estate.

Although VOY is unusual, it is by no means unique; there is a wider phenomenon of radical, alternative and principled youth organisations at the current time; we have already discussed Sarah's social enterprise in Chapter Two, for example. Local projects inspired by radical politics are too rarely written up, but a few accounts exist (see Batsleer, 2013a; Batsleer and Hughes, 2013). A notable example in the North West of England is Feminist Webs, a lively network of feminist youth workers and young women's groups (Feminist Webs, 2012). International examples include anti-racist youth organisers and feminist girls' work in the USA (Sheridan-Rabideau, 2008; Kwon, 2013) and grassroots work with street children in Brazil (De Oliveira, 2001). Alternative youth organisations build on a rich history that, in the UK, encompasses the socialist Clarion Clubs of the early twentieth century (Prynn, 1976), the experimental 'Branch Street' play project of the 1940s (Paneth, 1944), the libertarian Paint House youth club of the 1970s (Daniel and McGuire, 1972), and the explicitly anti-racist and feminist youth work of the 1970s and 80s (John, 2006; Irving, 2011; Feminist Webs, 2012; Batsleer, 2013b; Spence, 2014). Special mention must go to the Woodcraft Folk, a socialist and environmental youth movement founded in 1925 that remains active today (Davis, 2000).

This chapter aims to complement the small body of writing about radical, democratic, principled and alternative work with young people. We have attempted to write about VOY in the spirit of the way we work; as such, this chapter is different from the rest of the book in style as well as in content. At its core is a dialogue between myself and six of my colleagues, two of whom are local young people. It is not an unedited transcript; rather it is a carefully edited dialogue based on recordings of two long focus group discussions. This approach is inspired by other examples of dialogical writing, particularly the method employed in *A pedagogy for liberation*, which Paulo Freire and Ira Shor (1987) describe as their 'talking book'. This edited dialogue makes up the majority of the chapter, and focuses on how VOY's five core principles work in practice. Following the collectively written section, I reflect on how VOY's youth workers are engaged in creating an alternative way of working which could be seen as a form of prefigurative politics, and discuss the potential for idealistic grassroots youth work organisations as a form of resistance to neoliberal youth work.

Our first recorded conversation took place at a workers' and volunteers' training residential weekend in the summer of 2013. We started by taking some time as individuals to think about our five principles (provided below) after which a different person volunteered to start a discussion on each principle. The principles were then discussed in a self-facilitated conversation for 20 minutes each. When questions came up during the discussion that we thought were important but did not have time to address, we wrote them up on a large piece of paper. After agreeing these working practices, the focus groups were self-facilitating, and I was able to put my researcher role to one side and (as far as possible) take part as a member of the cooperative, attempting not to direct or shape the conversation – at least, not more than any other participant. Afterwards, however, I took responsibility for transcribing the conversation and completing the first version of the edited dialogue. The initial edit consisted mainly of reducing it in length and improving clarity, while attempting to retain participants' characteristic voices and the informal atmosphere. This was shared and discussed at a cooperative meeting, and some changes were made.

Our second focus group conversation took place later in 2013 and addressed the questions we had not had time for during the first discussion, as well as some issues we thought were missing after we read the edited dialogue. Here, I edited some of our responses into composite answers and presented these as 'frequently asked questions'. I sent the first draft of the piece to everybody and created subsequent drafts based on colleagues' feedback. We discussed the final draft together at a cooperative meeting, settling on the version presented here.

In contrast with the rest of the book, this chapter does not anonymise the individual workers and volunteers, nor does it anonymise our organisation. This was a deliberate choice discussed and agreed with the members, volunteers and young people of VOY, naming our organisation as a way of contributing to the history of alternative youth and community work organisations and inspiring current youth workers who may be interested in working in different ways – we wanted readers to be able to get in touch with us if they wanted to know more. Each cooperative member and volunteer in VOY had an informed choice about whether to take part in the discussions, and was given an information sheet and consent form, as well as the opportunity to discuss the research with me and with each other. Each had an individual choice over whether to use their real name, and we all agreed to respect the anonymity of any colleague who decided to use a pseudonym. Every worker and volunteer involved in VOY at that time was happy to take part (although some were eventually unavailable on the day) and all chose to use their real names.

Before our discussions, we agreed to be self-critical and reflective about VOY's work rather than portraying it in an unrealistically positive light; we wanted to share the challenges of practising against the status quo. We were also keen to share our successes and the aspects we are proud of. There is an important role for celebration alongside critical reflection when considering radical projects:

> The feelings of frustration, and sometimes cynicism, that many educators and community members experience are often the result of not hearing each others' stories. Failure seems to make better headlines than hard-won, slow success. (Apple and Beane, 1999, p 25).

What follows is a series of edited dialogues between seven of VOY's youth workers, discussing how our principles work in practice, and sharing the dilemmas, challenges, joy and excitement of running an idealistic youth work organisation. First, a short description of the authors (in alphabetical order):

Anna-Nina was the youngest founder member of the cooperative at age 16, having taken part in youth projects in the local area. She is currently on a break from VOY while studying for a degree in anthropology.

Carys lives in the local area and works in policy and campaigning. She had been a volunteer for several months by the time of this discussion and is now a cooperative member.

Emma lives locally and was a founder member of the cooperative. She also works as a social worker. Emma left VOY a year or so after this discussion but still keeps in touch.

Fionn grew up and still lives locally and has been a youth worker in the borough before. He joined as a placement student at the time of VOY's launch, and then became a cooperative member. He still works for VOY and for another organisation working with young trans people.

Julia was a founder member of the cooperative, also worked for a local youth charity, and is currently on a break from VOY while training to be a psychologist.

Keishaun took part in youth projects while growing up in the local area. He became a founder member of the cooperative as a young person and was heavily involved for many years. He currently works in computing and comes back to help out with specific projects.

Tania was a founder member of the cooperative, and a PhD student at the time of this discussion. She has remained involved on a voluntary basis while also working at a university.

This collective piece of writing and the rest of the chapter is substantially informed by all of the past and current young people, cooperative members, volunteers and supporters who have been part of VOY.

Doing something different in the world

This section was written collectively by Anna-Nina Koduah, Carys Afoko, Emma Heard, Fionn Greig, Julia Betancour Roth, Keishaun Decordova Johnson and Tania de St Croix in late 2013.

This piece is written by a group of youth workers who aim to challenge inequality and hierarchy through the ways we work with young people and each other. Voice of Youth (VOY) was formed in 2011 by youth workers and young people who wanted to do things differently. We began by talking about what we valued in youth work, and about the things that got in the way. After a few months of meetings we registered as a workers' cooperative (or co-op), working non-hierarchically with no bosses and a flat pay rate, and making decisions by consensus. We draw on traditions of youth work in which young people choose whether and how to get involved, without pre-planned outcomes or adult-imposed programmes. One of the first things we did was to develop our five core principles:

1. Young people choose whether and how to become involved with our groups and our work.
2. Our work starts from the needs and wishes of young people in Hackney and all funding bids will reflect this.
3. We involve young people in taking action to improve their own lives and the lives of their communities.
4. We promote equality and challenge oppressive structures in society, institutions, groups and individuals, including in our own organisation.
5. We promote cooperative decision making in our own work, in our youth groups and in the communities where we work.

This piece takes the form of short dialogues on each of our five principles. We try to do almost everything in groups so it seemed a good idea to write this piece collectively. We use conversation all the time within the cooperative and with young people – to build relationships, share perspectives, address conflict, reflect and learn, and decide what to do and how to do it – so it seemed appropriate to 'write' this piece through speaking. As Anna-Nina said, 'Talking's a really powerful tool. You can really get through to someone by having simple conversations.' We hope our experiences will be useful to others working towards principles of equality and cooperation, whether now or in the future – not because we think VOY is a perfect example to be copied (it is not), but because it is a real and creative attempt to challenge capitalist, authoritarian and hierarchical ways of working. Challenging the idea that 'there is no alternative', it could be seen as an example of utopian thinking in practice. VOY makes us feel hopeful, and perhaps our story can inspire others, too – not to do exactly as we have done, but to create diverse creative opportunities for anti-oppressive and cooperative work with young people.

Q. What does VOY do?

A. We work with young people in community buildings and on the streets of their local areas. Currently we work weekly in three neighbouring areas of Hackney, a diverse London borough that has many strengths and faces many challenges. We work with young people through conversation, getting to know them and learning together about the issues that affect their lives. We support them to organise activities and projects around their areas of interest.

Q. Why have principles and how do you use them?

A. When we started meeting to plan a new organisation, one of the first things we did was discuss and decide on five shared principles. These helped bring us together and clarify the values we shared as a group or that we wanted to aspire to. We discuss these principles with new workers and volunteers, and with young people in our groups. We have reflected that changing the world can be a massive and overwhelming challenge, and that exploring and revisiting our principles helps us to break it down into smaller tasks, make better decisions and check how our work is going. Read on as we discuss our principles in more detail, and see what you think!

Principle 1: Young people choose whether and how to become involved with our groups and our work

Julia: In a lot of settings young people *have* to come, maybe as part of youth offending orders or because it's part of their school day. In our groups, the young people come because they *want* to and they choose how to take part.

Emma: If they have the autonomy over what we do or how we do it, or how to become involved, it's also going to give them more energy to be part of it, isn't it? So you're not just getting dragged along because you have to do it – you actually really *want* to be there. But in a lot of places that's been forgotten. Is that because of funding? Or is that because people have that anxiety about young people, and the idea that they need to be engaged in 'positive activities' whether they like it or not?

Keishaun: For me, this principle is about building up confidence in our young people. You're told to go to school; it's not really your choice. But being allowed to go to a youth group and being allowed to choose whether you just want to sit in a corner with your friend on your phone and just sit there, do nothing – or whether you want to get involved, talk to the workers, start planning – it's building up their confidence within themselves. You're allowed to have your own mind, you're not forced to go to one place, and you don't have to act like everyone else. You might be playing cards, sitting down, doing cooking or having a discussion with a worker. It's not a space where everyone has to do exactly the same thing. Everyone can come and choose what they do within the club, which is why we try to provide a range of activities.

Carys: See, that's why I think choice is so important when you're young. It's about youth work not being the same as school. It's really important to have a space where you're treated as a person and you can choose.

Julia: You just reminded me of something I noticed the other day in one of the groups. A young person had just arrived a bit earlier with his cousin who was visiting, and then his cousin left because some of his relatives came by. And this young person who comes every week said, 'I'm gonna go home,' but looked a bit guilty at the same time. And I remember Fionn asking why, but in a very accepting way. And they

151

had a bit of a conversation about it and Fionn sort of acknowledged, 'Is it because your cousin went?', letting him know that it's completely fine. And the young person looked much more comfortable with it, and they both said, 'See you next week,' and he left. It sounds like such a tiny thing but I really loved that conversation.

Fionn: Maybe he felt a bit obliged to stay? Because he's really keen and he knows we appreciate his presence and his passion for the club. And so by leaving, does he feel like he's letting us down? It was really important for me to say, 'Great, you're going to see your cousin,' even though inside I *was* disappointed that he was going. They have the right to choose when and how to be involved.

Emma: I think it helps that we don't have targets for our work, like when young people have to get a certain qualification. When there's more freedom around the funding, young people get to choose whether to participate. When there's more autonomy for us workers, then there isn't a pressure of, 'You have to get it done,' or, 'You have to stay.'

Julia: I agree completely, and that's what I liked so much about the conversation Fionn had with that young person. But there's another way of looking at it. Some time ago I was working with a group outdoors. It was really cold, and two young people used to stay for the whole session, and they would ask, 'When are we gonna be done?' We would say to them, 'You can go whenever you want.' But I started thinking they were there because they felt a bit bad for us. And on the one hand I don't want them to come just for our sake, but on the other I felt it was a very beautiful sign of respect and trust as well.

Tania: Yeah. Young people choose whether and how to become involved, but that doesn't stop us workers from *encouraging* them to stay sometimes. It's great to make them feel comfortable to come and go as they please. But I also think it's really nice that we do encourage them to be there, and make them feel cared for, that we actually want to spend time with them. As long as they can go whenever they like, and they're free to leave.

Emma: In another one of our groups, someone came who we'd never seen before and that day it was all young women there so he was the only young man. He walked in and he looked like he didn't want to be there, and we said, 'Come and have a seat,' and he very casually, very shyly sat down. And then I said, 'Play a game of cards?' and he did. And by the end of the session he was cooking! For the first minute I really wanted to say to him, 'It's alright, you can go if you want; I understand,' because he looked so uncomfortable, but he stayed and he seemed to have a really good time! So I suppose that's an example of what you were saying. Yes, they *are* free to leave, but we do encourage them to stay and see what it's like!

Q. What actually happens in the VOY youth groups?

A. Young people plan what to do: it might be cooking, group games, hanging out, serious conversations, table tennis, football, drawing, film, colouring, drama, treasure hunts, walks, chatting, free running, art activities, trips, weekends away, more chatting, educational workshops and made-up games, for example. We often start with what comes up when we're talking, or with what's there in the environment. Youth workers also make suggestions. The activities are usually informal, but sometimes we decide to work together on a more focused project or campaign. After the 2011 London riots the young people created discussions and a participative community performance, to challenge perceptions of why the riots happened and challenge how young people are negatively portrayed. More recently, one group has made a brilliant short film about how schools (especially academies) often undermine their human rights and members of the group have taken it out to different groups to discuss rights in schools (see Mouth That Roars and Voice of Youth, 2013).

Q. What kind of young people do you work with?

A. They're all different! They're funny, brilliant, thoughtful, surprising. We sometimes find this question difficult because we do not want to put a label on the young people we work with. We work in social housing estates which are sometimes seen as disadvantaged or deprived, but we don't start from a deficit perspective – these places have their problems but they are also diverse, exciting and strong communities. We mainly work with 8–19-year-olds although we're flexible. The doors are open. Each person comes for their own reasons which they might or might not share – for example, they might come because it's a safe space, a free space, different from home or school, to take time out, to see friends, to have a break from their problems, and because they like activities or the youth workers or the other young people.

Principle 2: Our work starts from the needs and wishes of young people in Hackney and all funding bids will reflect this

Emma: Young people's needs and wishes are so diverse, and there's lots of stereotypes about what people think young people need. A lot of the time young people are categorised and not asked, 'What's important for you?' I enjoy asking young people one-to-one or in a little group, 'What do you want, what do you need?' I think it's a really good thing for young people to be listened to and know that their opinions count.

Fionn: And then to see it to fruition, a funding bid coming in or a project starting: we've listened and we've made something happen *together*. In one group they were talking about wanting food each week at the youth club, and I found out about a funding opportunity. We brought it to the club and wrote that application together, and got a healthy cafe off the ground. And they really have ownership over it, they all want to help in the kitchen. And if you'd imposed that, would they all be saying they want to help? Their enthusiasm is proof of the importance of that principle.

Tania: Yeah, and part of it is having young people involved as workers, running the organisation.

Anna-Nina: Yeah. I think the principle really goes well with the name of our co-op, Voice of Youth, which was a name young people chose and voted for. The name is about the voice of the young people and what they want to see happen or change, and what they want to do. They're the base of our work.

Emma: Sometimes there's a difficulty, though. Young people aren't often asked in their lives what they want or what they think they need, so when in groups we try and plan 'What do you want to do?', they can't think of anything.

Fionn: Yes, or they give a very limited range of answers. And is that because those answers are what they're used to from other clubs, or from school, or society?

Keishaun: I found it difficult recently when trying to organise a trip with some of our older ones, where I've asked them and they've had no ideas for weeks. So, at what point do we as workers – not stop asking – but just make a decision? That's something that I've found challenging because I didn't know when to stop asking them.

Emma: It's a challenge for us to work with them in a creative way to inspire new ideas. Remember when we got them writing ideas with chalks on the floor? That really worked, just being creative to help them explore what they want. Because a lot of them don't get listened to much outside of the group.

Tania: And sometimes asking a question can be limiting. It's also about being there, and reading between the lines of conversation. When we did a project about the riots it wasn't because we asked, 'What should we do a project about?' It was because everyone on the streets was talking about the riots. Everyone was like, 'What do you *think* about this?' From that, we workers asked young people, 'Would it be interesting to do a project about this?' And so many of them said, 'Okay, yeah, let's do it!'

Anna-Nina: I think the way the principle is worded is good. It says 'Our work *starts* from the needs and wishes of the young people.' So even something like asking their opinion on snacks for a picnic: they list sweets and chocolate, and then we also bring carrots and hummus for them to try and they end up liking that too. So we're there to encourage them to try new things as well.

Carys: Yes, because asking that open question people can just end up with the same things. Because otherwise, if you can't think of something new, you don't get to try new things.

Emma: One evening I decided we'd go down to Central London and do a walk, just spot things and talk about them, and I prepared a bit of a quiz. And they really enjoyed it. Probably if you'd put down on the table, 'Do you want a walk around central London?' they'd say, 'No'. But it was a giggle and they learned a few things and they taught us things.

Fionn: Recently we organised a trip to the theatre, and when I said the words gender and sexuality, being *proud* that the play was about that, then some of them thought, 'No way am I going to that!' Only two came but they loved it, and when the others hear back from their peers that'll be 10 times better. This principle for me is about balancing what we've all been talking about. So our work starts from their needs and wishes – whether we've been discussing it, whether they've identified it, or whether they've just been interested in it. And then it's about building *our* confidence that it *is* our job to suggest things and sometimes to just *do* things, but without ever contravening their needs and wishes.

Emma: There's something I wanted to point out with this principle which we've not discussed: we say that funding bids should reflect young people's needs and wishes. Young people *want* money to do projects or special things. How creative can we be to not compromise our values, not be stereotypical or targeted or oppressive, but get funding to do a bit more?

Julia: Tania and I were writing a funding bid a while ago and we were like, 'Oh no, we have to identify outcomes, argh!' But then we decided to write down outcomes that we actually do try to achieve, like challenging oppression. You can write it in quite a clear way and show examples of how this is done, and show that these things *are* difficult to measure but this is what we do, and we're very happy to talk about it and to show it.

Fionn: But that's the thing: who gets to choose the targets? A lot of funding bids will give you the targets and you have to just say, 'Yeah, we'll do them,' or you can't apply.

Emma: We're lucky that we don't need much money to run, but some groups need money to keep people's jobs. It's really difficult, isn't it? Because you don't want to sacrifice people's livelihood and ability to work with young people. I don't know, it's very difficult and we're in a fortunate position where we can keep to this principle and really strive for it.

Julia: I still want to believe that we might be able to do both!

Fionn: And maybe pay ourselves eventually!

Carys: I like what's built into this principle: the idea of maybe trying to challenge funding. In some charities there's a bit of a mentality of, 'This is what we have to do.' Well, no, you could actually push back, or you could *not* apply for that money. I think that's what's interesting about it.

Q. Is it possible to get funding while sticking to your principles?

A. We hope so ... We're new and small, and there's very little funding available for open access youth work, but we have found enough to keep three regular groups going every week and to pay our youth workers for some of their work. We can run on a limited income because we do a lot of voluntary work and because local groups support us, for example, with free access to buildings. We deliberately decided to stay small and grassroots, and we don't need funding for management or fancy premises. It would be great to be able to raise enough money to employ some of our workers more regularly so they could rely on the income and so we could do a bit more with young people. It's something we are still learning about.

Q. Do VOY workers and volunteers all share the same values and beliefs?

A. Yes and no. We don't always agree on everything and it would be a bit boring if we did! We have different backgrounds, experiences and ways of expressing our values and beliefs. Our shared principles are important, because they clarify what is most important to us as a group, and they protect VOY from agendas imposed from outside. When we discuss what we have in common we identify things like respect and care for young people and for each other, commitment to equality, passion for youth work and young people, and belief in cooperating.

Principle 3: We involve young people in taking action to improve their own lives and the lives of their communities

Keishaun: Speaking for myself, youth work has been so helpful and such an encouragement in my life, when I was a young person in the area and some of you were my youth workers, just the activities that were run and the opportunities that were given, even the discussions we had. And from that point I went from being a young person in the group, and I never thought I would become a youth worker, to becoming a volunteer and then becoming an actual full-blown youth worker. So I think this principle is about encouraging young people to take responsibility for their own lives, thinking about their future, their careers, and what they really want in life. It's just a nice thing. And the lives of their communities, because being a part of your community like I got involved in mine just opens up doors. So I want to involve and encourage other young people to take part and do the same with their communities, take leadership and take responsibility.

Emma: Often young people are very disheartened. But where you come from or how you've been brought up or the way you are, that doesn't have to impact on the rest of your future, and it's giving that confidence and hope that you can make things better for yourself, and we're all here to support that. And you need someone telling you, 'If you want to do that you can. You can make things better.' I just think it's a very special and lovely kind of ethos.

Julia: For me, this principle has to do with what you have already described but also on a different scale, like young people questioning what their lives are and what other people's lives are on a political level, because it doesn't have to be the way it is. To encourage them to see themselves not just as individuals but part of a group in society, and the potential of maybe not accepting certain roles that are given to them.

Anna-Nina: Where it says, 'improve their own lives and the lives of their communities', we want them to have a good life in a nice community. Then it also says, 'We involve young people in taking action,' and that's the whole point of VOY. Instead of us saying, 'We're gonna change your life,' we want them to realise that they can do it.

Fionn: And I think that's really important, to have the belief from us that they can do it. It's not just about 'positive activities' for young people, it's actually about being political. Because even just trying to get heard or trying to change your own life is an act of politics. It's different from that idea of other people swooping in to help or 'save' a group. For me this is not about philanthropy or charity, it's about empowerment.

Emma: That reminds me of a project we did with another group who wanted to celebrate Hackney and made their own book to show their feelings that, 'Hackney's actually okay and we're well-rounded young people living in Hackney.' And so when we talk about taking action it's not necessarily fighting the negative but promoting the positive as well. So that principle is very broad, isn't it?

Carys: Yeah, because you don't just want to create a great youth group where young people have a really great time and then when they're 18 we say, 'Bye, good luck with the rest of your life.' It's recognising that people are in a community and it's not just about creating a nice safe haven for people to come – we also want to help empower people to be able to do that in other bits of their lives. Taking the positive things they have in their youth group and trying to bring that to other things.

Tania: A lot of youth organisations have some sort of mission statement around 'changing young people's lives' and often it's too individualised. People have a certain amount of power, but it's only if you work together in groups, in communities, that you've got more chance to make a change. The project about the riots, I think it made everyone who took part feel a bit differently, not just about the riots but about themselves and the importance of having a say and being listened to and all the different ways they could express themselves. One of them said, 'I've never had a discussion like this at school or anywhere.' They created a space and time to discuss and question, and reflect, and think, 'Yeah, we can do something.'

Julia: Yes, and it doesn't even have to just be a political project. It can be through everyday youth work. It's the whole idea of communicating in a different way. It's the space of maybe learning how to challenge people, both young people and also adults, so you can actually be heard. And that can be on so many different levels, so it can be a big political project but it can be something completely unrelated that leads to a different approach in how you talk and discuss.

Fionn: Everything's political.

Julia: Everything's political, exactly.

Emma: I was just thinking, young people always end up talking about the police in our groups, and a young person came in one day and she said, 'You'll never guess, the police came to our school and I challenged them on a few things.' And we didn't encourage her to do that; we didn't tell her to do that. It all grew from our discussions, but she wanted to bring it up.

Carys: It was like she felt empowered because of those discussions, so when the police came in she could say, 'Well, this is what I think.' That's quite a cool thing because it means she doesn't need a youth worker to be there; it means that's how she's going to be always. You don't need to be there behind her, going, 'Go on, you can do it!'

Julia: I feel we go against certain norms and we challenge a lot of things that otherwise are the status quo within society, and that in itself is extremely empowering. We're not putting the thoughts in the young people's heads–– most of the time those thoughts are already there – but from feeling alone, all of a sudden there's a space where you can express yourself and feel, this is real.

Q. What do you do when young people disagree with youth workers' decisions?

A. We talk about it. We involve young people at every level of the cooperative. Decisions are ultimately the responsibility of the youth workers at cooperative meetings – some of the VOY workers and volunteers are young people who have grown up in the area so young people's views are always there in every decision – and then we also need to discuss decisions with the young people in our groups because they might have different views. We hope that the young people in our groups know that we want to hear their ideas and that we will take them seriously. If it's something where they disagree with us, we will keep listening, thinking and talking together about what to do, and see if we can compromise or agree somehow.

Q. What happens when co-op members disagree among themselves?

A. We discuss it and take time to think about it. We try to listen, understand other perspectives, and stay open-minded even while upholding our own personal values. If we tell each other when we disagree or feel angry or uncomfortable (and express this in a caring way) this shows our respect for each other. Even if we have the occasional difficult or frustrating moment, we hope it will make us stronger in the long run – and that we'll still be working together tomorrow, next week, and in the longer term.

Principle 4: We promote equality and challenge oppressive structures in society, institutions, groups and individuals, including in our own organisation

Carys: I like this principle because it's a value statement. It's like, there is oppression in the world, there is inequality in the world, and we're here to challenge it. So in the groups, that means things like when the boys are playing football and they're excluding the girls we don't stand by the side and go, 'That's alright.' We try and encourage them to let the girls play and we challenge them if they make sexist comments. And we're not going to have the female volunteers do all the washing up in the kitchen, the men will do it as well. I think it is maybe a more controversial principle but I think that's important because it's a statement of what we believe.

Julia: I think it's interesting that you used the word 'controversial'. It is kind of interesting that promoting equality and challenging oppressive structures is controversial in today's society!

Carys: I think promoting equality is less controversial, but I think saying we're 'challenging oppressive structures', saying that schools or the police are oppressive structures, that isn't something that is a widely accepted thing.

Emma: Can I ask: why do we personally promote equality and challenge oppression? I feel it's important because in my life I've seen people being treated unfairly. I've got a passion for history, I've got a passion for looking at oppressed societies, so that's why it's very important to me. But it's interesting why we feel this is important whereas lots of other youth groups don't feel promoting equality and challenging oppressive structures is part of their youth work.

Keishaun: You don't see equality any more; everyone is living their life based on labels or based on values that aren't themselves. No one seems to love or take care of themselves. They're only happy if they have the latest name-brand clothing. Everyone is being oppressed, and no one seems happy any more. As a youth worker I want young people to be happy within themselves. And not going to school and then being oppressed by teachers saying, 'Oh you're getting a D,' or, 'You're only getting a B; you should be getting an A.' Qualifications don't determine a young person's whole life. As youth workers we encourage people and say that no matter how you are doing in school, you always have a chance. I think everyone has the right to be equal. Whether you're black, whether you're light-skinned black or you're dark-skinned, whether you're white, in our youth clubs everyone has the right to be equal and to take part in everything, no matter their shape, size, background. And we promote our groups to be accessible to everyone. No matter what you like, whether it's different types of music, different types of clothing.

Fionn: For me it's really important to recognise how oppression works in society, not individualise things as if, 'You are homophobic,' or 'You are sexist.' It's more, 'Where do you think that belief or comment arises from, or why do you think that?' And actually recognising that we're affected by the society we live in, which is oppressive on many levels. And so, massively, are the children and young people we work with, who maybe don't have the tools yet to critique everything that they're being taught. So for me this is about saying, 'We challenge that view in a young person,' because we recognise that it's a homophobic view or a sexist view because of the structures in society. Just by saying, 'Hm, why is it "not natural" to be gay?' – just one question challenges the structure.

Julia: Personally, for me, it's intrinsic in youth work to challenge oppressive structures. But also I think it's something that we're constantly questioning and looking at in the way that we work as colleagues. For instance, I'm aware that I'm older and I might have a bit more experience in youth work, and there are younger workers in the organisation. Or, we all have different backgrounds. I'm very aware of that when I say things or in how I work.

Keishaun: We promote equality and challenge within our organisation. For me, being a younger worker, I feel my voice is equally heard to those who have more experience or even more qualifications than I do within the same field. If we were discussing a workshop, it's not that my voice wouldn't be heard. If I said something, my colleagues will understand where my point of view is coming from if they can't see it for themselves, because my background is growing up in the area and I'm closer to the young people's age, whereas some of my colleagues might have come from a different area and see it differently. It's understanding that we all have different views on things but in the end all our goals are the same, so we're trying to bring ourselves to an equal level to make sure that we bring the best to the young people.

Julia: Exactly! But it's also that we have a climate where we can challenge each other. If we say something, someone else can say, 'Mm, I'm not entirely convinced by that.' We would really want to work through something if we're not completely convinced by something someone's said. Without judging that person, but by having a conversation about it. The same way we would with young people.

Tania: I also like the fact that we are all paid the same hourly rate. Because sometimes organisations say, 'Yeah, young people have a full voice in our organisation; they're on the board,' but then you ask, 'Who's paid?' And people on the top pay are – to generalise – usually white, middle class and older. If you're really saying young people should have an equal voice or should run the organisation, then look at pay because it's a marker of how people are respected. The fact that we're all paid the same hourly rate in VOY, it's saying that if you're a young person who has that expertise of knowing what it's like to be a young person in that area, and putting in as much work as everyone else, why shouldn't you get paid the same?

Fionn: By doing that we're saying a massive thing about society. We are doing something different in the world and that's really exciting.

Julia: I also want to say that challenging oppressive structures can be something fun. Like, the other week we had a painting session and one of the male workers painted his bike pink!

Fionn: One of the best times for me about challenging structures is when young people feel free enough to be able to bring the question back to us. So when the young people asked for a meeting about whether or not we ban people, or who we choose to come on trips, for me their confidence in being able to ask for that is about saying that young people should be able to ask for things in their area, their space, their youth club. And the fact that we responded to that really positively shows that we're up for that, turning the world on its head and being challenged. I think that's really positive.

Q. How does it work in practice not having bosses or managers?

A. It's great! We can work in the interests of young people, and make decisions together, rather than being told what to do by someone at a higher level who is not accountable to us or to the young people. We are collectively accountable through cooperative meetings. We support each other informally, and each of us has regular one-to-one supervision meetings with an experienced youth worker. We share out tasks so we don't all have to think about everything all the time, and we work in pairs or small groups so we're not isolated.

Q. What does it mean to challenge oppressive structures in your own organisation?

A. We try to recognise, think about and act on potential and actual inequalities within VOY, through discussions, training and reflection. We are a diverse group (for example, in terms of gender, ethnicity, class, sexuality and age) and we see this as a strength; however, there is clearly the potential for the inequalities in wider society to be reflected by informal hierarchies in VOY, however much we try to work as equals. We are currently thinking about how to do more to recognise oppressive and unequal structures in VOY, and what we can do to change and challenge them on an ongoing basis.

Principle 5: We promote cooperative decision making in our own work, in our youth groups and in the communities where we work

Anna-Nina: We all bring something to VOY: different ages, different sexes, backgrounds. It's stronger when everyone comes together and when we're all different, because we can bring more to the group. We also work cooperatively with young people in their groups, because we don't want big hierarchical boundaries and we don't want them to see us as being like their teacher. We don't want to be seen as telling them what to do, or like we're better than them or more experienced. They learn from us and we learn from them. And in the community, working cooperatively helps build that kind of good relationship.

Keishaun: That just reminds me of how we first started. We could barely decide on where to start! It took us how many months? Just to figure out what area we wanted to start in, how many clubs we should open, where we should work.

Anna-Nina: Sometimes it is really long! But it's interesting. It takes a while because we all have to meet and then we all have to make decisions together. But it's better, I think, because we all know what we're doing and we've all chosen to do it. We've all said what we wanted to do and we've made it into one.

Emma: It can get tricky sometimes when trying to decide between our ways of working and what the young people want – for example, about banning. If there was a vote young people would vote to ban young people who misbehave, whereas we would not endorse that. It's about working cooperatively, giving them a space to talk about this, and giving our reasons as to why we don't want to do that. But it can get tricky at those points when you're in conflict.

Fionn: I think what's really beautiful about this is that we value time. Decision making cooperatively isn't encouraged by our world as it stands, a world that thinks efficiency and capitalism is the only answer, and if you do things efficiently then you're more successful. But who's excluded from that? Who's not heard? Who feels abused, or who feels ignored? And so I think that's key, having the time to discuss things through.

Anna-Nina: I think it's quality over quantity. We try and do better work rather than rushing it and doing more.

Tania: When we started I was really caught out by that, even though I was really inspired to be in a radical cooperative. In my working experience it was the norm that you had to get so much done and often as an individual. When we started, several times I would go off and do something on my own, and I've had to learn to be like, 'I think I'd like to do this, who wants to do it with me?' I'm still learning! We are really busy sometimes, but we always make space to consider, to talk to each other, to think and to try and work together.

Emma: We've also figured out on the way what works. For example, now there's two people responsible for every group or area of work, and those two can make a decision; we don't have to email all seven or eight members and get their responses before making a decision. If we're struggling or if it's a really big decision then we go back to the whole group. So it's finding out what works best for us and the way we work.

Julia: I feel as well there's a difference working with the young people when they know that nobody is the boss. I actually feel like the young people work more like that themselves when we have that approach.

Anna-Nina: I think you're inspired when you see something that works that you've never really thought about. I think a lot of the young people when they ask about the cooperative are quite fascinated that we all get paid the same and we haven't got a boss.

Julia: Now some of the young people have become young volunteers in a different group, and they are automatically taking responsibility. They just keep an eye out: 'What needs to be done?' It's this cooperative attitude. They are just doing all these things without us telling them.

Emma: It's by modelling; it doesn't need to be by instructing.

Carys: I guess that even if people aren't co-op members – and I'm a volunteer but not a co-op member – it's the culture that it creates: a flat culture, an inclusive culture. And that then affects how you deal with everyone. Also, I think one of the other big benefits of cooperative work is that everyone seems to be happier!

Emma: Yeah, we've been doing this for two years now and people are happy and people come to meetings every month. It's not a chore.

Tania: People ask me, 'What do you do about people who don't pull their weight?' And I'm like, 'Well, that doesn't happen.'

Fionn: We pre-empt that, because we're considerate and caring about what that means, to pull weight. It's voluntary participation as well, because I think we are all equally, in very different ways, passionate about VOY. So we want to be here. I want to do my work, I want to do well, I want to consider others, and that's because of the culture. Is it something about how these principles work, and cooperative decision making?

Julia: And caring as well. Because young people, if they feel heard and respected and seen and cared for, that does create an atmosphere. That's what's happening in the co-op with us workers and maybe that's what's being reflected with the young people as well – that we care for each other and we hear each other's needs.

Fionn: It makes you feel better to go to work, it makes you want to care for others.

Emma: But it's not a coincidence, is it? The reason why it's working is because we all needed this, wanted this, from the beginning.

Fionn: What is the spark with what we're doing? Is it about the principles as opposed to the cooperative structure? Or does the structure allow the principles?

Carys: I think for me it's also about linking it to our fourth principle, that there are certain structures that are oppressive in society. Cooperatives are not perfect, but it's a structure that is not as oppressive. This is the kind of world we want, so this is how we're going to work.

Postscript

The collectively written dialogue above was recorded as a conversation in summer 2013 and edited into its current form later that year. As this book is being finalised over two years later, VOY is still going strong and will soon celebrate its fifth birthday. Funding remains difficult to find, and most of the work is still done on a voluntary basis, with some part-time paid work for those who need it when funding allows. Some volunteers and cooperative members have left because of work, study or for personal reasons, but everyone keeps in touch and visits when they can. We have some fantastic new co-op members and volunteers, including more young people who have grown up in the local area and come through our groups, and we have just held a training residential for 10 young people who want to be youth workers. The film about human rights in schools (see Mouth That Roars and Voice of Youth, 2013) has been viewed many hundreds of times, and VOY young people have used it to run workshops with youth groups, teachers and other interested people.

Reflections on VOY

For the remainder of this chapter I write once more as an individual practitioner and researcher, drawing out how VOY's story contributes to understandings of grassroots youth work in a changing policy context. It is important to acknowledge again that I am writing here about an organisation I am practically, politically and emotionally invested in. My identity as an 'insider researcher' is hardly absent from the other chapters, and yet there is a different quality to writing about VOY. It is an organisation that I have been involved in setting up. My colleagues there are friends and (in some cases) young people I have known and cared about since they were children, and we are attempting to practise and organise youth work in ways I have always hoped and dreamed might be possible. I am immensely proud to be involved in VOY, even on our most difficult days. In these circumstances it is questionable how critical I can truly be about this organisation. Others involved in VOY would narrate this story differently – this is one of the reasons for including the collectively written dialogue, above, but of course the discussion would have included other perspectives if more colleagues had been able to come along, or if younger youth group participants had been included.

Throughout this book I have explored some of the barriers faced by grassroots workers in the context of dominant neoliberal policy. Youth workers are subject to marketised, performative and surveillant policy that is enacted differently depending on local and organisational contexts. Management is an important factor in how policy is experienced and mediated: volunteers and part-timers in this study identified some managers as supportive and willing to listen, while others were seen as authoritarian and lacking in understanding of grassroots practice. Managers themselves have limited room for manoeuvre in current policy contexts: they have little time for face-to-face practice, and are themselves held accountable to inflexible targets and financial imperatives (Spence and Devanney, 2006; Davies and Merton, 2009, 2010).

In this context, Voice of Youth provides a counter-hegemonic perspective. Grassroots workers are the creators of VOY alongside the young people they work with; unlike the part-timers and volunteers in most organisations, they do not have managers, which puts them collectively at the centre of both practice and decision making. VOY's formal structure as a workers' cooperative gives each worker an equal stake in decisions through cooperative meetings, and its participative structure is reinforced by the absence of hierarchical management and an equal hourly pay rate. This means that VOY's workers are in a different relation to their work than would be the case if they were conventionally managed. The workers clearly feel that the flat structure feeds through to the way they work with young people: 'It's the culture that it creates. A flat culture, an inclusive culture. And that then affects how you deal with everyone' (Carys).

VOY's flat structure challenges but does not remove informal hierarchies or power imbalances that might be reinforced by societal and structural inequalities, including those relating to gender, race, age, experience, class, sexuality and (dis)ability. Inequalities in the wider world are likely to affect relations in any group and this is recognised by VOY's fourth principle, which aims to 'promote equality and challenge oppressive structures ... including in our own organisation'. This includes being aware of and tackling interpersonal and social inequalities and valuing local knowledge and understanding. Local young people are at the heart of VOY. Keishaun suggests that his experience as a local young person is valued: 'My colleagues will understand where my point of view is coming from if they can't see it for themselves, because my background is growing up in the area and I'm closer to the young people's age.' It is likely that there will be times when the cooperative process works less well, and when some workers and volunteers feel their perspective is not valued or heard. If VOY is to continue to challenge internal hierarchies and inequalities, this will be an ongoing project; as Julia said, 'I think it's something that we're constantly questioning and looking at in the way that we work as colleagues.' Despite aiming to involve and listen to every worker and volunteer, it might be difficult for some to raise concerns, and the potential for conflict remains even when many principles and values are shared. VOY will need to make deliberate efforts in its aim to maintain a diverse team; a cooperative structure does not guarantee the enactment of diversity, equality, voice or participative decision making, it merely provides the grounds to make it more possible.

VOY was motivated by a positive vision of putting equality and worker participation at its heart. It was also formed to resist and struggle against what its workers feel are inappropriate funding mechanisms. Its unwillingness to accept funding that does not accord with its principles sets it apart from most mainstream voluntary and non-profit youth organisations, which understandably place financial sustainability at the forefront of their decisions. Throughout this book, workers speak of ways in which they are affected by funding that requires them to work towards targets that constrain their work and change their identities as workers. No organisation that is registered and accepts funding can ever escape policy constraints (INCITE!, 2007); however, VOY's willingness to turn down funding is an important factor in its principled independence. As a result, young people in VOY can choose whether and how to get involved rather than being required to attend. Their details are not shared with other organisations. They are fully involved in decisions. They are encouraged and supported to become volunteers and youth workers themselves. And they are rarely – if ever – asked to do something 'just for the paperwork'. VOY's youth workers position themselves on young people's side, supporting them (for example) in their campaign for young people's rights in school.

One of VOY's problems is its lack of sustainable funding to employ workers on reliable or significant contracts. At the time of writing, cooperative members undertake a great deal of unpaid work, often only being paid during special projects. The small amount of paid part-time work available means that nobody can expect to make a living from their work for VOY. This is not unusual for a small organisation, but is perhaps exacerbated by a principled stance that precludes accepting certain contracts or funding. Some of VOY's workers have jobs elsewhere and are satisfied with voluntary work or occasional part-time hours, but others do not, and if they were paid for more of their work they could contribute more to VOY. Having a genuine involvement in creating their own working conditions can compensate workers to some extent for lower pay and uncertain employment conditions (McGregor and Mills, 2014). However, it can also be seen as a form of self-exploitation:

Co-ops can struggle to pay their workers a sustainable wage, and members run the risk of replacing exploitation by a boss with a mentality of self-exploitation. In addition, surviving in a capitalist market whilst sticking by our ethical and political beliefs can be a real struggle, not just economically but also personally. Sometimes difficult compromises have to be made, and this can be emotionally challenging. (Radical Routes, 2012, p 14)

Self-exploitation and burnout can be a particular danger for organisations that organise themselves democratically while working in a field that has limited resources and seems to require almost endless amounts of care, commitment, patience and love. This resonates with the dilemmas around passion and emotional labour discussed in Chapter Three. The VOY workers discuss their caring and passionate commitment, which they suggest is reinforced by being part of a cooperative:

'I think we are all equally, in very different ways, passionate about VOY. So we want to be here. I want to do my work, I want to do well, I want to consider others, and that's because of the culture.' (Fionn)

'Sometimes it is really long! But it's interesting. It takes a while because we all have to meet and then we all have to make decisions together. But it's better, I think, because we all know what we're doing and we've all chosen to do it.' (Anna-Nina)

'Young people, if they feel heard and respected and seen and cared for, that does create an atmosphere. That's what's happening in the co-op with us workers and maybe that's what's being reflected with the young people as well – that we care for each other and we hear each other's needs.' (Julia)

The passion and caring expressed by VOY members echoes the language used by grassroots workers throughout this book. Consideration between workers feeds back into passion and care for young people and for youth work itself. Emotional satisfaction is frequently expressed at VOY meetings, although at times we also talk about feeling tired, overloaded and overwhelmed. Inevitably, it is difficult to sustain any radical organisation, particularly when it is dependent on the voluntary labour of a small number of people (Sheridan-Rabideau, 2008). Developing a wider network of support might mitigate some of the pressures involved in running our own organisation while retaining its positive aspects, and this is something we hope to work towards.

Resistance through alternatives

Idealistic groups such as Voice of Youth can be seen as both protest and experiment, formed in opposition to dominant policy while also trying something different. This is expressed by Carys in her closing remark in the VOY dialogues: 'This is the kind of world we want, so this is how we're going to work.' Paradoxically, difficult funding environments can open up spaces for organisations to experiment with different ways of working; perhaps in an era of drastic cuts there is 'little to lose' from trying something different. Several workers in my study had either set up their own organisations, or were hoping to do so in the near future, as discussed in Chapter Two. Sarah's small business supports young people to campaign on local issues, and to sit on the board of the company. Zandra and her colleague have a flexible, affectionate and human approach to working with young people, despite onerous targets and a payment-by-results contract. Billie's charity was set up in a neighbourhood with a historic lack of youth provision, and attempts to work in cooperation rather than competition with other local youth providers. Keiron and Diana are meeting a business advisor about their ideas, hoping to 'show that there can be a really good organisation there that really cares about young people'. Without denying the significant challenges experienced by small idealistic organisations, they can also be seen as enactments of hope, of 'becoming the change we wish to see – in all the small details of our lives' (B'Hahn, 2001, p 9).

Radical, idealistic and alternative youth work can be seen as an enactment of prefigurative politics, described as 'the embodiment ... of those forms of social relations, decision-making, culture, and human experience that are the ultimate goal' (Boggs, 1977, p 2). The thinking behind prefigurative politics is both visionary and practical, and involves protest as well as creative positive alternatives; the future is reimagined in opposition to the problems of the present, and elements of a preferred future are put into practice. Groups have adopted this stance for tactical as well as principled reasons: 'if the new society were to be characterised by participatory democracy, anti-authoritarianism and liberation, the political means of achieving these goals had to be consonant' (Breines, 1989, p 53).

Throughout history, radical groups have worked 'prefiguratively', creating alternatives while simultaneously opposing the status quo. During the English Civil War in the seventeenth century, the Diggers attempted to live non-hierarchically on common land in harmony with nature and in defiance of wealthy and powerful landowners (Hill, 1972). Villagers in the Spanish Civil War organised themselves according to democratic anarchist principles while fighting fascists (Bookchin, 2001). The Black Panthers in the USA in the 1960s organised neighbourhood health and education programmes, including free breakfasts for children (Newton, 1974). Women who organised against sexism in the 1970s formed consciousness-raising groups and rape crisis centres (Rowbotham, 1979). Prefigurative politics can be seen more recently in oppositional movements. For example, in anti-austerity and pro-equality Indignado and Occupy movements that took place across the world in the wake of the 2008 global financial crash, decisions were made inclusively through discussion and consensus rather than having leaders, hierarchies and predefined demands (Graeber, 2004, 2013).

Congruent methods of organising are not only prefigurative of an abstracted new and better future; there is an important element of living our present lives in the best ways we can, even (or especially) in difficult conditions. Working and living more fairly and openly can make a real qualitative difference to our day-to-day lives, while showing through practice that other ways of relating to each other are possible. This does not mean that working in idealistic ways is escapist – it is impossible to escape entirely the constraints we live under, even if we might want to.

Even the most radical youth organisations are implicated in, and reliant on, the oppressive power relations they oppose. The term 'non-profit industrial complex' is used in the USA to recognise the financial and structural power of philanthropic foundations (INCITE!, 2007). Poststructuralist theory points out that resistance can never take place outside of existing unequal power regimes (Foucault, 1978; Butler in Olson and Worsham, 2000), and Marxist and anarchist thinkers would add that subversive ideas tend to be recuperated back into mainstream profit-driven governance (Debord, 1977).

Breines (1989) writes about the emotions of disappointment and despair that arose in movements she studied when their attempts to organise differently did not always work smoothly in practice. There is an extra layer of emotional vulnerability when working on politically radical projects, partly because any 'failure' might be taken as evidence that there was, after all, no alternative. Instead, perhaps, we can at least hope that we do not become dogmatic or closed-minded, that we continue to care for each other and for the young people we work with, and that our politics and principles remain at the centre of our work and are not diluted or compromised. In the words of the Zapatista activist, Marcos: 'The nightmare would be that after all this, we would end up the same' (El Kilombo Intergalactico, 2007, p 53).

Conclusion

Like the other stories of resistance in this book, Voice of Youth's story challenges any argument that austerity, privatisation and marketisation have entirely captured the youth work field. Even if VOY and similar organisations are short-lived, they provide stories of hope in difficult times. As Kofman and Lebas (1996, p 21) argue, 'To think about alternative possibilities, we need utopias.' 'Real utopias' do not need to be perfect or out of reach; they can be enacted in practice:

> It would be impossible to come up with detailed plans of actual institutions which would fully embody all of our ideals. Our real task is to try to think of institutions which themselves are capable of dynamic change, of responding to the needs of the people and evolving accordingly, rather than of institutions which are so perfect that they need no further change. (Wright, 2010, p 3)

Real utopianism is about taking action now, even or especially when the situation is particularly desperate. In a discussion of socially just education policy, Gandin and Apple reproduce the following quote from a lecture by Zizek:

> True utopia emerges when there are no ways to resolve the situation within the coordinates of the possible and, out of the pure urge to survive, you have to invent a new space. Utopia is not a free imagination: utopia is a matter of innermost urgency: you are forced to imagine something else as the only way out. (Zizek, quoted in Gandin and Apple, 2012, 16)

This resonates with the story of Voice of Youth, born in an environment that is somewhat hostile to critical and democratic forms of youth work. VOY is not intended to be an 'ideal' model to be copied, and yet might inspire others who want to do things differently in their own contexts. My colleagues and I want to share our experiences with VOY partly because of the paucity of alternative stories:

> Whilst sociological work in education had been extremely effective in identifying social injustice in education, and in analysing the way in which education systems reproduce inequality, it had been less good at proposing alternative models. (Francis and Mills, 2012, p 3)

Because of the all-encompassing nature of neoliberalism, it could be that it is at small local levels that alternatives are most able to be practised, and many of these stories will be lost because those involved are often too busy and tired to write them up. Researchers can sometimes have a useful role here, as critical 'secretaries' or 'consultants' (Apple and Beane, 1999; Land and King, 2014). As youth work struggles to remain alive in a context of constraints, it seems particularly important to share stories of 'real' alternatives.

SEVEN

Reclaiming and reimagining youth work

This book celebrates the passionate commitment of grassroots youth workers who make a vital contribution to the lives of young people. Their work emerges from this study as a distinctive practice that takes place on young people's terms, takes their everyday lives seriously, celebrates fun and informal learning, values the unpredictable and the unmeasurable, and creates spaces for young people to build positive relationships with each other and with adults. Youth clubs, street-based work and anti-oppressive groups are historically significant forms of practice that continue to play an important role in a social and political context where young people are facing ever greater pressures.

It is clear that youth workers are operating in extremely challenging circumstances. The threat to their practice is most visible in the repeated rounds of spending cuts and the associated redundancies, project closures and organisational restructuring. However, these are not the only consequences of a neoliberal policy context. Other far-reaching developments have been more subtle, were introduced over a longer period, and have faced limited overt resistance. These changes, which might prove the greater threat to grassroots youth work, can be summarised under the following terms:

- **Managerialism:** Top-down managerial processes prioritise administrative procedures over human relationships.
- **Marketisation:** Youth work organisations are increasingly business-oriented in their operation and values.
- **Performativity:** Youth workers' and organisations' performance is monitored and managed in ways that transform how youth work is practised.
- **Surveillance:** Youth workers are increasingly brought into the surveillance and control of young people, while also experiencing greater surveillance themselves.
- **Precarity:** Youth work projects, jobs and volunteering opportunities are increasingly short-term and insecure.

This book has demonstrated the stark effects of these manifestations of neoliberal policy on grassroots youth work in England. Such policy developments are not unique to youth work or to England, however. They are experienced by a broad range of welfare and education workers across the globe, underpinned by dominant funding and policy regimes, informed by neoliberal ideologies that celebrate and promote market mechanisms in all aspects of life. The impact of these global changes is particularly stark in relation to open and anti-oppressive approaches to youth work, which are based on relationships and process, are led by young people, and have outcomes that are difficult to predict or measure – features that bring them into conflict with market and managerial priorities.

This book has been concerned with how youth workers experience, enact and resist policy in their everyday practice. It has looked at how their work is affected by policy and explored how workers are involved in negotiation, contestation and resistance against policy changes that they experience as damaging. Good youth workers are consistently emphasised as one of the most important resources of effective youth work, including by young people themselves (Strobel et al, 2008); alongside young people, grassroots youth workers' perspectives must be central to efforts to reclaim and reimagine grassroots youth work for the future.

In aiming to understand and contribute to grassroots youth work practice, this study and the book as a whole are underpinned by an activist scholarship approach. Activist scholarship is an orientation towards research that is informed by, and works in solidarity with, groups and communities that struggle against dominant norms and ideologies. This is not to suggest that the youth work field can be seen straightforwardly as a community in struggle, and youth work is not inherently a form of activism (although some of its forms could be understood in this way). Practice can be informed by a number of perspectives that may be conformist as well as critical, conservative as well as progressive. Nevertheless, it is the argument of this book that passionate grassroots youth work practice is, quite rightly, underpinned by a *critical* approach to both practice and policy. This does not mean simplistically that youth workers criticise and obstruct everything that they are asked to do, but rather that developing a questioning attitude and a critical orientation is central to the youth worker role.

This concluding chapter discusses the role of grassroots youth workers in reclaiming and reimagining youth work. There is also a vital role, of course, for young people, as well as for youth work educators, managers, policy makers, parents and carers, neighbours, community activists and researchers. However, the future development of youth work must include at its roots the active engagement of those people who have made it their passion: committed grassroots youth workers, many of whom are still young people themselves, and many of whom benefited from youth work when they were young. This chapter starts by summarising the key findings from the study. This is followed by a discussion on the different ways in which youth workers demonstrate their active engagement in the reclaiming and reimagining of grassroots youth work. Finally, the book concludes with recommendations for policy and practice.

Key findings

This book has discussed in detail the complex blend of passion and resistance that is involved in being a grassroots youth worker in a changing policy context. While the chapters allow for more complex and nuanced discussion, it is useful to summarise the key findings here:

1. Grassroots youth work is under threat – but is surviving.

It is well established that significant spending cuts in local and central government have disproportionately affected grassroots youth work: both directly through closures and service reduction, and indirectly through the demise of local authority youth services that previously provided structure, support, training and partnership as well as direct services. Local young people and communities have lost valued organisations and infrastructure, and it is questionable whether open access youth work is currently a viable career option. However, it would be inaccurate to claim that open access youth work has been lost, or that its loss is imminent and inevitable. This research shows that grassroots youth work survives, even in an insecure and difficult context. Some local authorities have maintained their youth clubs, street-based projects and anti-oppressive groups against the odds; some voluntary sector organisations continue to prioritise open access projects; and new grassroots youth groups are being set up. Without belittling these efforts, however, the current scale of the dismantling of services is momentous, and an active and continuing defence of open access and anti-oppressive youth work is of vital importance at the current time.

2. Market values, target cultures and top-down management obstruct grassroots youth work.

Committed grassroots youth workers speak consistently about how certain policy and organisational requirements obstruct their work with young people. In particular, they are critical of 'tick box' monitoring and 'bums on seats' approaches, in which young people seem to be reduced to numbers and required to meet predefined outcomes. Workers are also critical of top-down management systems, where senior managers do not seem to listen to frontline staff or involve them in decisions; this is particularly problematic when managers have little experience or understanding of face-to-face work, a situation that is increasingly common. Part-timers and volunteers are worried that experienced colleagues spend too much time in the office, and are concerned about their own futures in youth work if promotion means being distanced from face-to-face practice.

3. Part-timers and volunteer youth workers are passionate about their work, and yet vulnerable to exploitation.

The grassroots youth workers in this research expressed love and passion for their work, and emphasised their care for young people and enjoyment in spending time with them. Such emotional engagement can be the basis of genuine positive relationships which are greatly valued by young people. Youth workers, both paid and voluntary, are often prepared to 'go the extra mile' without material reward, working long unpaid hours and tolerating difficult working conditions. Such commitment can be exhausting, and leave workers vulnerable to exploitation and burnout. Because of their deep emotional engagement in their work, grassroots youth workers might be susceptible to negative feelings; however, they also experience their passion for youth work as a source of strength and sometimes as contributing to resistance against the commodification of youth work.

4. Grassroots youth workers are inadequately involved in decisions that affect their work.

Part-timers and volunteers are increasingly relied upon as the main providers of youth work; however, they are often marginalised from the decisions made about their work. Sometimes marginalisation is structural, such as when part-timers and volunteers are excluded from staff meetings, not funded for training, and unable to access organisational email or internet facilities. All too many feel that their views and experience are not respected, and this means they cannot act on the views of young people. Even in organisations where part-timers and volunteers are valued and included on a local basis, they feel disempowered in relation to some of the wider policy decisions that affect their work.

5. Grassroots youth workers work in precarious conditions, which obstruct long-term work with young people.

Grassroots youth workers' marginalisation is exacerbated by precarious working conditions, which directly obstruct their capacity to build long-term trusting relationships with young people. Increasingly they are employed through agencies, on zero-hour contracts or on a 'self-employed' basis, with very little job security. Many engage in a variety of roles to make ends meet, taking any extra hours offered to them and unable to rely on a regular income. Often the lines between paid and voluntary work are blurred. Sometimes workers are misled about whether they will be paid, and if they work on 'payment by results' projects their pay might depend on whether they have met their targets. Such chronic insecurity adds to their sense of marginalisation and obstructs effective long-term work in communities.

6. Grassroots youth workers engage in questioning and resistance that contributes to the survival of critical and anti-oppressive practice.

Youth workers assert the need for a focus on authentic relationships with young people and the value of informal approaches that are qualitatively different from more structured and 'establishment' services. Their experience tells them that such approaches are valued by young people, particularly those who are most marginalised from mainstream services. For this reason, most are critical of aspects of managerialism and market-oriented policy in their workplaces, such as targets that seem inappropriate or meaningless, negative labelling of young people, cuts and inadequate resources, and practices that are akin to more formal services such as schools and social work. Youth workers are actively involved in celebrating grassroots youth work and challenging aspects of policy they disagree with. For a minority, this involves organised workplace struggle such as strikes and trade union organising, or engagement in looser networks such as In Defence of Youth Work, Feminist Webs or the Federation for Detached Youth Work. For most, critique happens mainly in their own workplaces and communities. Everyday forms of resistance may be limited in impact, but nevertheless contribute to the survival and reimagining of critical open youth work.

7. There are alternatives!

Taken as a whole, this book challenges the Thatcherite creed that 'there is no alternative', a slogan that emphasises the hegemonic dominance of neoliberalism. Alternatives exist in the everyday practice of grassroots youth workers that has been discussed in many of the stories told throughout this book: valuing passion and fun rather than profit; working on young people's terms rather than from adult-defined agendas; challenging discrimination and labelling rather than contributing to it; working cooperatively rather than competitively; and using qualitative and creative forms of evaluation such as storytelling, rather than being restricted to 'tick box' methods. Some grassroots youth workers have set up their own organisations to put alternative principles into practice. Others contribute to existing organisations that have been working for some time in ways that are critical of the status quo. Even workers in mainstream organisations can carve out spaces for autonomous practice and engage in discourses of love and care that challenge the dominance of marketised and managerial systems. These organisations and workers are putting critical and passionate grassroots youth work into practice.

Developing critical passionate practice

Throughout this book, policy has been presented as a process that is enacted in complex and messy ways at the level of practice (Ball et al, 2012). Practitioners experience policy differently to politicians and policy makers. Sometimes their critiques are consciously political, while more often they are based on practical experiences of how certain policy technologies obstruct their ability to develop trusting relationships with young people. The future of youth work depends on workers taking a passionate and critical stance towards their practice. This sometimes requires them to negotiate, challenge and resist everyday manifestations of policy in ways that are sophisticated, complex and context-dependent.

Throughout this study, I have been inspired by the passion and resistance of grassroots youth workers who oppose, question or contest the dominance of market and managerial values in their work. The theme of everyday resistance has recurred in different forms throughout the book. Chapter Two explored some of the ambivalent positions that youth workers take up in the youth work market. Some were involved in collective opposition to spending cuts, while in other places this kind of resistance was obstructed by organisational policies as well as workers' doubts about its effectiveness. Resistance was more clearly and consistently present in everyday practice, when part-timers maintained their passion for youth work even while working in incredibly difficult and precarious circumstances, and when they set up new organisations that put young people at the centre. This focus on young people was also emphasised in Chapter Three, which discussed grassroots workers' love and passion for their work. Workers demonstrate genuine care for young people and enjoy spending time with them, going 'the extra mile' to keep youth centres open, create homely spaces and maintain warm relationships. Although passionate practice risks exploitation and exhaustion, it also contributes to an attitude that contrasts with the marketisation and commodification of youth work.

Chapter Four discussed how target cultures and performance mechanisms undermine youth workers' passion for their work. In this context, workers struggle for authenticity by speaking of their work in ways that challenge 'tick box' cultures; by asserting non-measurable and youth-centred outcomes for their work; by opposing particularly damaging targets or measurement systems; by engaging in 'tactical performativity', being 'good workers' and thus earning leeway to challenge or refuse particular aspects of their work; and through collective action and campaigning. Some of these themes were developed further in Chapter Five, which focused on surveillance in the practice of street-based youth work. Some workers refused to engage in elements of surveillance, such as working alongside the police, while in relation to electronic surveillance most were involved in a process of resistance and accommodation, conforming to elements of policy while also challenging them. I suggested that workers might join with young people and others to question assumptions about who and what 'the street' is for, perhaps taking inspiration from political movements to reimagine the street for the use and participation of everybody.

Chapter Six developed this idea of rethinking what we take for granted and reimagining our present and our future, focusing on a small, local workers' cooperative, Voice of Youth. The cooperative is based on critical youth work principles, avoids funding that involves the systematic surveillance of young people and is organised without managerial hierarchies. This story shows that idealistic organisations can make a difference in their own communities, while also demonstrating alternative ways of working that could inform and inspire practitioners in other areas and settings.

Taken as a whole, this study provides evidence that grassroots youth workers can – and often do – take young people's side, challenge oppression, oppose tick-box and pathologising methodologies, and question the centrality of market logic. Such resistance is essential to the survival of grassroots youth work and needs to be encouraged. Even when hope seems misplaced and the future looks bleak, it is always better to live our everyday lives in ways that resist domination (Anonymous, 2011). Perhaps youth workers can develop an activist spirit by sharing their experiences of resistance as they share other aspects of their practice, learning from each other as well as developing creative new forms.

Taking action

Grassroots youth workers value participative, collective and bottom–up approaches. As the Afterword will go on to discuss, these approaches overlap (to some extent) with practical anarchism, which emphasises both solidarity and freedom, and the potential for changing the world without taking power (Holloway, 2002). In youth work and the wider world, resistance is diversifying. It does not only encompass mass collective forms of action such as large demonstrations and occupations, it includes what is sometimes referred to as 'everyday' or 'micro' resistance (Weitz, 2001; Thomas and Davies, 2005a, 2005b). My aim here is not to privilege everyday resistance over more ambitious and collective forms of activism, but rather to acknowledge the importance of localised and subtle actions and inactions at a time when workers are governed in decentralised ways. In everyday forms of activism, people use the tools at their disposal to speak or act for what they believe to be right and against what they see as wrong. It could be that 'these everyday, apparently trivial, individual acts of resistance offer the potential to spark social change and, in the long run, to shift the balance of power between social groups' (Weitz, 2001, p 670).

Everyday resistance takes diverse forms in grassroots youth work. Workers and volunteers can be seen as resisting when they refuse to accept directives to work with the police, criticise target-driven work, avoid collecting young people's details on the streets, value love and care over profit, and set up alternative organisations. Understandably, they are not resisting all the time; sometimes they challenge the status quo and at other times they work inside it. When it takes place, their resistance is often fluid, diverse and creative. Inevitably it can also be isolated, dispersed, risky and inconsistent, often taking place at a small scale on a local level, and not necessarily leading to change. Despite its limitations, however, everyday activism by grassroots youth workers emerges from this research as a key element in keeping open access and informal approaches alive.

While some commentators have expressed regret that the youth workforce 'inclines to debate and disputation' (Wylie, 2004, p 27), most workers in my study celebrated youth workers' rebellious culture, even if not all of them would name such behaviour as resistance. Laura argued that, 'To be a good youth worker we need to break the rules.' Rachel said, 'There's not many wallflowers. You can't be, can you? It wouldn't work. Lots of kind of feisty spirits but that's fine, that's good.' Similarly, Louise saw youth workers as 'free spirits' who 'don't like laws and rules'. Rebellion was often a matter for critical reflection, and workers made thoughtful and tactical decisions about where to conform and where to rebel. This can be seen in Chapter Four, for example, where Lucy discusses how she and her colleagues were seen as 'easy, good employees' and that this gave them some leeway to take a principled stance against certain targets they disagreed with.

What I want to do here is map the everyday action and resistance that has been encountered during this research, with the aim of presenting workers' actual critical practices as resources for sharing, adapting and developing by others working and living in different places. These approaches might be useful for grassroots youth workers struggling with the tensions between what they believe in and what they are asked to do. They might also be adapted by critical practitioners in other positions – managers, commissioners, funders and policy makers – as well as by people in other fields such as health, social work, teaching and higher education. In the following section I have conceptualised critical practice under three headings:

• developing counter-discourses
• refusing and rebelling
• reimagining youth work.

The point here is not to create artificial boundaries as if these are entirely distinct kinds of action, and neither is there any implied 'hierarchy' in which some types of actions are preferred over others. This model is simply one way to understand the interrelated kinds of resistance that grassroots workers already engage in. The examples included here can be used as ideas and inspiration for creative reinterpretation and transformation, and to encourage reflective, confident and active practice.

Developing counter-discourses

Counter-discourses are ways of speaking, thinking and acting that go against what is dominant or taken for granted in society (Woolford and Curran, 2013). My research demonstrates that grassroots youth workers regularly employ counter-discourses in various contexts and for different purposes, for example, when they speak about their love and passion for their work, and when they value their relationships with young people over financial reward, as well as when they express doubt, uncertainty and overt critique. By speaking against oppressive policy regimes and in favour of care, cooperation and relationship, they are 'proceeding from a different field of judgement' (Lipman, 2013, p 13).

Emotional engagement in youth work might be seen as unremarkable in a caring occupation, particularly in an era when workers across all sectors are required to be passionate (Lazzarato, 1997). Critique might be dismissed, too, as part of the day-to-day complaint that tends to exist in organisations. I would suggest, however, that in a policy environment where returns on investment are 'what counts', expressions of emotional commitment, doubt, uncertainty and critique constitute a vital element towards reclaiming and reimagining grassroots youth work. Speaking about care rather than money, and cooperation rather than competition, goes some way towards rejecting or at least questioning the dominant neoliberal values we would otherwise take for granted. It is a way of unsettling ourselves and others (Ball, 2013, p 147), an unsettling that might contribute to the survival of critical grassroots youth work.

Counter-discourses have been a particularly important part of feminist, black and anti-colonial struggles. Hill Collins (1986, 1990) and bell hooks (1984) write that black women have made creative use of their marginal status and adopted alternative discourses around self-definition and self-validation. Thiong'o (1986) calls for African writers to 'decolonise the mind' by using their own languages in preference to the English of their colonisers. Part-time and volunteer youth workers, who may be seen as a marginalised occupational group and who often come from marginalised social groups, tend to question and reject the language of targets, outcomes and profit. Using non-dominant language can reinforce cultures that work against the grain of dominant power (Thiong'o, 1986) and might interrupt institutional definitions and narratives (Langhout, 2005). Youth workers in this research have engaged in counter-discourses in various ways, including by:

- prioritising young people's experiences, feelings and opinions over meeting targets;
- explaining to managers and funders that there are things about youth work that cannot easily be measured or explained;
- sharing professional and practice dilemmas with young people and colleagues;
- talking about young people as young people, rather than using pathologising labels;
- meeting with others to reflect on the current conditions of youth work practice and young people's lives.

Despite the importance of such actions, resistance through discourse can be limited in its possibilities. Using one's voice is particularly problematic for marginalised groups as it relies on being located where it is possible to speak and be heard (Spivak, 1988). Part-time workers are often excluded from meetings and other spaces of decision making, and may fear speaking out at a time when jobs and whole organisations are at risk. Many are in vulnerable positions, living on incredibly low incomes and with little or no job security, and may decide to keep their critique to themselves or only share it with trusted allies. In this context, the disputatious cultures of grassroots youth work are in danger of being lost. It has been suggested that youth workers could be more courageous and engage more readily in questioning:

> Amidst the tension and strain in the workplace there's often more space to question than we allow. It becomes easy to censor ourselves before the official censor even appears ... it is possible to say, 'here are the figures for this particular project in percentiles. The data is easy on the eye and ear, but in truth it tells us less than we used to garner from the project reports, our meetings with workers and young people in the past'. (Taylor and Taylor, 2013, p 13)

Using counter-discourses 'upwards' in the direction of managers, funders and politicians is a risky strategy, and yet many of the workers in this research do just this, even despite insecure employment conditions. Some of their views are ignored, while others have changed local policy and practice. It is difficult to assess the impact of thinking and speaking in divergent ways, but this does not mean that counter-discourses are ineffective. In trying to speak differently we will not always 'get it right'; doubt can itself be a counter-discourse, a challenge to the dominant insistence on proof and certainty.

Refusals and rebellion

While counter-discourses are widespread among grassroots youth workers, traditional larger-scale resistance such as strikes and demonstrations are less common. Youth workers are sometimes concerned about taking action that could be perceived as negative, and want to focus on being creative, innovative and positive. Part-timers also worry that getting involved in protests could put them at personal risk, and they are concerned that others might not join them. Through my involvement with In Defence of Youth Work I have often heard workers expressing fear that their employer might find out that they had been to one of our meetings, or that they had attended a conference workshop on radical youth work. Workers repeatedly tell stories of not being allowed to speak out against cuts to services, and being told not to support young people in having their say on issues identified by managers as 'political'.

Nevertheless, this research shows that many committed grassroots youth workers *do* exercise refusals and rebellion in their workplaces. Refusal can be compatible with passionate practice and does not necessarily need to be seen as negative. Although most of the workers involved in this study do not see themselves as politically active and few are affiliated to campaign groups or unions, nearly all have at some time acted in dissent. For example, it was common among street-based youth workers to avoid or refuse requirements to ask each young person to fill out a registration form on first meeting them (see Chapter Five). Such street-level rebellions are small-scale but important, and the widespread nature of these refusals led indirectly to a change in one market-leading database system, so that anonymous contacts can now be recorded. Such change is hardly revolutionary; nevertheless, this small but important reform suggests that refusal and rule-breaking, even when it is decentralised and uncoordinated, can lead to change. The research participants also demonstrated other forms of rebellion and rule-breaking, including:

- leaving a job or giving up a piece of work because of disagreements with managers or objection to a requirement;
- avoiding jobs that take them away from face-to-face work or that require extensive bureaucracy;
- discussing potential youth club closures and cuts with young people, despite being told not to;
- refusing to work alongside the police;

- refusing to 'out' young people by entering the details of LGBT youth group members on local government databases.

The space for overt refusals and rebellion is diminishing, and the dispersed acts of rebellion discussed here may have limited political impact at times. However, they have the potential to maintain and develop the kind of activist spirit that is essential for a critical workforce (Sachs, 2000; Avis, 2005). In a context of legal impediments which make traditional workplace organising difficult to sustain, trade unions have begun to think more openly and democratically about the kinds of actions that might be more effective and community-based. It is difficult to know in advance what forms of protest will make a lasting transformation, so it is important for unions and campaigning organisations to remain open-minded about the diverse tactics and possibilities for change, at least to disturb the boundaries of dominant norms by undermining and subverting their restrictions.

Creating alternatives

This study shows that grassroots youth workers are actively engaged in a process of reimagining youth work, whether by setting up alternative organisations, or by working innovatively within existing organisations. Creating these new alternatives is a process of praxis: of understanding our situation, thinking about how things could be different, putting those thoughts into practice and reflecting on these actions (Freire, 1988). Alternative organising and prefigurative practice can encompass both ambitious new projects and small-scale innovations. Youth workers in this research engaged in creating alternatives in a variety of ways:

- starting a youth work 'business' that questions and rejects market-oriented values and supports young people in campaigning;
- opening up a youth centre to young people as often as possible, rather than only at standard times;
- forming a non-hierarchical youth workers' cooperative based on principles of critical youth work and cooperation;
- using stories – in all of their ambiguity and uncertainty – to evaluate and describe youth work, rather than relying on statistical outcomes (IDYW, 2011, 2014b);
- claiming spaces for open access, anti-oppressive and critical work with young people.

While 'creating alternatives' has positive connotations whereas 'refusal' sounds negative and reactive, this is a false dichotomy. Questioning and perhaps rejecting what we have come to see as normal is necessary for the reinvention of our assumed ways of working, and the creation of positive alternatives depends on political engagement and critique. Refusals interact with new ideas to create alternatives, as suggested by Butler and Athanasiou when they discuss:

> how to become dispossessed of the sovereign self and enter into forms of collectivity that oppose forms of dispossession that systematically jettison populations from modes of collective belonging and justice. (Butler and Athanasiou, 2013, p xi)

What is important here is a valuing of the collective rather than the 'sovereign self', and a productive and optimistic rejection of norms in order to claim different ways of working – or simply freer spaces that allow more scope for young people to create as they wish. There are norms that we might need to rebel against, disconnect from or dispossess ourselves of, and our refusals might help us to reclaim, reconnect or repossess alternative forms of living, working and organising. As Ahmed (2010, p 163) articulates it, 'The utopian form might not make the alternative possible, but it aims to make impossible the belief that there is no alternative.' Inspiration for positive alternatives can come from a variety of sources: activist movements of the past and present; struggles over identity, equality, freedom and recognition; alternative organisational forms such as collectives, communes and cooperatives; radical community work, social work and education; art, music, dance and fiction; and critical theory and research. It can also come from the history, practice and theory of youth work itself, particularly in its radical, experimental and anti-oppressive forms. Stories and experiences from different countries and contexts, and from inside as well as outside youth work, can spark discussions between colleagues, young people, allies and wider communities. In the creative process of reimagining what and how our work might be (and we may or may not always name this as 'youth work') we can try out some of our ideas and learn more about the reality of alternatives through a process of trial and error, discussion and critical reflection.

While Chapter Six concentrated on the potential for new idealistic organisations, there were also examples in my research where workers reimagined and reinvented youth work *within* mainstream local authority and voluntary sector organisations. Alan, whose work is discussed in Chapters Three and Four, works for a local authority and is under pressure to meet bureaucratic requirements and inappropriate targets. However, he rejects the dominant managerial cultures of youth work by spending as little time as possible on administration; he insists on opening the youth centre to young people as often as possible, rather than only during formal opening times, and developing responsive and sensitive systems for dealing with challenging behaviour, rather than enforcing inflexible punitive policies.

Other workers also create spaces to practise differently. Louise challenges restrictive timeframes despite a culture of 'getting things done', and I described in Chapter Three how she worked for long periods with one young woman who needed intense support. Colleagues Laura, Bridget and Lucy insist on involving young people in decisions about funding, targets and whether to work with the police; by doing so they also assert their voices as part-timers, despite working in a normatively hierarchical organisation (see Chapters Four and Five). These workers are engaged in processes of creating autonomous spaces and a critical use of time within established settings where they reject cultures that are overly instrumental and controlling (Colley et al, 2012).

By discussing how youth workers are engaged actively and diversely in the enactment and contestation of policy, it is by no means my intention to tell youth workers what forms of action they should take. Such an exercise would be both futile and inappropriate:

> Resistance is local, arising on a specific site and a singular conjecture. It is therefore difficult to develop universal principles of resistance, even though common trends in different sites of power may lead to similar reactions. Every situation and age creates new forms, strategies and subjects. Resistance reacts to the concrete circumstances it finds itself in ... This process feeds into power, too. (Douzinas, 2014, p 89)

This study suggests that workers are *already* involved in discussing, debating and trying out different forms of questioning, contestation and resistance at local levels. My contention here is that such critical orientations to policy are *essential* if we are to reclaim and reimagine grassroots youth work.

Recommendations

This book is written in the spirit of engagement with all those involved in youth work and related practices, and aims to be useful rather than simply sitting on a shelf. However, the usefulness of research is not always direct, transparent or easily observable. Just as policy is interpreted and enacted in various ways, so research is received and used differently by those who come across it. Readers will come to their own conclusions about the implications of this research, depending on their values, principles and the diverse contexts in which they are working. There are limitations to the usefulness of a list of recommendations, particularly when research findings challenge the dominant policy context. Real change would require a much wider and deeper level of transformation than exists within the scope of this study. However, even small actions can have a genuine impact, perhaps opening up the cracks in a world dominated by capital (Holloway, 2010). The following recommendations are offered in the same spirit as the rest of the book: as resources for practice, reflection, discussion and debate.

Organisational change

Minimising bureaucracy

Celebrating and valuing grassroots work requires a steep reduction in bureaucratic practices that take skilled and experienced workers away from face-to-face work with young people. The bureaucratic burden of new and existing initiatives must be assessed and evaluated. Workers, organisations and funders could share ideas and practices that minimise high administrative workloads.

Democratising organisations

Youth, community and education organisations often claim a commitment to participation from young people and other community members, and yet overlook the importance of internal workplace democracy. Part-timers including volunteers should be invited to regular meetings and training, given choices over how much or how little information they would like to receive, and provided with space and encouragement to support each other, learn together, develop their own projects and share their concerns and ideas. Flatter structures and lower pay differentials that demonstrate (beyond policy statements) that workers at all levels are valued will result in more inclusive, dynamic and effective working practices.

Building alliances

The current policy context promotes individualising tendencies and a blame culture. Critical youth workers and organisations need to reclaim collective and associational practices, such as bringing groups of young people together; supporting and encouraging colleagues; making time for reflection and debate; building bottom-up networks; meeting informally to discuss issues in the workplace; engaging in existing campaigns and groups; working in cooperation rather than competition with other local organisations; and working in solidarity with young people, activists, community groups and practitioners in other settings.

Employing, supporting and empowering staff

Implementing fair employment

All employed youth workers, including part-timers, should be rewarded for their work in line with nationally negotiated pay scales, encouraged to join a union, and given long-term contracts wherever possible. This requires funders and senior managers to recognise the value of long-term work with young people and in communities. Fair employment – which includes paying part-timers to take part in training and evaluation as well as face-to-face work – is essential for good quality youth work.

Valuing staff development

All youth workers including volunteers need regular support, guidance, one-to-one supervision and training. Good quality youth work is underpinned by a well trained and well supported workforce, taking into account the complex emotional, practical and political pressures faced by youth workers. Introductory and part-time training routes are overdue a review. Grassroots workers need access to continuing professional development, including inexpensive training for individuals and teams, as well as support to access advanced courses at university level.

Enabling critical practice

Critique and democratic engagement are vital for the development of practitioners who have the courage to stand up for young people. Critical reflection on practice must be encouraged, and youth workers need space to discuss and debate a wide variety of issues with colleagues and young people, rather than feeling constrained and censored. Youth work that practises at a distance from mechanisms of control (such as policing and formal social services) should be valued, as it enables meaningful engagement with the most marginalised young people.

Policy change

Questioning target and outcomes cultures

While youth work needs to be accountable, its primary accountability must always be to young people and their communities. This research shows that target cultures tend to distort and obstruct practice and lead to excessive managerialism and surveillance. The outcomes of grassroots youth work are diverse, open-ended, and often emerge over a long time frame. Assuring good quality practice does not need to involve excessively prescriptive outcomes frameworks; it can be achieved through training, support, advice and meaningful contact.

Challenging market mechanisms

Grassroots youth work is poorly suited to a market framework. Funding mechanisms such as 'payment by results' distort the youth work method, encourage gaming, and give disproportionate advantage to larger charities and companies while small grassroots organisations cannot access longer-term sources of funding. Publicly accountable youth services have a vital role in providing open forms of youth work, and in supporting communities and young people to run their own youth clubs by providing grants (rather than commissioning) and free training and advice.

Supporting and funding grassroots youth work

Grassroots youth work – in the form of youth clubs, street-based projects, anti-oppressive projects, and groups for specific communities and social groups – is a distinctive practice that is highly valued by young people and communities. Youth work is not a 'luxury' for the young people who rely on it. It is a relatively inexpensive and vital resource that has been developed over many decades, and must be protected for the present and the future.

Conclusion

This book is rich in its stories and accounts of grassroots youth workers who are committed to building relationships with young people through informal and person-centred approaches. With their passionate practice, and their diverse forms of everyday action and resistance, these grassroots workers are contributing to a process of reclaiming and reimagining youth work. It is worth struggling to hold on to practices that have been highly valued by young people over decades, such as the voluntary principle, informal education, critical reflection, detached work and anti-oppressive practice. However, it is not enough simply to reclaim what we once had. Reclaiming needs to go along with reimagining, a process of challenging taken-for-granted policies and practices, and working creatively with young people to try out new methods and ideas.

Grassroots youth work faces many challenges. It is a practice that works with marginalised young people, many of whom are working class and from minority groups, and its workforce tends to mirror this demographic. It is hardly surprising, then, that youth work, its participants and its least senior workers have not occupied a powerful position in society or policy making, and have been marginalised over many generations. Despite these challenges, the passion of youth workers and young people has contributed to the survival – in adverse circumstances – of a principled and reflective practice that values equality, freedom and collective life. If we are to reclaim and reimagine youth work for the future, however, there remains much to do.

AFTERWORD

Research methodology

> Cycling between home and university, I travel through the neighbourhood where I am a youth worker. Has youth work become a place that I'm only passing through on my research journey? The metaphor is perhaps too obvious, but there might be something in it. Most researchers get closer to the world they are studying while they're doing field work, whereas for me, doing a PhD has also meant the opposite: a subtle loss, a slow pulling away. I still feel like a youth worker, but I am less immersed in the practice than I was two years ago, and feel guilty about it. Then, I feel guilty that I'm spending too much time doing youth work when I could be studying. Paradoxically, I am drawing on my youth work identity *for* my research at the same time as this identity is becoming weaker *because* of the research. (Research diary, December 2012)

The research for this book was completed between 2011 and 2014 as the study for a PhD in the Sociology of Education. My previous experience and identity as a youth worker was a starting point and ongoing resource for this study, even if it has sometimes been difficult to disentangle and navigate the dual roles of practitioner and researcher. However, the main focus of the book is the perspectives and experiences of the part-time and volunteer youth workers who took part in the research. My aim in this book has been to place their voices centrally, while attempting to make explicit how my own positioning as a researcher might influence, enhance and obstruct analysis and interpretation. The rationale throughout this study has been to develop a methodology that is consistent with youth work itself: being open to others' perspectives, while remaining principled; encouraging participation, while taking responsibility; and reflecting critically on my own practices, while acting collectively with others.

The study, while not a pure ethnography, is inspired by the ethnographic approach: the commitment to detailed and long-term immersion in a culture (in this case, grassroots youth work), using participant observation and interviews to develop rich and holistic insights into people's lived experiences. In this chapter I outline and discuss the methodological approach to the research, beginning with reflection on the research methods – in-depth interviews, focus groups and participant observation – and a discussion of data analysis and how the study was written up. This is followed by discussion on the study's theoretical and methodological underpinnings, and how these are informed by anarchism, activist scholarship and theory from a range of critical perspectives.

Research methods

The starting point for this research was a commitment to hear the experiences and perspectives of part-time and volunteer youth workers from a diverse range of work settings and social backgrounds. A qualitative approach enabled detailed and thoughtful engagement with how grassroots youth workers were experiencing their work in highly challenging times. Speaking to a relatively small number of research participants, combined with extensive participant observation and policy analysis, enabled the development of a detailed understanding of how youth workers experience their work in a changing policy context.

Research participants

I recruited research participants through short written adverts (one asking for volunteers to take part in interviews, and a later one advertising the focus groups), which I gave out at events and emailed to a range of local authority and voluntary sector youth organisations in England. Anybody who worked in England and described themselves as a part-time and/or voluntary youth worker was eligible to take part; I wanted to hear from those who self-defined as youth workers rather than closing this down in advance. Using a purposive sampling strategy, I selected a diverse range of research participants in terms of workplace characteristics, levels of experience and qualification, geographical location, and social identity.

The study involved 35 research participants: 22 from a range of English regions took part in interviews and 8 working in or near a northern city took part in a series of three focus groups. (One person took part in both an individual interview and the focus groups.) In addition, 6 colleagues from Voice of Youth in London took part in two focus groups and a collective writing process. These participants all worked in 'open' settings, including youth clubs, street-based projects, mobile bus provision, girls' work and LGBT groups. Several had more than one role as youth workers, and some of these roles involved casework or other more targeted forms of work with young people. They worked in a range of organisations: local government youth services, charities and social enterprises. Although there is a significant faith-based sector in UK youth work, most of the participants in this study worked in secular organisations; this reflects the study's focus on the enactment of government policy, which is most clearly experienced by youth workers employed, funded or directly regulated by the state or local government. One participant worked for an explicitly Christian charity that had received local government funding. The research participants were also a diverse group in terms of gender, social class, ethnicity, age and sexuality. Most had at least three years of youth work experience, even though many were still young people themselves. I have included a short description of each interviewee and focus group participant in the Appendix, including their youth work role, qualifications and aspects of their social identity that they chose to share.

Prospective interviewees were sent an information sheet and consent form, which explained the purpose of the research and safeguards such as confidentiality, anonymity and the right to withdraw. The names of people, places and organisations were changed, and information was occasionally omitted if either the research participant or I felt that it might risk them being identified. Participants chose a false name to be used in the writing up of the research, and were offered a copy of their interview transcript on request.

In-depth interviews

My approach to interviewing is inspired and influenced by feminist, ethnographic and constructivist grounded theory understandings of interviewing as a two-way conversation in which the interviewee has the opportunity to shape the interview (Oakley, 1990; Charmaz, 2006) This characterisation should not imply that an interview is an 'ordinary' chat; a research interview is a *particular kind* of conversation that is distinct from everyday talk and 'goes beneath the surface of ordinary conversation and examines earlier events, views and feelings afresh' (Charmaz, 2006, p 26). While acknowledging that an interview can (at least initially) provoke feelings of anxiety or self-consciousness in both interviewer and interviewees, there is also a positive potential for interviews, which can create a thoughtful space for critical reflection outside of day-to-day practice.

Aiming to minimise possible discomfort around the 'research interview' scenario, particularly given that many part-time and volunteer youth workers do not come from academic backgrounds, I aimed to create a relaxed atmosphere. Interviewees were generally given a choice of where to meet, and most chose to meet in a cafe or at their own workplace. I explained that the interview would take the form of a conversation about their work that could go in any direction they chose, that there were no wrong answers, and that I was interested in anything they had to say. I gave participants the option of being interviewed together with colleagues if they preferred; 17 of the interviews were one-to-one, one involved two workers who knew each other from a training course, and one was with a group of three colleagues.

The interviews were carried out over a period of two years between 2011 and 2013, and were semi-structured, with their structure evolving over the time of the research. I started each interview with the question, 'How did you get involved in youth work?', a familiar topic that tended to get the conversation flowing. This does not mean that participants' routes into youth work were necessarily easy to recount, and some of the stories shared in Chapter Three show that people come into youth work for a variety of reasons, some of which are deeply personal. The first six interviews were relatively unstructured and free-flowing from this point; this was because I wanted to keep the focus of the study relatively open, and to focus on participants' interests rather than on my own preconceived thoughts. After transcribing and analysing these early interviews I developed a flexible interview schedule, with a short list of topics selected either because they had elicited rich discussion amongst the initial participants, or (in the case of young people's and workers' identities) because I thought them important even though they had been relatively absent. The interview schedule is shown in Table 3.

These topics and questions were designed to be as open-ended as possible, to avoid prejudging the issues that might be important to interviewees, and to allow conversation to flow relatively freely. As a result, the interviews covered a wide array of topics and it has been impossible for the book to do justice to everything we discussed. The conversation often started before the tape recorder was switched on and continued long after it had been switched off. I made notes immediately after every interview, noting such aspects as body language, facial expressions and the setting where the interview took place, as well as my feelings about how the interview had gone. I transcribed each interview myself in full, spending many hours listening and writing

Table 3: Flexible schedule for in-depth interviews

Key theme	Explanation
Routes into youth work	How you came to be a youth worker
What you do	What kind of things you do at work, what a 'typical' day or week looks like
Young people	What kind of young people you work with, how you would describe them (perhaps including gender, class, ethnicity, sexuality etc.)
Your identity	How you would describe yourself, how young people see you, similarities and differences with the young people (perhaps including gender, class, ethnicity, sexuality etc.)
Being a part-time or volunteer youth worker	Differences between being part-time and full-time, paid and voluntary, advantages and disadvantages; would you rather be in a different position?
Likes/dislikes	What do you like about the work? What don't you like? What helps? What gets in the way? What changes have taken place in the time you've been a youth worker?
Training and education	Have you done youth work qualifications? What were they? What was your experience? How important are they?

out what each person said, which assisted me in getting to know the interviews (Charmaz, 2006).

Several participants told me that they had enjoyed their interview and that it had been less formal than they had expected, and even though some of them discussed issues that they clearly found upsetting, painful or enraging, many said that it was useful to have the chance to reflect on their work. I felt somehow both exhausted and energised after each interview and found the discussions incredibly satisfying, stimulating and engaging. While some interviewees expressed similar feelings, it is important to recognise that interviewees' experiences are not transparent to the researcher, and it might have been difficult to tell me if they had more negative or ambivalent feelings about taking part.

Research encounters include complex emotional and relational elements, and researchers have a responsibility to be reflexive in relation to their actions and identities. For example, I experienced feelings of fellowship with research participants because of our shared identities as youth workers, but this may not have been experienced in the same way by them. Commonalities between researchers and participants can build trust (Ochieng, 2010), and some participants seemed reassured or interested that I had been a youth worker for many years. In the earlier stages of research I was uncomfortable with my academic identity and presented myself mainly as a fellow youth worker; while I had no intention to be manipulative, it is important not to obscure the reality of power relations in the research process (Archer, 2002). Whether I saw myself as an academic or not, many of the participants identified me, reasonably enough, with the university – some interviewees told me guardedly that they were 'not academic', while others built common ground, saying that they volunteered to take part because they knew from their own experience as students that it can be difficult to find research participants. By the time of the later interviews I was more comfortable in my academic identity and began to feel more natural about being both practitioner and researcher.

Perceptions of the researcher's social identity are also likely to affect the research in complex ways that might not be transparent. For example, feminist researchers have discussed the ethical advantages of women interviewing women (Oakley, 1990), as well as the dangers of researchers 'trading on' shared identities by inviting confidences that interviewees may later regret (Finch, 1984). Shared social identity, then, is not a straightforward advantage or disadvantage, but is something to take account of in the practice and analysis of research. Social differences can be a barrier; for example, as a white researcher, I am aware that black interviewees might be guarded in sharing race-related experiences with me, especially as they may have been disbelieved or misrepresented by white people in the past (Gillborn, 2008). My class identity is mixed – my relatives are from a variety of class and occupational backgrounds. I grew up in social housing in a family receiving benefits and free school meals, and yet my accent, demeanour and academic role usually make me appear relatively middle class; this might restrict what working class participants are willing to share. While complex power-charged social relationships cannot be removed from the research process, I have attempted to be reflexive about how they might affect the findings.

Focus groups

The in-depth interviews were complemented by a series of three linked focus groups, which took place at monthly intervals in early 2013. Including a group discussion element in my research methodology felt important, as youth work is an associational activity that values group work and colleagues reflecting together. Eight youth workers took part in the focus groups, of whom one had also taken part in an individual interview. The focus groups followed an innovative methodology drawn from community philosophy approaches, in which participants take an active role in choosing issues and concepts to discuss (Tiffany, 2009). In community philosophy, the agenda is largely in the hands of the participants as they formulate, discuss and select the questions. In preparation for the focus groups I attended training on community philosophy facilitation, provided by SAPERE (The Society for the Advancement of Philosophical Enquiry and Reflection in Education). My role as facilitator was to guide the discussion, attend to group process and provide discussion stimuli. A fellow youth worker and facilitation trainee acted in the role of co-facilitator, as well as taking part in some of the discussions at times. Co-facilitating was enormously beneficial because we could take turns leading activities and discussions, and each of us noticed different opportunities to ask follow-up questions.

The first focus group started with an introduction to the research, the aims of the focus group and the community philosophy methodology. We then spent some time developing a group agreement, asking the group members to discuss and agree what would help them to take part. As part of this, it was important to discuss internal confidentiality to ensure that participants would not divulge the identity of any other member of the group (Tolich, 2004). We also agreed that it might be a good idea not to bring up extremely sensitive issues in the group, and I offered to meet with anybody outside of the group, either for an informal chat or an individual interview. After developing the group agreement, my co-facilitator and I ran a small group activity using Post-it notes to discuss and develop questions based on what the group members thought was good and bad about being a part-time and/ or volunteer youth worker. Most of the questions discussed over the next three sessions were derived from this activity, and some additional questions were devised during subsequent discussions.

The focus group met for two hours over three sessions, the content of which is outlined in Table 4.

The content and process of the focus group discussions was particularly rich and thoughtful, and the end of the final meeting felt like the culmination of a powerful process. Participants were keen to interact with each other and reflect on their views, and their words and body language showed a great deal of engagement, thoughtfulness and interest. Unlike in a traditional group interview, the participants responded mostly to each other rather than relating mainly to the facilitators, and the format and atmosphere of the discussions enabled them to support, develop, question and challenge each other's points. The community philosophy methodology was instrumental in the group members' ownership of the process. The process was identified

Table 4: Discussion group topics

Session	Discussion topics
One	Introduction to community philosophy, discussion on confidentiality, group agreement. Evaluating youth work (using Post-it notes): what do you think is good and bad about being a part-time and/or volunteer youth worker, and what would you like to change? Wrote and selected questions for future meetings. Philosophical inquiry using question identified by the group: 'Why are youth workers and young people under-valued?' Evaluation of the first session and discussion of future sessions.
Two	Reflection on previous session. Objects: each person brought an object which for them related in some way to youth work and the group used these as stimuli for discussion. Outlining an average day at work. What it is like to be part-time/voluntary and how it would be different to be paid/full-time. Returned to questions identified last time and decided as a group to discuss the question: 'Do youth workers share the same values?'
Three	Inquiry using a question chosen by the group which arose in previous discussions: 'Do we need to be driven by outcomes?' Inquiry using a question from the first session which the group wanted to return to: 'Where is equality in youth work?' Discussion on youth workers' backgrounds and identities, and whether/how these are important. Evaluation of the three sessions and the whole process.

by participants as useful in its own right, and they emphasised their learning from each other:

> 'There's been many times when I've sat here and thought one way, and then by the end of it I think something different. Definitely learned something from everyone in the group, changed my opinions on some of the things.' (Mark)

Mark's quote emphasises the dynamic nature of youth workers' understandings of their work, which change through experience and in conversation with each other. As another focus group participant said:

> 'When we stop questioning, when we stop being unsure, maybe that's the time we get complacent in our work, and that for me, that state of frustration, unsettlement, is not always comfortable, it's not always nice, but ... maybe it informs or it helps to do better work.' (Mickie)

The importance of questioning and uncertainty, eloquently expressed by Mickie, has also been an important part of my process as a researcher.

Participant observation

Alongside the interviews and focus groups, this study draws on three years of participant observation from my ongoing involvement in youth work. This brought insights from the highs, lows and sheer normality of everyday practice into the study, and (crucially) meant that the research, while focusing on the perspectives of *practitioners,* was also informed by regular, sustained and detailed encounters with *young people.* The aim of the participant observation was to record and reflect on everyday experiences of youth work, alongside discussions with colleagues, to contribute towards a body of youth work theory:

> ... the generation of knowledge to develop theory (i.e. knowledge that can develop our understanding of the social world and improve our explanations of how it changes, develops or remains the same) is a crucial responsibility for social researchers generally, and for practitioner-researchers in particular. (Cullen et al, 2012, p 11)

While this study is not a pure ethnography, it is inspired by ethnography in its approach: in particular the ideas of long-term immersion in a culture, and developing knowledge and theory through significant engagement with this culture (Hammersley and Atkinson, 1995). 'Practitioner ethnography' is a particular approach to ethnography that takes place in a practitioner's own workplace; practitioner ethnographers 'are more than just participants: they live and have lived the experience that they want to investigate' (Barton, 2008, p 11). This form of ethnography offers the benefits of depth of immersion in practice, although it also brings dangers such as over-familiarity, as I will go on to discuss.

As an experienced and active youth worker, my participant observation for this study took place in a neighbourhood where I had already worked for three years. During the first few months of my research, in summer 2011, I was employed as a part-time youth worker for six hours per week by a local charity. My role was to organise and work in a small weekly youth club, and work nearby as a detached (street-based) youth worker. Meanwhile, I was also meeting with fellow youth workers and young people to set up a small youth workers' cooperative, Voice of Youth. In early 2012 I left the charity to focus on Voice of Youth, for whom I worked several hours per week as a volunteer and occasionally on a paid sessional basis throughout the rest of the study. I continue to volunteer with Voice of Youth today. In both of these roles, my primary work was direct face-to-face work with young people, and I was also involved in planning, meetings, evaluation and ongoing administration.

One of the challenges of practitioner research is that practitioners are wholly engaged in practice settings where they are likely to have primary responsibilities that are more important, or at least more pressing, than the 'observational' role of the observer. The 'distance' recommended for traditional ethnographic research can be difficult for insider researchers to maintain:

> There must always remain some part held back, some social and intellectual 'distance'. For it is in the space created by this distance that the analytic work of the ethnographer gets done ... If and when all sense of being a stranger is lost, one may have allowed the escape of one's critical, analytic perspective. (Hammersley and Atkinson, 1995, p 115)

Practitioner ethnography is, in this sense, somewhat contradictory: it would be difficult if not impossible to carry out youth work, which relies on building relationships, while maintaining a sense of being a 'stranger'. However, this is not unique to insider research, and all ethnographers face the challenging balance of building trust and rapport while keeping their critical faculties. While ethnographic distance may be difficult to maintain in the hurly-burly of practice, it can be regained through the meticulous keeping of a research diary or journal, which promotes 'precisely the sort of internal dialogue, or thinking aloud, that is the essence of reflexive ethnography. Such activity should help one avoid lapsing into the "natural attitude" and "thinking as usual" in the field' (Hammersley and Atkinson, 1995, p 192). My research diary, quoted at times throughout this book, encompassed straightforward 'field notes' alongside diagrams, lists, charts and more creative forms of writing. It also included reflections and questions in an attempt to think through and beyond my taken-for-granted grounded knowledge of youth work.

Despite these attempts to look objectively at my practice experiences, particularly through the research diary, there are clearly ongoing challenges to maintaining critical distance in relation to a setting that I was (and remain) actively engaged in. A more disinterested researcher would, perhaps, have noticed aspects of practice that I missed; however, being less engaged in practice would have had different drawbacks, and long-term ongoing experience brings particular insights to a study. Some aspects of youth work are rarely discussed in interviews and yet arose repeatedly in practice: the long-term, slow-burn, up-and-down nature of relationships; the informal chats with colleagues and young people; the times when we don't see anyone and not much is happening. The research in this book was enriched by writing regularly about these elements of the everyday, the normal and the boring that are best captured by 'being there' over a long period.

As well as challenges around critical distance, practitioner researchers who draw on their own practice reflections need to think carefully about how they represent themselves in their research. While 'treating the self as a unit of analysis' (Coffey, 1999, p 123) remains somewhat controversial, even in qualitative research, there is a growing body of auto-ethnographic research that uses personal experience as data (Ellis and Berger, 2003). The aim is not self-indulgence, but rather the explicit interrogation of one's own experience as a resource for building knowledge. My youth work experience was used extensively in the process of analysis and in early drafts, and yet appears more sparingly in finished writing. I was cautious to avoid excessive self-analysis, often 'writing in and then crossing out autobiographical details of my own life' (Reay, 1996, p 445). Theorists and activists from critical traditions have long argued that self-understanding is an important aspect of developing wider societal and political analyses:

> The starting-point of critical elaboration is the consciousness of what one really is, and is 'knowing thyself' as a product of the historical process to date which has deposited in you an infinity of traces, without leaving an inventory. The first thing to do is to make such an inventory. (Gramsci, 1971, p 324)

Researchers writing about other people in the context of their own experience need to be particularly aware of the ethical implications and the power relations involved (Tolich, 2010), and this became a key challenge in this study. I had informed and consulted colleagues and young people about my research, and asked their permission to include reflections on youth work practice from the setting. However, they primarily saw me as their colleague or youth worker. How could I be sure that they did not mind me writing about what was happening, without intrusively reminding them all the time that I was doing research? Making extensive use of a 'permission to observe' would have felt coercive and disruptive, because they relate to me on the basis of our primary professional and personal relationships. At first I had intended to share any research diary entries I was hoping to use in my written work with those involved, but even this felt compromised because of formal power relationships (I might later write a colleague's reference, or decide whether a young person is given a place on a trip), and informal relationships and loyalties (they might feel personally obliged to agree, wanting to support my research, even if they felt uncomfortable). These ethical issues were all the more salient because my place of work could be discovered with a few clicks of a mouse, so I began to feel that the potential for true confidentiality was limited.

As a result, we discussed the idea of naming the cooperative in the study rather than keeping it anonymous, and agreed that I would restrict the inclusion of research diary extracts to relatively low-risk subjects. Colleagues and young people were happy for Voice of Youth to be named, keen to share learning from involvement in this unusual organisation. This meant that many field notes could not be used, particularly those involving sensitive issues with young people. It is for this reason that I wrote a series of vignettes which appear at the beginning and end of Chapters Two to Five. Creative writing has been used by others in educational research to protect anonymity while honouring 'the rawness of real happenings' (Clough, 2002, p 8). The characters and events in the vignettes are derived from real youth work situations and experiences over many years, but none of them are exact representations of events, and the characters are imaginary and not based on real people. Of course, the vignettes are not perfect; although they are an attempt to portray the nuance and uncertainty that is inherent in youth work practice, they inevitably lack the authenticity of 'real' field notes. Nevertheless, they are an attempt to portray some of the complexities of youth work in practice in a way that is complementary to the interview and focus group quotations and research diary excerpts.

In discussing the role of participant observation here it has been particularly important to think carefully about its dilemmas and challenges; perhaps in doing so, however, I have not given enough space to its positive contribution. Ongoing engagement in youth work practice has been an integral aspect of every stage of this study. Practitioner researchers have advantages in terms of access, grounded knowledge, shared understandings and rapport with research participants (Barton, 2008). In addition, we are likely to have a deeper, longer and broader engagement with our research setting than most researchers. During my research I have worked with hundreds of young people, some of whom I have known well for years; taken part in and facilitated meetings, training and supervision; worked on the streets, in parks, on housing estates and in community halls; been incredibly busy and wasted time; worked alongside and learnt from many different colleagues; helped facilitate drama, art, sports, games, more than twenty day trips, and two residential weekends; had fun, been bored; felt happy and sad; filled in a *lot* of forms; and taken part in thousands of conversations with young people and with colleagues. This is the stuff of youth work, and I am certain that my research is richer for my everyday involvement in practice.

Analysis and writing

In common with most PhD studies, there were times when I felt overwhelmed by the sheer quantity and complexity of data – 300,000 words of transcripts (more than three times as long as this book), as well as 12 notebooks full of field notes. Here I aim to be explicit about how this material was analysed and how conclusions were drawn, without falsely presenting it as a wholly scientific process of coding.

The analytical strategy was similar to that used in ethnography, in which analysis is not a distinct stage of research that happens 'after' data collection, nor a process that is confined to formal coding (Hammersley and Atkinson, 1995). Analysis was not separate to the process of interviewing and participant observation; it began in discussion with a research participant during an interview, continued during the careful transcribing of audio recordings, and was developed in doctoral supervision and through informal conversations with youth workers and others.

In the early stages of the research I used detailed line-by-line coding alongside content analysis, developing themes derived from the interview and discussion group transcripts, and from field notes. Coding was a useful process for learning the habits of close reading and attention to detail, and I continued to use it at times, but as a main strategy it felt somewhat reductive, as data were chopped into smaller parts and were in danger of losing their overall narrative sense. Over time, I moved towards a more open form of analysis, focusing on concepts, themes and narratives (Coffey and Atkinson, 1996). This involved careful reading and rereading of transcripts and field notes, listening and re-listening to audio recordings, and looking out for rich, descriptive content, narrative insights and overall themes, as well as silences and absences. In order to develop the themes, I wrote and rewrote short pieces, known in grounded theory as memos (Lambert, 2007, p 249), as well as drawing diagrams and mind maps. I focused in particular on commonalities, differences, tensions and contradictions, both between and within different parts of the data. Through this collection of methods I built up deep familiarity with the research materials, aiming to develop understanding, find connections, generate ideas, identify uncertainties, explore tensions and make sense.

This open-ended and in-depth approach to analysis was made possible by the three years I had to conduct this study, and its relatively small number of participants. Having been involved in much briefer projects with similar numbers of interviewees, the lengthy and detailed process of analysis involved in this study felt much more meaningful and rigorous than is possible to achieve in a shorter time frame. I felt I was 'getting to know' the research participants in listening to the recordings, transcribing them, and repeatedly listening and reading again. This process was a joy and a privilege. Nevertheless, the weight of information was sometimes overwhelming and occasionally it became difficult to see a way through. I tried to see analytic difficulty as productive even if it was frustrating. Perhaps it has become a cliché to emphasise messiness in the research process, but it is recognisable.

No researcher comes to their study as an 'empty vessel', free of ideas and preconceptions on their topic, and it is important to reflect critically on how 'who we are' informs the decisions we make and the understandings we develop. As an experienced part-time youth worker, I recognised many of the experiences and feelings shared by fellow youth workers in the interviews and discussion groups. However, there was always the risk of over-identification, of making the assumption that I understood and could relate to the research participants' experiences, and thereby failing to listen fully to what they were actually saying. I noticed this happening at times when I listened back to the interviews, hearing moments where I was in my comfort zone, joining in with celebrations of youth work practice and recognising well-worn criticisms of paperwork and targets, and missing the chance to ask good enough questions. As part of a thorough and rigorous approach, then, it was important to be more critical later when poring over transcripts and field notes: for example, by engaging in particular with the aspects of interviews and focus groups that I could least relate to, by avoiding assumptions about common experiences, and by questioning shared understandings and opinions.

Writing my PhD thesis and this book could be seen as a continuation of analysis, as well as a process of communication. I write rather slowly, with a great deal of redrafting, restructuring and editing, clarifying and refining my thoughts as I go. Each chapter in this book is based on a key theme that was identified through the analysis of interviews, focus groups and participant observation. The writing process, like all aspects of research, involves ethical decisions around respecting and valuing research participants. I gave participants a pseudonym of their choice so they would recognise and identify with themselves in finished writing, and many seemed to enjoy choosing their 'false name'. Of course, naming is not enough: they will only 'see themselves' in my writing if I engage fully and respectfully with what they have said rather than 'decorate' my work with their words.

The first half of Chapter Six is written as a series of edited dialogues, collectively written by myself and six of my colleagues in Voice of Youth (two of whom are young people who were recent participants in youth work, and are now working in the cooperative). My colleagues were fully involved in deciding on the topics for discussion and in contributing to editing decisions, although I took overall responsibility for the transcribing and editing. As co-writers, they were given the choice of whether to use pseudonyms for the purposes of the research, but all were keen to use their real names.

Theoretical and practical underpinnings

In this section I discuss the productive and sometimes contradictory relationship between practice, activism and research that is at the heart of this study, and how this interacts with feminist, poststructuralist and Marxist theory to provide the theoretical underpinnings of the study. My reading, writing and thinking are substantially informed by experiences in play, youth and community work, and (less obviously) my involvement in environmental and social activism. These influences have been central to the approach taken to this research, although at first I was not entirely conscious of this, or at least did not feel confident that it was valid to be informed by theory derived from practice and experience more than from books. I had an impression that novice researchers should 'pick' a theoretical and methodological framework as if from a menu, although I could not understand how this was meant to happen and the 'choice' felt rather unreal and arbitrary.

As an activist and youth worker I was informed and inspired by discussions, debates, disagreements and arguments on practical matters rather more than by written theory. Studying for a Community and Youth Work diploma and, later, an Education Studies degree, I started to read more widely, and became interested in a wide range of critical perspectives including feminism, poststructuralism, Marxism, critical race theory, queer theory and critical disability studies. Scholars and activists from different critical orientations provide vital critiques and insights in understanding the world; the use of a variety of critical world views can be seen as consistent with anarchism and activist scholarship, which tend to be based on practical and strategic questions rather than adhering to the views of a single thinker (Graeber, 2004).

Practical anarchism

Anarchism means 'without rulers'; it is based on the principles of self-organisation, voluntary association and solidarity, underpinned by a rejection of domination, inequality and structural violence (Graeber, 2004). Practical anarchism is the everyday living of these values; it is an active attempt to 'change the world without taking power' (Holloway, 2002). The way I understand and live in the world today is fundamentally shaped by deep involvement as a younger woman in anarchist-informed social and environmental activism. This began when I became involved in a campaign against a local road development from the age of 12, writing letters and going on demonstrations. A few years later the road building started, and local people pledged to take direct action by locking ourselves to bulldozers, setting up protest camps on the land, and squatting threatened buildings. I spent my early adulthood involved in this and other protests, living on camps, squats and people's floors, while also volunteering on playschemes and in a youth project. Eventually I moved into a youth support project (a foyer) and began working part-time as a play worker and youth worker. These part-time jobs were a means of earning enough to live on (and to stop claiming benefits) while maintaining my involvement in political action; they were also rewarding in their own right.

Playing, chatting and hanging out with children and young people provided a grounding contrast to my often manic activism, especially as I began to feel burned out. While my political beliefs had not changed and I remained involved in campaigns, it increasingly felt as though I was living two lives. Juggling them was mentally and physically exhausting. Without making any conscious decision I became less intensely involved in activism; I have enormous respect for those who integrate their activism with work, family and rest over the long term, but I rarely found a balance. However, the political life I experienced as a young activist continues to inspire me every day in my work, research, campaigning and personal relationships.

This research is underpinned, then, by 'anarchism in practice rather than in theory' (Roth, 2014, p 303). This is a political and theoretical approach that does not primarily come from books but rather from the daily experience of collective organising, living and action, taking direct action against elements of the state and big business and (perhaps more successfully) educating and organising without formal hierarchies.

> Whilst many articulate their Anarchism thanks to the written word it's rare, in my experience at least, that many decide to become anarchist through it. Rather the most powerful 'propaganda' is that 'by the deed' – lived experience, either through involvements in resistance or through meeting the love and lived ethics of anarchist communities. (Anonymous, 2011, p 90)

As an activist I was part of a community aiming to create the change we wanted to see in the world, rather than making demands or asking those in power to change things for us. We made decisions through consensus, questioned everything, challenged formal and informal leadership structures, cared for and loved each other, met and talked endlessly, were inspired by activists from previous generations and other places in the world, and created our own ways of living. By no means was it perfect or idyllic. However, lived anarchism continues to infuse my life, and provides a grounded basis for my practice as a youth worker and researcher.

Practical anarchism can be consistent with some of the practices of youth work, for example, when workers and young people work together to make collective decisions without formal leadership structures, take thoughtful action in their neighbourhoods and wider world, and combine care, question and challenge. In turn, youth work informed my political activism, making me more committed to taking people's different lived experiences and priorities into account, more conscious of inequalities and informal hierarchies, and more open-minded about how the world should be and how we might get there. In learning to be a researcher, my approach has been informed by both anarchism and youth work, while theory and research methodologies have begun to influence my youth work practice and clarify my political beliefs. Some of these relationships are summarised in Table 5.

Activist scholarship and its dilemmas

Research that is undertaken in solidarity or alignment with struggles against dominant norms and ideologies is sometimes known as activist scholarship (Hale, 2008) or public sociology (Burawoy, 2004). Activist scholarship might mean collaborating on research with community organisations; making evidence available to campaign groups;

Table 5: Practice, research and activism relationships

	How can youth work ideas influence and inform...	How can research theories and methodologies influence and inform...	How can anarchism influence and inform...
... youth work practice?	Clarity on purpose and methods. Critical reflection on own practice.	Understanding wider context for individual/local issues. Questioning taken-for-granted practices.	Political context of everyday life. An understanding that people working together at the grassroots can change things.
... research practice?	Open-minded, open-ended, improvisational and conversational approaches. Concern with relevance to practitioners and listening to practice perspectives.	Building on the accumulated knowledge and experience of other researchers. Awareness of researcher reflexivity and situated ethics.	Understanding inequality and domination and how they might change. Focus on diverse forms of resistance.
... political principles and actions?	Knowing and working with a variety of people. Awareness of how inequalities work even within apparently progressive groups.	Ways to articulate beliefs and understand them more deeply. Combining strong political commitment with openness to challenge.	Creating the change we want to see in the world, rather than asking for change from above. Solidarity with other struggles.

contributing to public conversations; negotiating boundaries of race, gender and difference; bringing less visible issues to light; and putting aside the researcher role where human or political considerations are more important (Lipman, 2011). Activist scholarship methodologies have been useful and inspiring in my research, and I was lucky to visit a community of activist scholars in Chicago during my PhD. They were not 'outsider' researchers or maverick academics looking to improve their own reputations and careers; instead, they were collectively engaged in struggles for public education and social justice, and it was often difficult to see the boundaries between their activism, research, teaching and learning.

Even as I identify with activist scholarship, I am also somewhat uncomfortable with it. When I was a full-time activist, the theory I found most inspiring and thought-provoking was developed collectively through discussions at our meetings and gatherings, and sometimes written down in pamphlets about strategy and organising, our own journals and newsletters, and information shared about movements from the past and from other parts of the world. Many activists are engaged in the interpretation and creation of theory outside of the academy (Bevington and Dixon, 2005). I wonder whether celebrating the activist scholar might risk lending status to those from the relatively protected world of the university, giving academics an undue influence on movements, or salving the consciences of those (like myself) who have become tired or burned out from everyday involvement in more risky political struggle. Although activist scholars tend to experience somewhat marginalised working situations in relation to more conventional academics (Hale, 2008), they may nevertheless benefit from association with activists, while full-time activists' lives are far more risky, precarious and financially challenging. In addition, the individuality and reputation that are sometimes dominant in mainstream academia clash with anarchist and activist cultures and principles of collectivity and anonymity.

Whether or not it is used in relation to scholarship, the word 'activist' must also be subject to critical questioning, because 'defining ourselves as activists means defining our actions as the ones which will bring about social change, thus disregarding the activity of thousands upon thousands of other non-activists' (X, 2000, p 160). Activism is an arena of power like any other, and can exclude; as Luu (2004, p 423) asks, 'who has the power to decide what is "radical" in the first place and who gets left out because of that definition?' As a full-time activist I once subtly disapproved of those who were not 'committed enough', a condescending attitude I am now embarrassed to admit to. Now I often fail to engage in important youth work campaigns and events because of being busy working in the university and the youth club. Politics rather than career advancement inspired me to study; however, my options have been widened by my university education and I am not always sure whether I am using these new opportunities for the most effective purposes.

For all of these reasons it is important to use the term 'activist scholarship' with caution, humility and critical reflection. Nevertheless, it is a useful concept for those of us who are attempting to combine study with activism. It helps to honour my learning from involvement in anarchist activism as a young woman, and more recent involvements in the youth work campaign In Defence of Youth Work and workers' cooperative Voice of Youth, both of which overtly challenge neoliberal versions of youth work.

Using theory

While the methodological and theoretical approach of this study is shaped by my lived experience as an activist and youth worker, it is also influenced by engagement with a variety of critical theoretical traditions, including poststructuralist feminism, critical race theory, Marxism, critical disability studies and queer theory. I am greatly inspired by theorists and activists who, while coming from a variety of traditions and disciplines, have in common the ability to combine strong anti-oppressive political principles with an openness to challenge, complexity and contradiction. It is important not to use inconsistent theories out of context or without thinking about their possible contradictions; however, the differences between diverse radical theoretical approaches can sometimes be exaggerated, and activist scholars have always learned from one another. In addition, using a variety of critical theoretical perspectives can help guard against entrenched thinking.

One misconception of politically informed scholarship is that it must equate to a predetermined view of how the world works. Adopting a fixed perspective could obstruct learning from youth workers who are active in creating their identities in what might be seen as hostile circumstances; it would also be antithetical to an ethics in both youth work and anarchism of understanding people's lived experiences and perspectives. Open mindedness does not equate to moral relativism. My core (anarchist) principles, which could perhaps be expressed as freedom, equality, solidarity and care, are non-negotiable; however, there is much here that remains open to question. Are these values meaningful, expressed in such vague terms? What might they exclude or obscure? How do anarchist values both reinforce and contradict each other (Suissa, 2010)? What do they mean when translated into practice in a neoliberal world (Clark, 2013; crow, 2014)?

As Judith Butler (2000, p 41) writes in relation to discussions over political tensions, 'The point ... is not then to answer these questions, but to permit them an opening, to provoke a political discourse that sustains the questions and shows how unknowing any democracy must be about its future.' In terms of research, this means combining political principles with a genuine regard for the perspectives of others. It is vitally important to listen carefully to the grassroots youth workers who were involved in this research, inviting them to challenge and develop my understanding, rather than using their words to illustrate or 'prove' something I already believed to be true.

As a youth worker, activist and researcher, then, I try to question my assumptions and 'live in the anxiety of that questioning without closing it down too quickly' (Butler in Olson and Worsham, 2000, p 736). Being open to question and challenge is inherent to anarchist politics, but this does not mean being a blank slate with no preconceptions. It would be too easy to hide behind notions of open-ended practice and say, 'I just listen to the research participants,' as if the researcher has no view. As the author of this research, it is important to acknowledge my perspectives, influences, values and positioning, and reflect carefully and ethically on how these influence the research (Gewirtz and Cribb, 2006). For me this was best supported by keeping a research journal and through supervision. Having access to experienced and supportive researchers as PhD supervisors was an absolute privilege and pleasure, made all the more valuable because it was a space where I could be honest, doubtful and uncertain. In both youth work and research, a combination of reflective writing and conversation can be a process of rehearsing ideas, trying different approaches and following creative paths. The ability and willingness to improvise is part of an open-ended approach to research that allows it to be more democratic than if everything had been decided beforehand.

Conclusion

In this chapter I have attempted to write authentically about my research choices, making explicit the ways in which they are influenced by experience as a youth worker and activist, as well as how they are informed by theory and research. It has been important to reflect on the possible contradictions in my research methodology, and to ask questions rather than being complacent. Such questioning is an ethical responsibility that is somewhat safeguarded by participation in communities of scholars, activists and practitioners who are very likely to challenge and hold me to account in different ways.

The challenge of combining an open approach with strongly held political principles is common to activist scholars and critical youth workers. Being open to, and thoughtful about, the questions and challenges of others – young people, practitioners, researchers, activists, community members – is not a threat to principled research and practice; it is essential for its development.

APPENDIX

Research participants

Below are short descriptions of the youth workers who took part in the interviews and focus groups for this book, in alphabetical order using their chosen pseudonyms. The descriptions focus on their work roles, youth work qualifications and experience, as well as some aspects of their social identity. Because I did not explicitly ask participants about their social identities in the early interviews or in the first two discussion group meetings, and because I do not want to make assumptions, I have only included such information where it was explicitly discussed.

Alan is a part-time assistant youth worker in a local authority youth service in London, working in youth clubs and in community outreach. Aged 30, he has been a youth worker for 10 years and has a master's degree in youth work. He is white and middle class. (Individual interview)

Arimas is setting up a social enterprise after being made redundant when her local youth service shut down. She is studying for a youth work degree in her northern city where she has been a youth worker for several years. She is a Muslim of North African descent. (Discussion groups 1, 2, 3)

Billie volunteers for a charity at a youth club attended mostly by Roma young people in a northern city. She is relatively new to youth work and has a degree but no youth work qualification. Billie is white with a working-class background, and is a community development worker for a housing association. (Individual interview)

Bridget works part-time on a self-employed basis for a charity, supporting young people to find work and running a weekly youth club. She has a second part-time job at another community youth club. She is black with Caribbean heritage. (Interviewed with Laura and Lucy)

Callie works part-time on a mobile youth bus for a local authority in the South West, and runs a weekly youth club for a village council. She volunteers as a guide leader and works part-time in a school, and was previously a careers advisor. She is white and middle class. (Individual interview)

Diana is a part-time youth worker on a housing estate in a northern city, employed on a temporary basis by a charity. She became a youth worker after starting a university access course and was previously a beauty therapist. She is studying for a youth work diploma. She is white and working class. (Interviewed with Keiron)

Forde is a part-time outreach and detached youth worker for a London borough council, working on a mobile youth bus and running a girls' group. She has been involved in youth work since volunteering aged 18. She has a youth work NVQ. She is 24 years old and black. (Individual interview)

John works four nights per week in youth clubs and detached work for a rural local authority in the South East. He became a peer educator at his local youth club when he was 15. He is now 22, is in the second year of a youth and community work degree, and also works as a carer. (Individual interview)

Keiron works part-time at a large youth centre run by a charity in a northern city. He is also involved in sports and music ventures, and works at his local youth club where he started volunteering aged 15. He moved to England from Africa as a teenager. He is studying for a youth work diploma. (Interviewed with Diana)

Laura has been a part-time detached youth worker for three years, working for a charity in London. She studied for a psychology degree and has started a youth work diploma. She grew up in another European country and feels she is seen as middle class and white, although her parents were refugees. (Interviewed with Bridget and Lucy)

Leo is a part-time detached youth worker in a northern town and his 'day job' involves supporting young people who are out of work or education. He has been a youth worker for several years and has a degree in youth and community work. (Discussion groups 1, 2)

Lorenzo is a part-time youth worker for a charity in a large youth centre in a northern city. He became a youth worker after being made redundant as an electrician. He is in the second year of a youth and community work degree. He is 27 years old and working class with a mixed ethnic background. (Individual interview)

Lorne is a part-time youth worker for a cooperative in London, and is studying for a youth work degree. He has been a youth worker for 10 years and has mainly worked in LGBT and trans youth work. He is 29 years old, white and middle class, and grew up in the multicultural disadvantaged borough where he works. (Individual interview)

Louise is a volunteer with a local authority detached youth work team in a southern city centre, working mainly with young adults. She has also worked at youth clubs in a village and on a social housing estate. She is in the second year of her degree in youth and community work. (Individual interview, 2011)

Lucy is employed by a charity two evenings per week doing detached youth work and supporting young people to find work. She is studying for a social work master's degree. She became involved in youth work after volunteering in her local youth club. (Interviewed with Laura and Bridget)

Mahad is a part-time detached youth worker for a London local authority. He also works as a gym instructor. He initially became a youth work volunteer through a family member who was involved in a community action project. (Individual interview, 2011)

Mark is a part-time youth worker for a mentoring and youth leadership charity in a northern city. He is in the final year of a degree in youth and community work. He is black and describes his class in relation to the BBC Great British Class survey as 'below working class, one above the bottom'. (Discussion groups 1, 2, 3)

Mickie volunteers for an LGBT youth organisation in a northern city. She also works four days a week at a youth volunteering organisation. She is in the second year of a youth and community work degree. She defines herself as a feminist, bisexual, white woman from a working-class family with Irish traveller heritage. (Individual interview, discussion groups 1, 3)

Nevaeh is a volunteer in a youth club in the northern town where she grew up. She is relatively new to youth work and is in the first year of a degree in youth and community work. She is a white, working-class

25-year-old who looks younger and often refers to herself as young. (Discussion groups 1, 2, 3)

Nicola is a volunteer for a northern inner-city youth club run by a local charity. She has been involved in youth work for 10 years and is currently in the final year of a community and youth work degree. She is black and working class. (Discussion groups 1, 2, 3)

Olly works part-time in a youth club and as a detached worker in a predominantly rural local authority in the South East. He became a youth worker 13 years ago and was previously a decorator. He has a Level 3 NVQ in youth work. He is white and working class. (Individual interview, 2012)

Ox works part-time at a local authority youth club in London and has an NVQ in youth work. Until recently he had a day job as a telephone fundraiser. He is black and defines himself as middle class with working-class roots. (Individual interview)

Quincie works for a London local authority as an outreach and mobile bus youth worker and is currently in the second year of a youth and community degree. She became a youth worker after volunteering in youth theatre. (Individual interview)

Rachel has recently left her role as a detached youth worker for a local authority in a large southern town, where she had worked part-time for four years. She previously worked for the Connexions careers service, and has an NVQ in youth work. (Individual interview, 2011)

Reema is a volunteer youth worker in a large northern city. She recently completed a degree in social work and mental health nursing. (Discussion group 1)

Sam volunteers at an after-school youth group in a northern town, and works as a teaching assistant. She is on the first year of a youth and community work degree, is white and working class, and describes herself as 'a bit more mature at 41'. (Discussion groups 1, 2, 3)

Sarah runs a small business in youth work. She has two degrees including one in youth work. She grew up in the borough where she works, is from a working class background and describes herself as 'white and black African', although she is not keen on labels and categories. (Individual interview)

Tracey was led to do youth work as a Christian, and is currently coordinating a street-based project for a charity with a Christian ethos. She is also a qualified teacher, and combines supply teaching with part-time youth work. She is white and middle class with a working-class background. (Individual interview)

Zandra works part-time for a small business working with young people who are not in education, employment or training, and also runs a weekly youth club for a charity. She is black and says she would currently be seen as 'working class, very poor' although she previously had a more middle-class job as a youth housing manager. (Individual interview)

References

Ahmed, S. (2010) *The promise of happiness,* Durham, NC: Duke University Press.

Anderson, K. (2011) 'Brits baffled by Big Society', YouGov, http:// yougov.co.uk/news/2011/01/31/Brits-baffled-by-Big-Society/

Anonymous (2011) *Desert,* St. Kilda: Stac an Armin Press.

Apple, M. (2006) *Educating the 'right' way: Markets, standards, God, and inequality* (2nd edn), New York: Routledge.

Apple, M. (2013) *Can education change society?* New York: Routledge.

Apple, M.W. and Beane, J.A. (eds) (1999) *Democratic schools: Lessons from the chalk face,* Buckingham: Open University Press.

AQA (2014) 'Youth services: how the Unit Award Scheme (UAS) helps your learners', Guildford: AQA, www.aqa.org.uk/programmes/ unit-award-scheme/youth-sector

Archer, L. (2002) 'It's easier that you're a girl and that you're Asian: interactions of race and gender between researchers and participants', *Feminist Review* 5(4): 108–32.

Austin, J.L. (1976) *How to do things with words* (2nd edn), Oxford University Press.

Avis, J. (2005) 'Beyond performativity: reflections on activist professionalism and the labour process', *Journal of Education Policy,* 20(2): 209–22.

Ball, S. (2001) 'Performativities and fabrication in the education economy', in D. Gleeson and C. Husbands (eds) *The performing school,* London: Routledge Falmer, 50–72.

Ball, S. (2003) 'The teacher's soul and the terrors of performativity', *Journal of Education Policy,* 18(2): 215–28.

Ball, S. (2008a) *The education debate,* Bristol: The Policy Press.

Ball, S. (2008b) 'Performativity, privatisation, professionals and the state', in B. Cunningham (ed) *Exploring professionalism,* London: Institute of Education, 52–68.

Ball, S. (2012) *Global education inc.: New policy networks and the neoliberal imaginary,* Abingdon: Routledge.

Ball, S. (2013) *Foucault, power and education,* New York and London: Routledge.

Ball, S., Maguire, M. and Braun, A. (2012) *How schools do policy: Policy enactments in secondary schools,* Abingdon: Routledge.

Ball, S.J. and Olmedo, A. (2013) 'Care of the self, resistance and subjectivity under neoliberal governmentalities', Critical Studies in Education, 54(1): 85–96.

Banks, S. (2011) 'Ethics in an age of austerity: social work and the evolving new public management', *Journal of Social Intervention: Theory and Practice*, 20(2): 5–23.

Barton, T.D. (2008) 'Understanding practitioner ethnography', *Nurse Researcher*, 15(2): 7–18.

Barton, T. and Edgington, T. (2014) 'Youth services spending down by one third', BBC News, 25 March, www.bbc.co.uk/news/uk-26714184

Batsleer, J. (2008) *Informal learning in youth work*, London: Sage.

Batsleer, J. (2013a) 'Youth work, social education, democratic practice and the challenge of difference: a contribution to debate', *Oxford Review of Education*, 39(3): 287–306.

Batsleer, J. (2013b) *Youth working with girls and young women in community settings: A feminist perspective* (2nd edn), Farnham: Ashgate.

Batsleer, J. and Hughes, J. (2013) *Looking from the other side of the street: Youth work, participation and the arts in the edgelands of urban Manchester*, (draft paper).

Bazeley, E.T. (1969) *Homer Lane and the Little Commonwealth*, New York: Schocken.

BBC (2014) 'Devon Youth Service faces £1m budget cut', BBC News, www.bbc.co.uk/news/uk-england-devon-25977379

Bell, M., Gray, L. and Marron, A. (2013) 'It's business as usual: Newcastle, commissioning and cuts', *Youth and Policy*, 110: 88–95.

Bentham, J. (1995) *The Panopticon writings*, London: Verso.

Bessant, J. (2012) 'Youth work and the education of professional practitioners in Australia', in D. Fusco (ed) *Advancing youth work: Current trends, critical questions*, New York: Routledge, pp 52–68.

Bevington, D. and Dixon, C. (2005) 'Movement-relevant theory: rethinking social movement scholarship and activism', *Social Movement Studies*, 4(3): 185–208.

B'Hahn, C. (2001) 'Be the change you wish to see: an interview with Arun Gandhi', *Reclaiming Children and Youth*, 10(1): 6–9.

BIS (Department for Business, Innovation and Skills) (2014) 'Young enterprise partners with Virgin Money and Department of Business to launch new enterprise challenge for primary school children' (press release), London: BIS and Prime Minister's Office, https://www.gov.uk/government/news/young-enterprise-partners-with-virgin-money-and-department-for-business-to-launch-new-enterprise-challenge-for-primary-school-children

Bjerke, B. and Ramo, H. (2011) *Entrepreneurial imagination: Time, timing, space and place in business action*, Cheltenham: Edward Elgar Publishing.

Board of Education (1939) *In the service of youth: Circular to Local Education Authorities for Higher Education*, Circular 1486.

Boggs, C. (1977) 'Marxism, prefigurative communism and the problem of workers' control', *Radical America*, accessed at LibCom, https://libcom.org/library/marxism-prefigurative-communism-problem-workers-control-carl-boggs

Bolger, S. and Scott, D. (1984) *Starting from strengths: The report of the panel to promote the continuing development of training for part-time and voluntary youth and community workers*, Leicester: NYB.

Bolton, S.C. (2005) *Emotion management in the workplace*, Basingstoke: Palgrave Macmillan.

Bolton, S.C. and Boyd, C. (2003) 'Trolley dolly or skilled emotion manager? Moving on from Hochschild's Managed Heart', *Work, Employment and Society*, 17(2): 289–308.

Bookchin, M. (2001) *The Spanish anarchists: The heroic years 1868–1936*, Oakland, CA: AK Press.

Booth, C., Cameron, D., Cumming, L., Gilby, N., Hale, C., Hoolihan, F. and Shah, J.N. (2014) *National Citizen Service 2013 evaluation*, London: Ipsos Mori.

Bowling, B. and Phillips, L. (2007) 'Disproportionate and discriminatory: reviewing the evidence on police stop and search', *Modern Law Review*, 70(6): 936–61.

Breines, W. (1989) *Community and organization in the new left, 1962–1968: The great refusal*, New Brunswick, NJ: Rutgers University Press.

Brent, J. (2004) 'Communicating what youth work achieves: the smile and the arch', *Youth and Policy*, 84: 69–74.

Brew, J.M. (1957) *Youth and youth groups*, London: Faber & Faber.

Burawoy, M. (2004) For public sociology, *American Sociological Review*, 70(1): 4–28.

Burgess, M. and Burgess, I. (2006) *Don't shoot: I'm a detached youth worker!*, Lyme Regis: Russell House.

Butler (1990) *Gender trouble: Feminism and the subversion of identity*, New York and London: Routledge.

Butler, J. (1997) *The psychic life of power: Theories in subjection*, Stanford, CA: Stanford University Press.

Butler, J. (2000) 'Restaging the universal: hegemony and the limits of formalism', in J. Butler, E. Laclau and S. Zizek (Eds) *Contingency, hegemony, universality*, London: Verso, pp 11–43.

Butler, J. (2004) *Undoing gender*, New York and London: Routledge.

Butler, J. (2006) 'Preface', in *Gender trouble: Feminism and the subversion of identity* (2006 edn), New York and London: Routledge.

Butler, J. and Athanasiou, A. (2013) *Dispossession: The performative in the political*, Cambridge: Polity Press.

Butters, S. and Newell, S. (1978) *Realities of training: A review of the training of adults who volunteer to work with young people in the youth and community service*, London: National Youth Board.

Cabinet Office (2014) *Local authority youth services survey 2013*, London: Cabinet Office.

Cameron, D. (2010) 'Big society speech', London: GOV.UK, 19 July, https://www.gov.uk/government/speeches/big-society-speech

Cameron, D. (2011) 'PM's speech on Big Society', London: GOV.UK, https://www.gov.uk/government/speeches/pms-speech-on-big-society

Capita One (2013) *Uniting youth services: One youth* (product brochure), https://www.capita-one.co.uk/files/one/downloads/one_youth_brochure_update_jun13_4_lr.pdf

Career Vision (2015) 'Core+ IYSS youth activity', Northwich, Cheshire: Career Vision, http://careervision.co.uk/products/youth-activity/

CCCS (Centre for Contemporary Cultural Studies) (1981) *Unpopular education*, London: Hutchinson.

Chadderton, C. and Colley, H. (2012) 'School-to-work transition services: marginalising "disposable" youth in a state of exception?' *Discourse: Studies in the Cultural Politics of Education*, 33(3): 329–43.

Challenge Network (undated) 'Our people', London: Challenge Network, http://the-challenge.org/index.php/about-the-challenge-programmes/who-we-are/our-people

Charmaz, K. (2006) *Constructing grounded theory: A practical guide through qualitative analysis*, London: Sage.

Civil Exchange (2013) *The Big Society audit 2013*, Civil Exchange, www.civilexchange.org.uk/the-big-society-audit-2013

Clark, J.P. (2013) *The impossible community: Realizing communitarian anarchism*, New York: Bloomsbury.

Clough, P. (2002) *Narratives and fictions in educational research*, Buckingham: Open University Press.

Coburn, A. (2012) *Learning about equality: A study of a generic youth work setting* (PhD thesis), Glasgow: University of Strathclyde.

Coffey, A. (1999) *The ethnographic self: Fieldwork and the representation of identity*, London: Sage.

Coffey, A. and Atkinson, P. (1996) *Making sense of qualitative data: Complementary research strategies*, Thousand Oaks: Sage.

Coleman, R. (2005) 'Surveillance in the city: primary definition and urban spatial order', *Crime Media Culture,* 1: 131–48.

Coleman, R., Tombs, S. and Whyte, D. (2005) 'Capital, crime control and statecraft in the entrepreneurial city', *Urban Studies*, 42(13): 2511–30.

Colley, H., Henriksson, L., Niemeyer, B. and Seddon, T. (2012) 'Competing time orders in human service work: towards a politics of time', *Time and Society*, 21(3): 371–94.

Commission on Big Society (2011) *Powerful people, responsible society*, London: Acevo.

Conservative Party (2010) *Big Society not big government*, London: Conservative Party.

Corbett, S. and Walker, A. (2013) 'The Big Society: rediscovery of "the social" or rhetorical fig-leaf for neoliberalism?', *Critical Social Policy*, 33(3): 451–72.

Corporate Watch (2012) 'How to beat up refugees the Serco way', Corporate Watch, 30 March, https://corporatewatch.org/printpdf/4264

Cooper, C. (2012) 'Understanding the English "riots" of 2011: mindless criminality or youth "Mekin Histri" in austerity Britain?', *Youth and Policy*, 109: 6–26.

Cribb, A. (2011) 'Integrity and work: managing routine moral stress in professional roles', *Nursing Philosophy*, 12: 119–27.

Crimmens, D., Factor, F., Jeffs, T., Pitts, J., Pugh, C., Spence, J. and Turner, P. (2004) *Reaching socially excluded young people: A national study of street-based youth work*, York: Joseph Rowntree Foundation.

crow, s. (2014) *Black flags and windmills: Hope, anarchy and the common ground collective* (2nd edn), Oakland, CA: PM Press.

Crowe, D., Gash, T., and Kippin, H. (2014) *Beyond big contracts: Commissioning public services for better outcomes*, London: Institute for Government.

Cullen, F., Bradford, S. and Green, L. (2012) 'Working as a practitioner-researcher', in F. Cullen, S. Bradford and L. Green (eds) *Research and research methods for youth practitioners*, Abingdon: Routledge, pp 5–24.

CYWU (Community and Youth Workers' Union) (2011) 'Fighting destruction: overview of government vandalism', *Rapport*, January: 6–10.

CYWU (Community and Youth Workers' Union) (2013) 'Youth work activists assemble', *Rapport*, August: 16.

Daniel, S. and McGuire, P. (eds) (1972) *The paint house: Words from an East End gang*, Harmondsworth: Penguin.

Davies, Bernard (1999a) *A history of the youth service in England, volume 1, 1939–1979: From voluntaryism to welfare state*, Leicester: Youth Work Press.

Davies, Bernard (1999b) *A history of the youth service in England, volume 2, 1979–1999: From Thatcherism to New Labour*, Leicester: Youth Work Press.

Davies, Bernard (2005) *Youth work: A manifesto for our times*, Leicester: National Youth Agency.

Davies, Bernard (2013) 'Youth work in a changing policy landscape: the view from England', *Youth and Policy*, 110: 6–32.

Davies, Bernard (2014) 'Independence at risk: the state, the market and the voluntary youth sector', *Youth and Policy*, 112: 111–22.

Davies, Bernard (2015) 'Youth work: a manifesto for our times, revisited', *Youth and Policy*, 114: 96–117.

Davies, Bernard and Merton, B. (2009) 'Squaring the circle? The state of youth work in some children's and young people's services', *Youth and Policy*, 103: 5–24.

Davies, Bernard and Merton, B. (2010) *Straws in the wind: The state of youth work practice in a changing policy environment (phase 2)*, Leicester: De Montfort University.

Davies, Bronwyn (2005) 'The (im)possibility of intellectual work in neoliberal regimes', *Discourse*, 26(1): 1–14.

Davis, A. (2005) *Abolition democracy: Beyond prison, torture and empire*, New York: Seven Stories Press.

Davis, M. (2000) *Fashioning a new world: A history of the woodcraft folk*, Loughborough: Holyoake Books.

Day, C. (2004) *A passion for teaching*, London: Routledge Falmer.

Debord, G. (1977) *Society of the spectacle*, London: Rebel Press.

De Oliveira, W. (2001) *Working with children on the streets of Brazil: Politics and practice*, New York: Routledge.

de St Croix, T. (2009a) 'Informal educators or bureaucrats and spies? Detached youth work and the surveillance state', in B. Belton, *Developing critical youth work theory*, Rotterdam: Sense Publishers, pp 109–18.

de St Croix, T. (2009b) 'Swimming against the tide', in B. Belton, *Developing critical youth work theory*, Rotterdam: Sense Publishers, pp 119–30.

de St Croix, T. (2011) 'Struggles and silences: policy, youth work and the National Citizen Service', *Youth and Policy*, 106: 43–59.

de St Croix, T. (2012) 'If someone is not a success in life it's their own fault: what Coalition youth policy says about young people and youth workers', In Defence of Youth Work, 15 August, downloadable at http://indefenceofyouthwork.com/2012/08/15/if-someone-is-not-a-success-in-life-its-their-own-fault-coalition-youth-policy-revisited/

de St Croix, T. (2013) 'Keeping it real? Part-time youth workers at the centre and periphery', *Concept*, 4(2): 1–9.

DfE (Department for Education) (2011) *Positive for youth: A new approach to cross-government policy for young people aged 13 to 19*, London: HM Government.

DfES (Department for Education and Skills) (2002) *Transforming youth work: Resourcing excellent youth services*, London: DfES/Connexions.

Douzinas, C. (2014) 'Notes towards an analytics of resistance', *New Formations*, 83: 79–98.

Duffy, S. (2014) *Counting the cuts: What the government doesn't want the public to know*, Sheffield: Centre for Welfare Reform.

ECYC (European Confederation of Youth Clubs) (undated) 'Open youth work', Brussels: ECYC, www.ecyc.org/about-us/open-youth-work

EHRC (Equality and Human Rights Commission) (2010) *Stop and think: A critical review of the use of stop and search powers in England and Wales*, Manchester: EHRC.

El Kilombo Intergaláctico (2007) *Beyond resistance: An interview with Subcomandante Insurgente Marcos*, Durham, NC: Paperboat Press.

Ellis, C. and Berger, L. (2003) 'Their story/my story/our story: including the researcher's experience in interview research', in J. Gubrium and J. Holstein (eds) *Postmodern interviewing*, Thousand Oaks, CA: Sage, pp 849–875.

Farrell, S. (2014) 'Serco shares fall under warning that scandal will hit profits', *Guardian*, 30 January, www.theguardian.com/business/2014/jan/30/serco-shares-fall-warning-scandal-hit-profits

FDYW (Federation for Detached Youth Work) (2007) *Detached Youth Work Guidelines*, Leicester: FDYW.

Feminist Webs (2012) *The exciting life of being a woman: A handbook for women and girls*, Bristol: HammerOn Press.

Finch, J. (1984) '"It's great to have someone to talk to": the ethics and problems of interviewing women', in C. Bell and H. Roberts (eds) *Social researching: Politics, problems, practice*, London: Routledge and Kegan Paul, pp 166–80.

Forkby, T. and Kiilakoski, T. (2014) 'Building capacity in youth work: perspectives and practice in youth clubs in England and Sweden', *Youth and Policy*, 112: 1–17.

Foucault, M. (1977) *Discipline and punish: The birth of the prison*, London: Penguin.

Foucault, M. (1978) *The history of sexuality, volume 1: An introduction* (trans. R. Hurley), New York: Pantheon Books.

Francis, B. and Mills, M. (2012) 'What would a socially just education system look like?' *Journal of Education Policy*, 27(5): 577–85.

Freire, P. (1988) *Pedagogy of the oppressed* (trans. M. Ramos), New York: Continuum.

Freire, P. (1998) *Pedagogy of freedom: Ethics, democracy and civic courage* (trans. P. Clarke), Lanham, MD: Rowman and Littlefield.

Freire, P. and Shor, I. (1987) *A pedagogy for liberation*, Basingstoke: Macmillan.

Fusco, D. (2013) 'Is youth work being courted by the appropriate suitor?' *Child and Youth Services*, 34: 196–209.

Fusco, D., Lawrence, A., Matloff-Nieves, S. and Ramos, E. (2013) 'The accordian effect: is quality in afterschool getting the squeeze?' *Journal of Youth Development*, 8(2): 5–12.

Gandin, L.A. and Apple, M.W. (2012) 'Can critical democracy last? Porto Alegre and the struggle over "thick" democracy in education', *Journal of Education Policy*, ifirst article, 1–19.

Gewirtz, S. (2002) *The managerial school*, London: Routledge.

Gewirtz, S. and Cribb, A. (2006) 'What to do about values in social research: the case for ethical reflexivity in the sociology of education', *British Journal of Sociology of Education*, 27(2): 141–55.

Gewirtz, S., Mahony, P., Hextall, I. and Cribb, A. (eds) (2009) *Changing teacher professionalism: International trends, challenges and ways forward*, London: Routledge Falmer.

Gill, R. and Pratt, A. (2008) 'In the social factory? Immaterial labour, precariousness and cultural work', *Theory, Culture and Society*, 25(7–8): 1–30.

Gillborn, D. (2008) *Racism and education: Coincidence or conspiracy?* Abingdon, Oxon: Routledge.

Goetschius, G. (1962) 'Club work recording: an introduction', *Youth Service*, 2(1).

Goetschius, G. and Tash, J. (1967) *Working with unattached youth*, London: Routledge and Kegan Paul.

Goffman, E. (1959) *The presentation of self in everyday life*, Harmondsworth: Penguin.

Graeber, D. (2004) *Fragments of anarchist anthropology*, Chicago, IL: Prickly Paradigm Press.

Graeber, D. (2013) *The democracy project: A history, a crisis, a movement*, London: Penguin.

Gramsci, A. (1971) *Selections from the prison notebooks*, London: Lawrence & Wishart.

Hale, C.R. (ed) (2008) *Engaging contradictions: Theory, politics and methods of activist scholarship*, Berkeley and Los Angeles, CA: University of California Press.

Hall, S. (1988) *The hard road to renewal: Thatcherism and the crisis of the left*, London and New York: Verso.

Hall, S. and O'Shea, A. (2013) 'Common-sense neoliberalism', *Soundings*, 55: 8–24.

Hammersley, M. and Atkinson, P. (1995) *Ethnography: Principles in practice* (2nd edn), London: Routledge.

Harris, J. (2013) 'Serco, the company that is running Britain', *Guardian*, 29 July, www.theguardian.com/business/2013/jul/29/serco-biggest-company-never-heard-of.

Harvey, D. (2008) 'The right to the city', *New Left Review*, 53, (September–October), http://newleftreview.org/II/53/david-harvey-the-right-to-the-city

Hayes, D. (2013) 'Hurd hails young generation at CYP Now Awards but says some youth services are "ok to lose"', *Children and Young People Now*, 28 November, www.cypnow.co.uk/cyp/news/1140794/hurd-defends-council-youth-service-closures

Heathfield, M. (2012) 'A Chicago story: challenge and change', in D. Fusco (ed) *Advancing youth work: Current trends, critical questions*, New York: Routledge, pp 85–99.

Hier, S.P. (2003) 'Probing the surveillant assemblage: on the dialectics of surveillance practices as processes of social control', *Surveillance and Society*, 1(3): 399–411.

Higham, R. (2014) 'Free schools in the Big Society: the motivations, aims and demography of free school proposers', *Journal of Education Policy*, 29(1): 122–39.

Hill, C. (1972) *The world turned upside down: Radical ideas during the English revolution*, London: Penguin.

Hill Collins, P. (1986) 'Learning from the outsider within: the sociological significance of Black feminist thought', *Social Problems*, 33: 14–32.

Hill Collins, P. (1990) *Black feminist thought: Knowledge, consciousness and the politics of empowerment*, Boston: Unwin Hyman.

Hillier, A. (2012a) 'National Citizen Service might cost £110m in 2014, says Cabinet Office', *Third Sector Online*, 15 February, www.thirdsector.co.uk/Finance/article/1117240/National-Citizen-Service-cost-110m-2014-says-Cabinet-Office/

Hillier, A. (2012b) 'Serco consortium takes six National Citizen Service contracts', *Third Sector Online*, 13 September, www.thirdsector.co.uk/Social_Enterprise/article/1149871/Serco-consortium-takes-six-National-Citizen-Service-contracts/

Hillier, A. (2013) 'Cost of a place on the National Citizen Service went up by £100 last year', *Third Sector Online*, 31 July, www.thirdsector.co.uk/go/volunteering/article/1193627/cost-place-national-citizen-service-went-100-last-year/

Hochschild, A.R. (2003) *The managed heart: Commercialization of human feeling* (20th anniversary edn), Berkeley and Los Angeles, CA: University of California Press.

Hollander J.A. and Einwohner, R.L. (2004) 'Conceptualising resistance', *Sociological Forum*, 19(4): 533–54.

Holloway, J. (2002) *Change the world without taking power: The meaning of revolution today*, London: Pluto.

Holloway, J. (2010) *Crack capitalism*, London: Pluto.

Home Office (2009) 'Operation Staysafe weekend: do you know where your child is?', Home Office press release, 23 February.

hooks, b. (1984) *Feminist theory: From margin to centre*, Boston, MA: South End Press.

hooks, b. (1994) *Teaching to transgress*, New York: Routledge.

House of Commons Education Committee (2011a) *Services for young people*, London: The Stationery Office.

House of Commons Education Committee (2011b) *Services for young people: The government response*, London: The Stationery Office.

Hudson, S. (2011) 'Most people think the Big Society will not be achieved, polls suggest', *Third Sector Online*, 14 April, www.thirdsector.co.uk/news/1065620/

Hurd, N. (2014) 'Youth services: question to Cabinet Office', House of Commons debate, 29 January, TheyWorkForYou, www.theyworkforyou.com/debates/?id=2014-01-29a.844.3&s=speaker%3A11792#g844.6

IDYW (In Defence of Youth Work) (2009) 'The open letter', IDYW, http://indefenceofyouthwork.com/the-in-defence-of-youth-work-letter-2/

IDYW (2010) 'Oppose closures: support Oxford, Haringey, Warks and Crawley', IDYW, http://indefenceofyouthwork.com/2010/12/03/oxford-closures-support-the-witney-protest/

IDYW (2011) *This is youth work: Stories from practice*, London: UNISON/UNITE, available at http://indefenceofyouthwork.com/the-stories-project/

IDYW (2014a) 'IDYW statement 2014', IDYW, http://indefenceofyouthwork.com/idyw-statement-2014/

IDYW (2014b) 'Story-telling in youth work', Story-Telling in Youth Work, http://story-tellinginyouthwork.com/

INCITE! Women of color against violence (ed) (2007) *The revolution will not be funded: Beyond the non-profit industrial complex*, Cambridge, MA: South End Press.

Ingram, G. (1987) 'Youth workers as entrepreneurs', in T. Jeffs and M. Smith (eds) *Youth work*, Basingstoke: Macmillan, pp 114–32.

INQUEST (2015) 'BAME deaths in police custody', London: INQUEST, www.inquest.org.uk/statistics/bame-deaths-in-police-custody

Introna, L.D. (2003) 'Opinion: workplace surveillance "is" unethical and unfair', *Surveillance and Society*, 1(2): 210–16.

Irving, S. (2011) 'Gus John and the Moss Side Defence Committee', *Manchester's radical history*, https://radicalmanchester.wordpress.com/2011/10/01/gus-john-and-the-moss-side-defence-committee/

Islington Council (2014) 'Invitation to market warming events for the provision of integrated youth work in Islington', London: Islington Council.

Jeffs, T. (2006) 'Too few, too many: the retreat from vocation and calling', Infed, www.infed.org/talkingpoint/retreat_from_calling_and_vocation.htm

Jeffs, T. and Smith, M. (2008) 'Valuing youth work', *Youth and Policy*, 100: 277–302.

John, G. (1981) *In the service of black youth*, Leicester: National Association of Youth Clubs.

John, G. (2006) *Taking a stand: Gus John speaks on education, race, social action and civil unrest 1980–2005*, Manchester: Gus John Partnership.

Jones, K. (2003) *Education in Britain: 1944 to the present*, Cambridge: Policy Press.

Jones, K. (2010) 'Crisis, what crisis?', *Journal of Education Policy*, 25(6): 793–8.

Justice Select Committee (2011) *The role of the Probation Service*, London: House of Commons.

Kaufman, S. (2001) 'Detached youth work', in F. Factor, V. Chauhan and J. Pitts (eds) *The RHP companion to working with young people*, Lyme Regis: Russell House, pp 246ff.

Keddie, A. (2012) *Educating for diversity and social justice*, London: Routledge.

Kelly, P. J., Campbell, P.B.E. and Harrison, L. (2013) '"Don't be a smart arse": social enterprise-based transitional labour-market programmes as neo-liberal technologies of the self', *British Journal of Sociology of Education*, 36 (4): 558–76.

Khan, M.G. (2013) *Young Muslims, pedagogy and Islam: Contexts and concepts*, Bristol: Policy Press.

Kofman, E. and Lebas, E. (1996) 'Introduction', in H. Lefebvre, *Writings on cities*, Hoboken, NJ: Wiley-Blackwell, pp 3–62.

Kwon, S.A. (2013) *Uncivil youth: Race, activism and affirmative governmentality*, Durham: Duke University Press.

Ladson-Billings, G. (2012) 'Through a glass darkly: the persistence of race in education research and scholarship', *Educational Researcher*, 41: 115–20.

Lambert, L.B. (2007) 'Asking questions of the data: memo writing in the grounded theory tradition', in A. Bryant and K. Charmaz (eds) *The Sage handbook of grounded theory*, London: Sage, pp 245–64.

Land, C. and King, D. (2014) 'Organizing otherwise: translating anarchism in a voluntary sector organization', *Ephemera*, 14(4): 923–50.

Langhout, R. D. (2005) 'Acts of resistance: student (in)visibility', *Culture and Psychology*, 11: 123–58.

Layton, L. (2002) 'Cultural hierarchies, splitting and the heterosexist unconscious', in S. Fairfield, L. Layton and C. Stack (eds) *Bringing the plague: Toward a postmodern psychoanalysis*, New York: Other Press, pp 195–223.

Lazzarato, M. (1997) 'Immaterial labor' (trans. P. Colilli and E. Emery), Generation Online, www.generation-online.org/c/fcimmateriallabour3.htm

Lefebvre, H. (1996), *Writings on cities*, Hoboken, NJ: Wiley-Blackwell.

Lehal, R. (2010) 'Targeting for youth workers', in J. Batsleer and B. Davies (eds) *What is youth work?* Exeter: Learning Matters, pp 90–103.

Lepper, J. (2013a) 'Inquiry to examine police-youth relations', *Children and Young People Now*, 17 July, www.cypnow.co.uk/cyp/news/1077787/inquiry-examine-police-youth-relations.

Lepper, J. (2013b) 'Inspectors criticise police custody in Essex', *Children and Young People Now*, 20 June, www.cypnow.co.uk/cyp/news/1077539/inspectors-criticise-police-custody-essex.

Lepper, J. (2015) 'Youth services face axe in Brent', *Children and Young People Now*, 16 February, www.cypnow.co.uk/cyp/news/1149742/youth-services-axe-brent.

Lindgren, M. and Packendorff, J. (2007) *Konstruktion av entreprenörskap: Teori, praktik och interaktion*, Örebro: Forum för Småföretagsforskning.

Lipman, P. (2011) *The new political economy of urban education: Neoliberalism, race, and the right to the city*, New York: Routledge.

Lipman, P. (2013) 'Economic crisis, accountability, and the state's coercive assault on public education in the USA', *Journal of Education Policy*, 28(5): 557–73.

Loeb, J. (2013) 'Race row after Hackney "whitewashes" Narrow Way', *Hackney Citizen*, 18 July, http://hackneycitizen.co.uk/2013/07/18/race-row-whitewashing-narrow-way/

Lowe, J. (1975) *Youth leadership: A survey of leaders, attitudes, training and work patterns*, London: ILEA.

Lumby, J. (2009) 'Performativity and identity: mechanisms of exclusion', *Journal of Education Policy*, 24(3): 353–69.

Luu, H. (2004) 'Discovering a different space of resistance: personal reflections on anti-racist organising', in D. Solnit (ed) *Globalise liberation: How to uproot the system and build a better world*, San Francisco, CA: City Lights Press.

Lyotard, J. (1984) *The postmodern condition: A report on knowledge*, Minneapolis, MN: University of Minnesota Press.

Mackie, A. (2015) 'Young people and the budget: worse than we imagined?', *Exploring Youth Issues*, https://oldmanmackie.wordpress.com/2015/07/11/young-people-and-the-budget-worse-than-we-imagined/

Macpherson, W. (1999) *The Stephen Lawrence Inquiry report*, London: HMSO.

Mahadeven, J. (2009) 'Charity to test concept of National Citizen Service', *Children and Young People Now*, 2 April, www.cypnow.co.uk/print_article/cyp/news/1039088/charity-test-concept-national-citizen-service?print=true

McGimpsey, I. (2013) *Youth work assemblage: Youth work subjectivity and practice in the context of a changing youth service policy* (PhD thesis), London: UCL Institute of Education.

McGregor, G. and Mills, M. (2014) 'Teaching in the margins: rekindling a passion for teaching', *British Journal of Sociology of Education*, 35(1): 1–18.

McNeil, B., Reeder, N. and Rich, J. (2012) *A framework of outcomes for young people*, London: Young Foundation

Mellor, D. and McDonnell, F. (2010) *A picture worth millions: State of the young people's workforce*, Leeds: Children's Workforce Development Council.

Ministry of Education (1960) *The youth service in England and Wales* (The Albemarle Report), London: HMSO.

Møller, V., Mthembu, T. and Richards, R. (1994) 'The role of informal clubs in youth development: a South African case study', *Journal of Social Development in Africa*, 9(2): 5–29.

Mooney, G. and Law, A. (eds) (2007) *New Labour/hard labour: Restructuring and resistance inside the welfare industry*, Bristol: Policy Press.

Morse, M. (1965) *The unattached*, Harmondsworth: Penguin.

Mouth That Roars and Voice of Youth (2013) *School and our rights* [film], http://voice-of-youth.org/2014/01/26/do-schools-respect-human-rights/ and http://www.oureverydaylives.tv/blog/school-and-our-rights/

MPA (Metropolitan Police Authority) (2008) *Seen and heard – young people, policing and crime: An MPA report*, London: MPA.

NatCen (2012) *Evaluation of National Citizen Service pilots: Interim report*, London: NatCen Social Research.

NatCen (2013) *Evaluation of National Citizen Service: Findings from the evaluations of the 2012 summer and autumn NCS programmes*, London: NatCen Social Research.

National Audit Office (2013) *Managing government suppliers*, London: Cabinet Office.

NCVYS (National Council for Voluntary Youth Services) (2013) *Youth report 2013*, London: NCVYS, www.ncvys.org.uk/sites/default/files/Youth%20Report%202013v2.pdf

NCVYS (2014) *Funding update*, February (no longer available).

Neilson, B. and Rossiter, N. (2005) 'From precarity to precariousness and back again: labour, life and unstable networks', *Fibreculture*, 2005: 5.

Newton, H. P. (1974) *Revolutionary suicide*, London: Wildwood House.

Nicholls, D. (2009) *Building Rapport: A brief history of the Community and Youth Workers' Union*, Coventry: Bread Books.

Nicholls, D. (2012) *For youth workers and youth work: Speaking out for a better future*, Bristol: Policy Press.

NPC (New Philanthropy Capital) (2012) *New Philanthropy Capital's well-being measure: Show the difference you make to young people's lives* (presentation),www.well-beingmeasure.com/media/35455/about_npc_s_well-being_measure_2012.pdf

North Devon Journal (2014) 'A sad day for democracy as young people from North Devon are refused to have their say over cuts', *North Devon Journal*, 21 February, www.northdevonjournal.co.uk/sad-day-democracy-young-people-North-Devon/story-20677507-detail/story.html.

Oakley, A. (1990) 'Interviewing women: a contradiction in terms', in H. Roberts (ed) *Doing feminist research*, London: Routledge, pp 30–61.

Ochieng, B. (2010) '"You know what I mean": the ethical and methodological dilemmas and challenges for black researchers interviewing black families', *Qualitative Health Research*, 20(12): 1725–35.

Olmedo, A. (2013) 'From England with love... ARK, heterarchies and global "philanthropic governance"', *Journal of Education Policy*, 29(5): 575–97.

Olson, G. and Worsham, L. (2000) 'Changing the subject: Judith Butler's politics of radical resignification', *Jac*, 20(4): 727–65.

Ord, J. (2009) 'Thinking the unthinkable: youth work without the voluntary principle', *Youth and Policy*, 103: 39–48.

Ord, J. (2014) 'Aristotle's phronesis and youth work: beyond instrumentality', *Youth and Policy*, 112: 56–73.

Orpin, H. (2011) *A burning love of humanity: Is this an appropriate definition of the professional identity of the youth worker in the twenty-first century?* (MA dissertation), London: University of Greenwich.

Ozga, J. (2000) *Policy research in educational settings*, Buckingham: Open University Press.

Paddison, N. (ed) (2015) 'How youth work changed my life', *Council of Europe Youth Partnership*, http://pjp-eu.coe.int/en/web/youth-partnership/compendium

Paneth, M. (1944) *Branch Street*, London: George Allen and Unwin.

Peck, J. and Tickell, A. (2002) 'Neoliberalizing space', *Antipode*, 34(3): 380–404.

Perryman, J. (2006) 'Panoptic performativity and school inspection regimes: disciplinary mechanisms and life under special measures', *Journal of Education Policy*, 21(2): 147–61.

Pidd, H. (2013) 'Youth clubs shut down as councils slash spending on their future', *Guardian*, 25 March, www.theguardian.com/society/2013/mar/25/drime-focus-youth-services-cuts

Power, M. (1994) *The audit explosion*, London: Demos.

PricewaterhouseCoopers (2006) *Overarching report on children's services markets*, London: Department for Education and Skills Children's Services.

Prynn, D. (1976) 'The Clarion Clubs, rambling and the holiday associations in Britain since the 1890s', *Journal of Contemporary History*, 11: 65–77.

Puffett, N. (2012a) 'UK Youth seals partnership with Microsoft', *Children and Young People Now*, 9 July, www.cypnow.co.uk/cyp/news/1073850/uk-youth-seals-partnership-microsoft

Puffett, N. (2012b) 'Serco consortium wins six NCS contracts', *Children and Young People Now*, 13 September, www.cypnow.co.uk/cyp/news/1074613/serco-consortium-wins-ncs-contracts.

Radical Routes (2012) *How to set up a workers' co-op* (3rd edn), Leeds: Radical Routes

RBKC (Royal Borough of Kensington and Chelsea) (2014) 'The feeling's mutual: exciting times for Royal Borough's youth service' (press release), Royal Borough of Kensington and Chelsea.

Reay, D. (1996) 'Dealing with difficult differences: reflexivity and social class in feminist research', *Feminism and Psychology*, 6(3): 443–56.

Reclaim the Streets (1997) 'Reclaim the Streets!', *Do or Die*, 6: 1–10.

Roberts, J. (2004) 'The significance of Circular 1486 – the service of youth', London: infed, www.infed.org/youthwork/circular1486.htm.

Robertson, S. (2005) *Youth clubs: Association, participation, friendship and fun*, Lyme Regis: Russell House.

Rochester, C. (2013) *Rediscovering voluntary action: The beat of a different drum*, Basingstoke: Palgrave Macmillan.

Rose, N. (1996) 'The death of the social? Re-figuring the territory of government', *Economy and Society*, 25(3): 327–56.

Rose, N. (1999) *Governing the soul? The shaping of the private self* (2nd edn), London: Free Association Books.

Roth, G. (2014) 'Review of "Demanding the impossible: A history of anarchism" by Peter Marshall', *Critical Sociology*, 40(2): 301–4.

Rowbotham, S. (1979) 'The women's movement and organising for socialism', in S. Rowbotham, L. Segal and H. Wainwright (eds) *Beyond the fragments: Feminism and the making of socialism*, London: Merlin Press.

Sachs, J. (2000) 'The activist professional', *Journal of Educational Change*, 1: 77–95.

Sanguinetti, J. (1999) *Within and against performativity: Discursive engagement in adult literacy and basic education* (PhD thesis), Geelong, Victoria: Deakin University.

Sedgwick, E.K. (2003) *Touching feeling: Affect, pedagogy, performativity*, Durham, NC: Duke University Press.

Sercombe, H. (2010) *Youth work ethics*, London: Sage.

Sheridan-Rabideau, M.P. (2008) *Girls, feminism, and grassroots literacies: Activism in the Girlzone*, Albany, NY: State University of New York Press.

Sheil, F. and Breidenbach-Roe, R. (2014) *Payment by results and the voluntary sector*, London: NCVO.

Sikes, P. (2012) 'Some thoughts on ethics review and contemporary ethical concerns in research in education', *Research Intelligence*, 118: 16–17.

Siurala, L. (2014) *Autonomy through dependency: Histories of cooperation, conflict and innovation in youth work*, Concept paper for 5th Seminar on History of Youth Work and Policy in Europe, Helsinki.

Smith, M. (2002) 'Transforming youth work: resourcing excellent youth services, a critique', *Infed,* http://www.infed.org/youthwork/transforming_youth_work_2.htm

Smith, M. (2013) 'What is youth work? Exploring the history, theory and practice of youth work', London: infed, www.infed.org/mobi/what-is-youth-work-exploring-the-history-theory-and-practice-of-work-with-young-people/

Smith, P. (2012) *The emotional labour of nursing revisited: Can nurses still care?* (2nd edn), Basingstoke: Macmillan.

Solnit, R. (2014) 'Diary', *London Review of Books*, 36(4): 34–5.

Spence, J. (2014) 'Feminism and informal education in youth work with girls and young women, 1975–85', in S. Mills and P. Kraftl (eds) *Informal education, childhood and youth: Geographies, histories, practices,* Basingstoke: Palgrave Macmillan, pp 197–215.

Spence, J. and Devanney, C. (2006) *Youth work: Voices of practice,* Leicester: NYA.

Spivak, G. (1988) 'Can the subaltern speak?' In C. Nelson and L. Grossberg (eds) *Marxism and the interpretation of culture*, Urbana-Champaign, IL: University of Illinois, pp 271–316.

Steinberg, R.J. and Figart, D.M. (1999) 'Emotional labor since the Managed Heart', *The Annals of the American Academy of Political and Social Science*, 561: 8–26.

Strobel, K., Kirshner, B., O'Donoghue, J. and McLaughlin, M. W. (2008) 'Qualities that attract urban youth to after-school settings and promote continued participation', *Teachers College Record*, 110(8): 1677–705.

Suissa, J. (2010) *Anarchism and education: A philosophical perspective,* Oakland, CA: PM Press.

Taggart, G. (2011) 'Don't we care? The ethics and emotional labour of early years professionalism', *Early Years,* 31(1): 85–95.

Taylor, T. (2010) 'Defending democratic youth work', *Concept*, 1(2): 3–10.

Taylor, T. (2012) 'Barclays teach money skills to the young unemployed!?' In Defence of Youth Work, http://indefenceofyouthwork.com/2012/07/05/barclays-teach-money-skills-to-the-young-unemployed/

Taylor, T. (2015) 'The cuts run deeper and deeper', In Defence of Youth Work, http://indefenceofyouthwork.com/2015/11/19/the-cuts-run-deeper-and-deeper/

Taylor, T. and Taylor, M. (2013) *Threatening youth work: The illusion of outcomes*, In Defence of Youth Work, www.indefenceofyouthwork. org.uk/wordpress/wp-content/uploads/2013/09/Threatening-YW-and-Illusion-final1.pdf

Thiong'o, N. (1986) *Decolonising the mind: The politics of language in African literature*, Nairobi: East African Educational Publishers Ltd.

Thomas, R. and Davies, A. (2005a) 'Theorizing the micro-politics of resistance: New Public Management and managerial identities in the UK public services', *Organization Studies*, 26(5): 683–706.

Thomas, R. and Davies, A. (2005b) 'What have the feminists done for us? Feminist theory and organisational resistance', *Organization*, 12(5): 711–40.

Tiffany, G. (2007) *Reconnecting detached youth work: Guidelines and standards for excellence*, Leicester: Federation for Detached Youth Work.

Tiffany, G. (2009) *Community philosophy: A project report*, York: Joseph Rowntree Foundation.

Tlili, A., Gewirtz, S. and Cribb, A. (2007) 'New Labour's socially responsible museum: roles, functions and greater expectations', *Policy Studies*, 28(3): 269–89.

Tolich, M.B. (1993) 'Alienating and liberating emotions at work: supermarket clerks' performance of customer service', *Journal of Contemporary Ethnography*, 22: 361–81.

Tolich, M. (2004) 'Internal confidentiality: when confidentiality assurances fail relational informants', *Qualitative Sociology*, 27(1): 101–6.

Tolich, M. (2010) 'A critique of current practice: ten foundational guidelines for autoethnographers', *Qualitative Health Research*, 20: 1599–1610.

Towers, V. (2011) 'Probation officers don't need telling off', *The Guardian: Comment is free*, 29 July, www.theguardian.com/commentisfree/2011/jul/29/probation-officers-government.

Unison (2014a) *Community and voluntary services in the age of austerity: Unison voices from the frontline*, London: Unison.

Unison (2014b) *The damage: The UK's youth services, how cuts are removing opportunities for young people and damaging their lives*, London: Unison.

Verschelden, G., Coussée, F., Van de Walle, T. and Williamson, H. (2009) 'The history of European youth work and its relevance for youth policy today', in G. Verschelden, F. Coussée, T. Van de Walle and H. Williamson (eds) *The history of youth work in Europe: Relevance for youth policy today*, Strasbourg: Council of Europe, pp 132–46.

Wacquant, L. (2013) 'Constructing neoliberalism: opening Salvo', *Nexus*, 25(1): 1, 8–9.

Weitz, R. (2001) 'Women and their hair: seeking power through resistance and accommodation', *Gender and Society*, 15(5): 667–86.

Whelan, M. (2010) 'Detached youth work', in B. Davies and J. Batsleer (eds) *What is youth work?*, Exeter: Learning Matters.

Wild, J. (1982) *Street mates*, Liverpool: Merseyside Youth Association.

Williams, L. (1988) *Partial surrender: Race and resistance in the youth service*, Lewes: The Falmer Press.

Williams, R. (2011) 'Teens are left to their own devices as council axes more youth services', *Guardian*, 23 August, www.theguardian.com/society/2011/aug/23/norfolk-axes-youth-services-effect.

Williams, Z. (2012) *The shadow state: A report about outsourcing of public services*, London: Social Enterprise UK.

Williams, Z. (2013) 'Strivers v. skivers: The argument that pollutes people's minds', *Guardian*, 9 January, www.theguardian.com/politics/2013/jan/09/skivers-v-strivers-argument-pollutes.

Wilson, D., Rose, J. and Colvin, E. (2010) *Marginalised young people, surveillance and public space: A research report*, Melbourne: Youth Affairs Council of Victoria and Clayton: School of Political and Social Enquiry, Monash University.

Winnett, R. and Kirkup, J. (2010) 'General election 2010: David Cameron: what Eton taught me about citizenship', *Daily Telegraph*, 9 April, www.telegraph.co.uk/news/election-2010/7569486/General-Election-2010-David-Cameron-what-Eton-taught-me-about-citizenship.html.

Woolford, A. and Curran, A. (2013) 'Community dispositions, neoliberal dispositions: managing non-profit social services within the bureaucratic field', *Critical Sociology*, 39(1): 45–63.

Wright, E.O. (2010) *Envisioning real utopias*, London and New York: Verso.

Wylie, T. (2004) 'How Connexions came to terms with youth work', *Youth and Policy*, 83: 19–29.

X, Andrew (2000) 'Give up activism', *Do or Die*, 9: 160–66.

Youdell, D. and McGimpsey, I. (2015) 'Assembling, disassembling and reassembling "youth services" in Austerity Britain', *Critical Studies in Education*, 56(1): 116–30.

Young Foundation (2011) *Growing interest? Mapping the market for social finance in the youth sector*, London: Young Foundation.

Index

and marketisation 71–2
and resistance 73–8
Peck, J. and Tickell, A. 27
performance indicators (REYS outcomes) 85, 86
performativity, theories of 96–7, 98
Perryman, J. 103
'philanthropic' emotion management 74, 75
play work 45
police
 deaths in custody 123
 Independent Advisory Group 124
 and racism 123
 working with 122–30
policy, definition of 14
poststructuralism 172
'powers of freedom' 24
practical anarchism 182, 210–11
'practitioner ethnography' 203–4
'precarious labour' 43–7, 175, 179
'presentational' emotion management 74, 75
PricewaterhouseCoopers 27
private sector contractors 32
privatisation 82
professional knowledge, loss of 48, 49
psychoanalytic theory 98
public spending cuts 21–2, 23
 and neoliberalism 27–8
 opposition to 36–9
 and threat to service 2–3, 14

R

race
 and emotional labour 69
 and shame 104
 and social identity of researcher 200
 and surveillance 113, 116, 123
radical groups, historical 172
Radical Routes 170
Realities of training report 1978 9
Reay, D. 205
'Reclaim the Night' 142
'Reclaim the Streets' 142
religion, and surveillance 116
research methodology 195–215
 focus groups 200, 201–2, 203
 interviews 197, 198–200
 participant observation 203–6, 207
 participants 196–7
 and social identity of researcher 200
resistance
 and alternatives 188

and anti-oppressive practice 179
and counter-discourses 184–5
everyday 182–3
and passionate practice 16, 73–8
and performativity 83
against police in youth work 128, 129–30
refusals and rebellion 186–7
target cultures and performativity 110–12
tracking and databases 137–9
REYS outcomes *see* performance indicators
Robertson, S. 67
Rochester, C. 30
Roma, stigmatisation of 49
Rose, N. 85, 124
Roth, G. 210

S

Sanguinetti, J. 53
SAPERE (The Society for the Advancement of Philosophical Enquiry and Reflection in Education) 201
Sedgwick, Eve Kosofsky 96, 98, 103
self-employment 43–5, 127, 179
self-exploitation 169, 170
Serco 30, 32
Smith, P. 64, 69
social control, and neoliberalism 27
social investment model 30
Solnit, R. 52
Spence, J. and Devanney, C. 88
staff development 191
Starbucks 34
Starting from strengths report 1984 9
stop and search 123
surveillance 103, 113–44
 as challenge 175
 and demonisation of young people 115, 116
 and higher education 114, 115
 of marginalised young people 141
 and neoliberalism 27, 114, 115
 and tracking and databases 130–8
 urban 116, 142

T

Taggart, G. 62
target cultures and performativity 81–112
 and administration 94, 95–6